T0271112

Asian Agribusiness Management

Case Studies in Growth, Marketing, and Upgrading Strategies

Asian Agribusiness Management

Case Studies in Growth, Marketing, and Upgrading Strategies

Editors

Ralph D. Christy (Cornell University, USA)

Joselito C. Bernardo (Asian Productivity Organization, Japan)

Aimée Hampel-Milagrosa (Asian Development Bank, Philippines)

Lin Fu (Cornell University, USA)

World Scientific

NEW JERSEY · LONDON · SINGAPORE · BEIJING · SHANGHAI · HONG KONG · TAIPEI · CHENNAI · TOKYO

Published by

World Scientific Publishing Co. Pte. Ltd.

5 Toh Tuck Link, Singapore 596224

USA office: 27 Warren Street, Suite 401-402, Hackensack, NJ 07601

UK office: 57 Shelton Street, Covent Garden, London WC2H 9HE

Library of Congress Cataloging-in-Publication Data
Names: Christy, Ralph D., editor. | Bernardo, Joselito C., editor. |
  Hampel-Milagrosa, Aimée, editor. | Fu, Lin, 1984– editor.
Title: Asian agribusiness management : case studies in growth, marketing, and upgrading strategies /
  edited by Ralph D Christy (Cornell University, USA), Joselito C Bernardo (Asian Productivity
  Organization, Japan), Aimée Hampel-Milagrosa (Asian Development Bank, Philippines),
  Lin Fu (Cornell University, USA).
Description: New Jersey : World Scientific, [2018] | Includes bibliographical references.
Identifiers: LCCN 2018011141 | ISBN 9789813233133 (hc ; alk. paper)
Subjects: LCSH: Agricultural industries--Asia--Management--Case studies. |
  Produce trade--Asia--Management--Case studies.
Classification: LCC HD9016.A2 A75 2018 | DDC 630.68--dc23
LC record available at https://lccn.loc.gov/2018011141

British Library Cataloguing-in-Publication Data
A catalogue record for this book is available from the British Library.

For any available supplementary material, please visit
http://www.worldscientific.com/worldscibooks/10.1142/10793#t=suppl

Desk Editors: Anthony Alexander/Karimah Samsudin

Typeset by Stallion Press
Email: enquiries@stallionpress.com

Printed in Singapore

Foreword

The Asian Productivity Organization (APO), a regional intergovernmental organization with a network spanning the Asia-Pacific, and Cornell University, a world-class institution with strong global research and outreach programs, began a partnership in 2012 to offer the Advanced Agribusiness Management Workshop for Executives and Managers series. In the 2012–2018 period, this partnership resulted in six highly successful workshops that engaged excellent agribusiness companies and dedicated policymakers in discussions on the major forces shaping the supply of, demand for, and distribution of food. Those discussions were guided by the case study method, a practical approach based on real-world examples, to facilitate greater understanding of effective business strategies that enhance the productivity and competitiveness of Asian economies. While those joint workshops served as forums to address the critical issues of the times, this volume of case studies represents a resource for long-term use to sustain debate and learning.

Agriculture is an engine of growth for the majority of Asian economies. Agribusiness, comprising multiple economic activities on both the input and output sides of farming, not only links food production to dynamic urban demand for food, fiber, and fuel but also embraces global markets to earn foreign exchange for many Asian economies. In previous decades, the national economic objective of agriculture was expressed in terms of self-sufficiency in food. Today, however, the role of private-sector actors in the global economy is expected to meet the national policy objectives of food security and safety. The missions of the APO and Cornell University are to contribute to greater efficiency, higher productivity, enhanced food safety, and a more environment-friendly approach to sustainable agriculture and agribusiness.

This volume of case studies and associated workshops on which it was based can contribute immensely to efforts to fulfill those missions. Having had opportunities to support, participate in, and observe several workshops, I know firsthand that the dedicated professionals from both within and beyond the APO region who were involved in those capacity-building endeavors were engaged in labors of love. Their efforts to promote sustainable productivity in agriculture and the competitiveness of agribusinesses for a better quality of life will have enduring impacts on economic growth and development in the Asia-Pacific and elsewhere.

Dr. Santhi Kanoktanaporn
Secretary-General
APO
Tokyo
29 March 2018

Preface

In 2012, the Asian Productivity Organization (APO), in collaboration with the Cornell International Institute for Food, Agriculture and Development (CIIFAD), held a workshop on Advanced Agribusiness Management for Executives and Managers of SMEs in Bangkok, Thailand. Following that inaugural workshop, there were three more in Bangkok, one in Bali, Indonesia, and one in Manila, the Philippines. In total, over 150 companies have participated in the APO-Cornell Advanced Agribusiness workshops. This volume of case studies is but one product of the workshops, and it is our hope that it will serve as a vehicle to continue important discussions beyond those official events for students, managers, and public policy-makers globally.

The APO-Cornell Advanced Agribusiness workshops offered an excellent opportunity for managers and owners of Asian agribusiness companies to become better acquainted with the forces shaping the food industry, management tools to plan company growth, and marketing strategies to fulfill company objectives and customer needs. The agribusiness space is growing, dynamic, and complex. It stands at the intersection of three sectors of the economy: agriculture, manufacturing, and service. For this reason, developing an understanding of the forces that drive change is critical to the success of any agribusiness company. The rapidity and complexity of change facing Asian agribusiness industries merit investments in forums that periodically bring together industry participants to network, share information, and learn new management strategies. With rising incomes and increasing populations in Asia, the region's agribusinesses that position their companies for those and other trends will be better able to meet the growing demand for food and food services.

In each of our workshops, we framed the discussions around the question, "What should every agribusiness manager know about strategy?" In choosing this provocative title, we are well aware that many companies do not always avail themselves of business management tools that can aide and guide their growth and marketing strategies. Managers commonly cite lack of time as the prime reason they do not make use of strategic management tools. In reality, modern management tools are not used because managers are unfamiliar with formal strategy frameworks and often lack the time and the skills necessary to employ and implement them. It has also been widely observed that strategic thinking tools are not employed because the culture of many companies is not conducive to fostering open and bottom-up discussion among the various levels within the organization. It takes trust and openness to make full use of many of the tools in the modern management toolkit. Within some organizations, the corporate culture, unfortunately, simply does not allow for such an exchange of ideas about the direction of the company. We encouraged participants to think strategically, utilize strategic thinking tools, and create an environment for strategic thinking within their own organizations. At least four critical questions are common to most strategic planning processes: Who are we? Where are we going? How will we get there? How long do we want the business to live?

Beyond these "big picture" topics, we felt it necessary to acquaint and reacquaint the managers and owners with contemporary marketing strategies. The marketing concept holds that the key to achieving organizational goals involves determining the needs and wants of target market consumers and delivering the desired products and services more effectively than competitors. An effective marketing strategy requires both careful planning, implementation, and continuous updating of pricing, product development, marketing channel decisions, and promotion. Most companies have developed a marketing plan as part of their overall strategic plan. Developing an effective marketing strategy requires thinking through three key elements: segment, target, and position, otherwise known as the STP process, or target marketing. Thus, we also encouraged participants to think about market segmentation, targeting, and product positioning. How should we divide the market into groups according to various criteria that are likely to influence consumer behaviors and patterns? How do we select one (or a few) of the market segments to be a primary focus? Is the market segment attractive — one that is growing, with relatively few competitors? Is the market segment a good fit — can the company produce enough for the particular segment and can we compete with already existing companies? How do we position, advertise, and display the product to engage customers in the market and to distinguish ourselves from our competitors?

This collected volume of case studies is organized around three major themes from the APO-Cornell Advanced Agribusiness workshops, namely growth, marketing, and upgrading strategies. A unique feature of the APO-Cornell workshops was the use of highly relevant and timely case studies that supported the workshop's instruction and group discussions. The three cases on upgrading were developed by Aimée Hampel-Milagrosa, initially during her sabbatical at Cornell in 2014, building on research that she began at the German Development Institute. The first eight case studies focus on growth and marketing strategies and were developed for the workshop by graduate students at Cornell University as part of Cornell's SMART Program. SMART (Student Multidisciplinary Applied Research Teams) is a program that brings together teams of students and faculty from diverse disciplines and pairs them with firms, organizations, or community groups in emerging markets. Students and faculty leaders work together to document and analyze companies, working directly with managers, employees, and stakeholders. We are indebted to all the companies who graciously provided us with their time and resources to host our students, researchers, and faculty. We are especially appreciative of the help and support of Cornell alumni across Asia in advancing the SMART Program: Jack Ho '81 and his daughter Kelly Ho '14 in Taiwan; Dr. Kittipong Kittayarak, LLM'83 in Thailand; and Ben Zehr '15 and the Barwale family in India.

Without the support of many individuals, perhaps too many to name, the workshops and these case studies would not have been possible. From APO, we would like to thank Secretary-Generals Ambassador Mari Amano and Dr. Santhi Kanoktanaporn, Directors Joselito Bernardo and Muhammad Saeed. We are indebted to our workshop facilitators and the many guest speakers who contributed immensely to the success of the APO-Cornell Advanced Agribusiness workshops: Kit Chan, Louie Divinagracia, Carlos Da Silva, Darunee Eduards, Mohammad Karaan, Suwimon Keeratipibul, Paradon Munro, and Rosa Rolle. Special mention goes to Kit Chan, an intrepid and intellectual businessman-cum-farmer from Kuala Lumpur. With Kit on our team, it was impossible for our presentations to drift off into the world of theoretical constructs about management and markets.

Kit insisted that we "keep it relevant," making sure at every turn to chime in with a perspective that was not only pertinent, but also profound with gems of insightful information that grew out of his business dealings with large European buyers, small-scale Asian farmers, and traders.

We owe a great deal of thanks to the Thailand Productivity Institute International Relations Department. From our very first meeting in 2012, Tassaneeya "Tassa" Trakoonsatjawat embraced the APO-Cornell collaboration and worked tirelessly to give tangible meaning to our vision of having our respective organizations partner in this important and impactful work. In the years that followed, Ratchada "Lek" Asisonthisakul stepped up and offered steady and reliable input to help the APO-Cornell workshop mature into an annual event. In March 2017, the APO-Cornell workshop moved to Bali, Indonesia under the leadership of Dr. Harjito, Ida Ayu Ratih, and Cordelia Ervina of the Ministry of Agriculture, Indonesia.

In preparing the cases in this volume, we greatly appreciate the excellent partnership with Kasetsart University in Bangkok, Thailand. With the unwavering support of Dean Nuchanata Mungkung and Professors Ravissa Suchato and Kulapa Kudilok, three case studies were completed that included both Cornell University and Kasetsart University students. Pita Limjaroenrat (CEO Agrifood, Thailand) was also very supportive of Cornell's SMART program and was the first company in Thailand to host students. Pita paved the way for other companies and serves as a shining example of university–company collaboration.

We also owe a special thanks to Helen del Rosario (Soyuz Foods, Philippines), Dalis and Vimol Chhorn (Kirirom Food, Cambodia) and Alit Artha Wiguna and Surya Prasetya Wiguna (Cau Chocolates, Indonesia) for not only allowing our team to document their companies, but for their willingness to allow us to use the case studies of their companies in our Advanced Agribusiness Workshops. In each instance, Helen, Dalis, Vimol, Alit, and Surya, presented their case to workshop participants and answered a barrage of questions. It takes a special company to subject itself to a roomful of inquisitive minds and critical eyes from around Asia.

A project of this nature, one that involves many researchers and spans multiple countries, requires a clear-headed taskmaster. Dr. Krisztina Tihanyi performed this role with exceptional good judgment and gentle reminders from the beginning of the initiative to the culmination of this volume. Her excellent organizational and technical editing skills were much appreciated by the editors and individual authors of this collection of case studies.

Our team of editors attempted to capture the courage and commitment required to own and manage an agribusiness in Asia. Through our journey of preparing the case studies in this volume and facilitating the workshops, we saw and were impressed by the sacrifice, commitment, and vision required of the women and men who own and manage agribusiness companies in Asia. We only hope that we captured their stories in this volume of cases studies in a manner that will inspire learning.

Ralph D. Christy
Ithaca, NY

Joselito Bernardo
Tokyo, Japan

Aimée Hampel-Milagrosa
Manila, Philippines

Lin Fu
Ithaca, NY

About the Editors

 **Ralph D. Christy** is the founder of Market Matters, Inc. and Professor of Emerging Markets at Cornell University in Ithaca, New York, where he teaches and conducts food marketing research and educational programs on the economic performance of markets and distribution systems. He has advised industry leaders and public policymakers on food marketing strategies, economic development, and the organization of the global food economy. A Ph.D. graduate of Michigan State University's Department of Agricultural Economics, Christy is past President of the American Agricultural Economics Association and past Board Member of the Winthrop Rockefeller Foundation, WinRock International, and the Agribusiness Capital Fund.

 **Joselito Cruz Bernardo** is a freelance management consultant based in Manila. He was affiliated with the Asian Productivity Organization (APO) for 13 years. He served as Director of the Agriculture Department for about six years and as Director of the Research and Planning Department for two years. He worked with various NPOs and agriculture ministries and in academia and SMEs in agribusiness in Asia in developing and managing capacity enhancement programs. Prior to APO, Mr. Bernardo was a Director at the National Economic and Development Authority (NEDA) and concurrently served as the Deputy Head of the Secretariat of the Philippine Council on Sustainable Development in Manila.

Aimée Hampel-Milagrosa is an economist in the Economic Research and Regional Cooperation Department of the Asian Development Bank. Prior to joining ADB, she was a Senior Researcher at the Department of Sustainable Economic and Social Development of the German Development Institute (DIE), the think tank of the German Ministry for Economic Cooperation and Development (BMZ). She has been a consultant for various research projects for UNIDO, UNCTAD, DANIDA, and BICC. Her specializations include the gender dimensions of business environment reform and private sector development, development of agricultural value chains, and financing for development.

Lin Fu is a research fellow with Cornell University's Emerging Markets Program, housed in the Dyson School of Applied Economics and Management. She was previously affiliated with the Cornell International Institute for Food, Agriculture and Development (CIIFAD) and has also been a visiting fellow at the Brookings Institution. Her research interests include political economy, economic development, entrepreneurship and small and medium enterprise growth, and food security. Prior to Cornell, she worked for a number of years in finance and project management consulting.

Contents

Chapter 1

Key Trends and Drivers in Asian Agribusiness

Lin Fu[1], Ralph D. Christy[1], and Joselito Cruz Bernardo[2]

Introduction

With the region's rising incomes and increasing populations, the outlook for Asian agribusiness is strong. This is a dynamic and complex space due to evolving macro factors (e.g. regional trade liberalization) and micro-level developments (e.g., changing consumer preferences). Agriculture remains a vital sector in all economies for national priorities like food security as well as for strategic reasons such as trade competition. While agricultural policies may vary across countries, they can generally be grouped into three categories that correspond to three different but often overlapping objectives: (1) increasing agricultural productivity; (2) increasing farmers' income; and (3) protecting farmers' land (Pinstrup-Anderson and Watson 2011).

Most national agricultural policies now also include "upgrading" efforts that try to capture more from the agricultural value chain within national borders — increasing the farm product processing capability and capacity of local firms, for example. Governments' agricultural policies as well as the food and agribusiness industry's practices and offerings are adapting to changing consumer profiles and demands, which represent both challenges and opportunities for small and medium enterprises in this space. This research note provides an overview of the key trends and drivers that will shape Asian agribusinesses in the coming years.

[1]SMART Program, Cornell University.
[2]Asian Productivity Organization.

1

Supermarket Revolution

Supermarket diffusion

Asian consumers, in increasing numbers, are shopping for their groceries in supermarkets. From a global perspective, the "supermarket revolution" reached Asia relatively late. The dissemination of supermarket food retail from North America and Europe outward currently consists of three waves. The first wave, which took place in parts of Latin America and Central Europe as well as South Africa, saw an increase in this "modern" food retail from 5-10% of overall food retail in the early 1990s to more than 50% by the mid-2000s. The second wave took place during the mid- to late 1990s in Southeast Asia, Central America, and Mexico. In these second-wave countries, supermarket retail as a share of total food retail ranged from 30% to 50% by the mid-2000s. The third wave occurred during the late 1990s and throughout the 2000s in China, India, and Russia. The supermarket revolution is taking hold in China at a faster pace than in any other country in the world. Supermarket sales grow on average 30-40% per year. Diffusion rates vary across other parts of Asia: for example, the average processed/packaged food retail share is 33% in Indonesia and Thailand, but is 63% in Taiwan and the Philippines (Reardon *et al.* 2012; Hu *et al.* 2004).

Several factors influence the pace at which supermarket diffusion occurs. Among the most important determinants are urbanization, income growth, foreign direct investment, and logistics technology.

Urbanization, by its very definition, is a population shift from rural to urban areas. As more people move to cities, patterns of work and leisure change such that shopping for fresh produce on a daily basis becomes a less viable habit. Additionally, as more women enter the labor force outside the home, the opportunity cost of their time increases and thus, there is greater incentive to seek shopping convenience and processed foods in order to save food preparation time.

Per capita income growth in many Asian countries during the 1990s, along with the rapid rise of the middle class, contributed to the rise of supermarket shopping. Consumers with more money but less time value convenience, resulting in the increased demand for processed foods. Processed foods have been the entry point into the food retail market for supermarkets: supermarkets are able to offer a greater variety of processed foods at a lower cost than traditional retailers due to economies of scale in procurement (Reardon *et al.* 2003).

Foreign direct investment (FDI) was critical to the takeoff of supermarkets starting in the 1990s. Multinational supermarkets sought to invest and/or establish their brands in developing markets due to saturation in their home markets and higher profit margins in these new markets. For example, the French supermarket chain Carrefour saw three times higher margins on average in Argentina than in France in the 1990s (Reardon *et al.* 2003).

Logistics technology advancements and the resulting revolution in retail procurement have made supermarkets more competitive compared to traditional food retailers. New practices such as Efficient Consumer Response (ECR), a consumer- and process-oriented supply chain optimization model, and inventory management methods that minimize the use of inventory control are examples of such advancements. Importantly, they all contribute to enabling supermarkets to better meet shoppers' demands (Seifert 2003).

Food retail industry consolidation

With increased economic development, markets have changed from fragmented, local and village markets to larger, centralized wholesale markets. In the supermarket sector, consolidation took place primarily through foreign acquisition of local chains and secondarily through absorption of smaller chains by larger domestic chains. Main players in Asia include global retail multinationals such as Ahold, Carrefour, and Wal-Mart and regional multinationals like Hong Kong-based Dairy Farm International.

Within the food industry, consolidation is proceeding at different rates. The takeover of food retailing in developing regions has occurred more quickly in processed, dry, and packaged foods such as noodles, milk products, and grains, products for which supermarkets have an advantage due to economies of scale. The entry of supermarkets into the fresh food market has been slower and penetration rates vary greatly due to differences across countries based on local tastes. The first fresh food category in which supermarkets typically gain a majority share are "commodities" (e.g., potatoes) where the difference between what is available at the supermarket and what is on offer by traditional retailers is not significant. Industry segments that are beginning and will likely to continue to see additional consolidation are those that involve primary processing of livestock, e.g., chicken, beef, pork, and fish (Brown 2005).

Trends in supermarket procurement systems

Centralization of procurement: As the number of stores in a given supermarket chain grows, there is a propensity to move from a per-store procurement system to a distribution center serving several stores within a given zone, district, country, or region. This requires centralized warehouses with fewer procurement and distribution officers.

Logistics improvement: Procurement modernization in processed and semi-processed products and staples seems to be happening early and rapidly in Asia, as it has elsewhere. To cover some of the additional transport costs that arise when procurement centralization occurs, supermarket chains have implemented best-practice logistical technology. For example, Ahold instituted a supply improvement program for vegetable suppliers in Thailand, specifying postharvest and production practices to assure consistent supply.

Logistics and distribution partnerships: Retail chains are increasingly outsourcing their logistics and wholesale distribution function, entering joint ventures with other firms. For instance, Wu-mart of China built a large distribution center that is operated jointly with Tibbett and Britten Logistics, a British firm with global operations.

Trends in the local food industry

Consolidation among medium and large food processing firms: Modern retailers sourcing processed foods, staples, and dairy from medium and large companies developed with the rise and consolidation of the processing sector in many Asian countries in the 1980s and 1990s, spurred by the FDI of multinational chains and domestic investment in agro-processing during that same time period.

Building domestic brands: The presence of multinational food processors spurred competitive investment and brand-building by national companies. Domestic brands from Asia that have successfully expanded internationally include Nissin of Japan, CP of Thailand, and Wilmar of Singapore.

Urbanization

Urbanization in Asia

Urbanization in Asia is occurring rapidly as a result of rural-to-urban migration. The reasons for such internal migration are the same world-wide: the search for economic and social opportunities. The world's urban population is currently around 3.9 billion and will reach 6.3 billion by 2050. Although it has a lower level of urbanization than North America and Europe, Asia is already home to 53% of the urban population in the world. Over the next four decades, the Asian continent will see a steady increase in its urban population and will continue to be home to more than half of the urban population of the world (52%) in 2050 (UN DESA 2015).

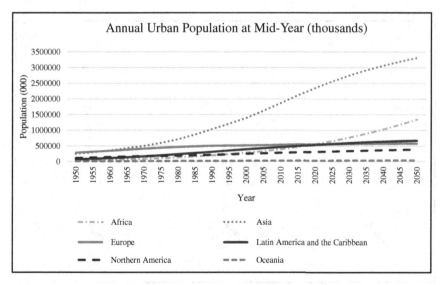

Fig. 1: Majority of urban population lives in Asia (UN DESA 2014).

Changes in consumption patterns

Diet diversification: Income growth leads to major shifts in demand across different types of food and the process of urbanization brings about new dietary preferences and more generally, lifestyle changes. As a result, consumer preferences and consumption patterns are changing. Urban consumers are shifting away from cereals and starchy food commodities, still common staples in rural areas, toward more high-value foods, e.g., horticultural and livestock products, and processed foodstuffs. This preference for the consumption of high-value food products will influence food production, processing and marketing, thus creating new opportunities, generating employment, and increasing incomes.

Increased demand for feed: Animal protein consumption in Asia is highly diverse with particularly high overall consumption in Malaysia, South Korea, China and Vietnam (see Figure 2). As the demand for high-value food such as livestock products increases, the demand for feed grain will also rise. Although cereal producers are negatively impacted by the decline in direct consumer demand for cereal, they benefit from a greater increase in indirect consumer demand for cereals as feed. The increased

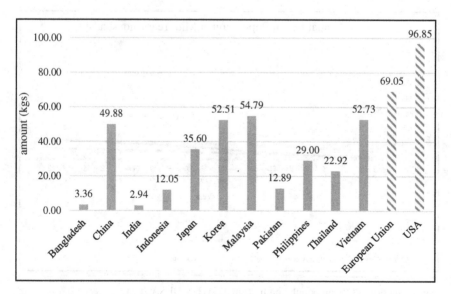

Fig. 2: Per Capita Meat Consumption of Select Asian Countries in 2016.

demand for feed means upward pressure on cereal prices (OECD 2017; Claxton 2013).

Emerging preference for organic products: Food safety is a growing concern for Asia's rising middle class. They are wary of residual pesticides and other contaminants in their produce. Rising per capita incomes mean that middle class consumers are able to pay more for that peace of mind. A growing number are willing to do so: organic farming has started to take off across the region (Yoshida 2016).

Biofuel and related products: With the rising affluence of the urban middle class and the consequent growing number of automobile owners, there has been an increased demand for rubber (for tires) as well as palm oil and other agricultural products like corn and sugar cane (for biofuel). This will positively impact the rubber and palm oil producing countries of Southeast Asia, namely Indonesia, Thailand, and Malaysia.

Changes in production patterns

Income diversification: Smallholders, who make up the majority of agricultural producers in Asia, have benefited from urbanization due to the increased opportunities for small farms to diversify into non-farm sources of income. In China, nonfarm income shares for farm households increased from 33.7% in 1985, to 63% in 2000, to 70.9% in 2010 (Huang *et al.* 2012), while in other Asian countries, non-farm income shares have reached 40% or more and are often much higher for the smallest farms (Haggblade *et al.* 2007).

Farmland consolidation: With increased income diversification, smallholder farm sizes are shrinking. Due to urban migration, rural households now commonly lease out their farmland as young people prefer to seek jobs in urban areas and are not available to work these family plots. As remaining rural households acquire land released by their neighbors, the average Asian farm size will increase. Farmland consolidation in Asia combined with their increased proximity to urban markets will likely lead to higher average outputs per farm in Asia.

Regional Integration

Increased trade within ASEAN

Intraregional trade has increased within Asia, particularly within South-east Asia. In November 2002, the member countries of ASEAN committed to the establishment of an ASEAN Economic Community by 2020. Additionally, ASEAN states are linked through the ASEAN Political-Security Community and the ASEAN Socio-Cultural Community. Such ties have facilitated trade between member states such that intraregional trade among ASEAN countries increased from less than 20% in 1990 to around 25% by 2011, a greater increase than was experienced by the South Asian Association for Regional Cooperation (SAARC). Intraregional trade in East and Southeast Asia increased by around 10% within that same period of time (Moinuddin 2013). Intra-ASEAN trade has been hovering around the 25% mark for the past few years while intraregional trade within SAARC and within ASEAN+3 have both risen slightly (see Figure 3).

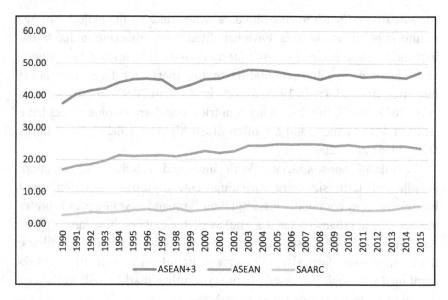

Fig. 3: Intraregional trade within SAARC, ASEAN, and ASEAN+3.

Other Asian trade agreements

Despite unresolved historical grievances and ongoing territory disputes, economic cooperation has been increasing steadily in the Asian region as a whole. As a result, trade between ASEAN countries and other Asian countries has also been steadily increasing and should continue to do so given the additional trade agreements now in place. Among the trade agreements already in effect are: the Regional Comprehensive Economic Partnership, ASEAN–Australia–New Zealand Free Trade Area (AAN-ZFTA), ASEAN–China Free Trade Area (ACFTA), ASEAN–India Free Trade Area (AIFTA), ASEAN–Japan Comprehensive Economic Partnership (AJCEP), and ASEAN–Korea Free Trade Area (AKFTA).

Impact of regionalization on agriculture and food sectors

Given increased intraregional economic cooperation and the spread of intraregional trade agreements, trade and investment activity has picked up. The opportunities are many and varied. South Korea's Lotte is taking its food retail expertise outside its home country, setting up supermarkets across Southeast Asia and in China as well. Japan, with its rapidly aging population and shrinking active labor force needs to maintain high-productivity and high-wage employment in order to combat its low growth rate; to this end, the country sources lower-value agricultural products elsewhere, hence Japanese investments in Thai food production companies. Chinese food and agricultural companies, in order to meet domestic demand, are engaging in more and more merger and acquisition activities abroad, including in Southeast Asia. Regional integration, at least when it comes to economic activity, means more competition, but also more opportunities as well for agribusinesses across Asia.

Climate Change

Climate change in Asia

Existing climate change studies vary in their models and scenarios, but most have average temperatures increasing globally by at least 1° C by 2050 (and by anywhere from 2° C to 4° C by 2100). The effects of climate change in the Asia Pacific region will vary depending on the country. As a whole, the region is expected to become warmer, but higher latitude areas will experience greater temperature increases than lower latitude areas. Pacific Island nations will likely see smaller changes in temperature and in annual rainfall, however, they will be significantly impacted by rising sea levels to the point where some of the smaller islands may no longer be livable. The coastal areas of South and Southeast Asia as well as parts of China will be threatened by changing precipitation, higher temperatures, and rising sea levels (ADB 2009, 2017; Nelson *et al.* 2010).

Impact on agriculture and food security

As agriculture is dependent on climate and weather, the entire agricultural sector is particularly vulnerable to climate change. Changes in tempera-ture and precipitation threaten agricultural productivity and consequently, the food supply. Extremes from desertification and droughts to typhoons and flooding will most likely have a devastating impact on farmers' liveli-hoods and regional food security.

Various studies commissioned by the Asian Development Bank forecast a decrease in crop yields across the Asia Pacific region. Climate change is expected to reduce both maize and wheat yields, but it is rice yields that will be particularly affected. Without any adaptation or technological improvements, rice yields may decline by up to 50% by 2100 from 1990 levels in Indonesia, the Philippines, Thailand, and Vietnam. In South Asia, the estimated average decrease in yield of all crops is about 8% by 2050, with potential yield reductions for maize and sorghum of 16% and 11%, respectively (ADB 2009, 2017).

The projected negative effects of climate change on crop productivity could lead to higher food prices and as a result, a decline in total demand for cereal and other crops and a reduction in calorie availability across the

Asian region. Central Asia will likely be the most heavily impacted, with projected declines in calorie availability ranging from 15% to 18%. Since childhood malnutrition levels are directly linked to calorie availability, the number of malnourished children is also projected to increase dramatically under climate change. From a geopolitical standpoint, population displacement and conflict as a result of these socio-environmental changes will present the region, and indeed the world, with a new set of challenges (Nelson *et al.* 2010; ADB 2017).

Technology

Internet and mobile phone use

Internet connectivity in the developing world has increased dramatically within the last two decades. Mobile broadband is particularly popular. Most countries in the developing world have skipped fixed-line infrastructure and leapfrogged directly to mobile technology. Driven by income gains and expanding networks in Asia and Africa, mobile phone penetration in developing countries is steadily increasing. By 2010, with its number of mobile phone users reaching 2.6 billion, the Asia-Pacific region accounted for over half the world's mobile cellular subscriptions, making mobile phones the most popular mode of communication. It is estimated that from 2015 to 2020, there will be an additional one billion people in the world using mobile phones. Sixty percent of that growth will come from just six Asian countries with India contributing the largest increase in numbers, followed by China, and rounded out by the newer, fast-growth markets of Indonesia, Pakistan, Bangladesh, and Myanmar (ITU Statshot 2011; GSMA Intelligence 2016).

In East and Southeast Asia, the internet has overtaken traditional media outlets such as TV, radio, or print. This presents new opportunities for customer engagement. According to the 2011 Nielsen Southeast Asia Digital Consumer Report, Singaporeans spend more than 25 hours online each week, followed closely by Filipinos and Malaysians, who respectively spend 21.5 hours and 19.8 hours a week online. Most of these people spend their time online reading, sending email, and accessing social networking platforms. Like in North America and Europe, social networking sites have become an important conduit between companies and consumers in Asia. Sixty-five percent of Filipinos, 60% of Malaysians, and 56% of Singaporeans interact with brands, products or companies via social media. A majority of consumers in Malaysia, Philippines, Singapore and Thailand read and post product reviews online. Given that companies in the region still spend relatively little on online advertising, this is an area that marketers will need to explore in the coming years in order to keep up with the increasing amount of time consumers spend online.

Moreover, Asian consumers, like consumers elsewhere, are increasingly using their phones to access the internet. In 2014, about 30% of the population of Asia, or 1.3 billion people, were mobile internet subscribers. By 2020 the number of mobile internet subscribers in Asia is expected to increase to 2 billion, which would account for over 50% of the worldwide total. As most people in the region access the internet using mobile devices, successful online marketing strategies need to include mobile phone-specific plans (Nielsen 2011; GSMA Intelligence 2015, 2016).

Internet connectivity and agriculture

On the primary producer side, internet connectivity can also help mitigate many of the problems associated with poor communication infrastructure. Farmers often have no way of knowing prices before they travel to the market with their goods. Having accurate and timely market information, especially as it pertains to perishable items, greatly reduces transaction and travel costs. According to one estimate in Sri Lanka, the "cost of information" constitutes 11% of farmers' total cost of production. With internet connectivity, farmers can also more easily share relevant information. They can use SMS to send critical local agricultural information like incidences of pests or crop yields, information that was previously difficult to obtain without expensive research surveys (De Silva 2008; George 2011).

Through leveraging mobile technology, farmers can overcome the barrier of imperfect information. The expansion of open access software has enabled grass-roots community organizations to share information such as extension and advisory services via publicly and privately provided mobile services. Farmers can tap into collective knowledge through crowdsourcing data using mobile phones. For example, Vietnamese state telecom company VinaPhone has a subscription service called Nong Thon Xanh (Green Country) that provides farmers with weather forecasts, pricing information, plant disease alerts, guidelines on relevant state policies, and notifications of abnormal conditions affecting agriculture, all for 10,000 dong (45 cents) per month. In Indonesia, startup 8 Villages offers similar services (George 2011; Yoshida 2016).

AgTech

Applying technology to agriculture in order to improve quantity, quality, and efficiency at various points along the supply chain is nothing new. The past couple of years, however, have seen a surge in interest in the agricultural technology space, allowing many more new and exciting ideas to be tried out. Prior to 2013, the conversation (and the investment) in agtech was predominantly about biotechnology and seed genetics. The agtech sector experienced a "breakout year" in 2014, receiving over $2.36 billion of investment across 264 deals globally (LeClerc and Tilney 2015).

Though agricultural biotechnology remains controversial in many parts of the world since the anti-GMO movement has not abated, it is still considered by many governments to be a valuable technological innovation given expectations of declining yields and extreme weather conditions. The research on high-yield, drought-resistant, and flood-resistant crop varieties could prove very useful in the future. In fact, the governments of China and Brazil have spent significant resources on creating their own domestically researched and developed ag biotech crop varieties. Agtech, however, is more than just ag biotech; it encompasses many other technologies, including:

- Farm management software, sensors, and IoT (Internet of Things), e.g. ag data capturing devices, decision support software, big data analytics.
- Robotics, mechanization, and equipment, e.g. on-farm machinery, automation, drones, grow equipment.
- Novel farming systems, e.g. indoor farms, insect, algae and microbe production.

- Supply chain technologies, e.g. food safety and traceability tech, logistics and transport, food processing.
- Bioenergy and biomaterials, e.g. non-food extraction and processing, feedstock technology.
- Innovative food, e.g. alternative proteins, novel ingredients, and supplements.
- Food marketplace/e-commerce, e.g. online farm-2-consumer, meal kits, specialist consumer food delivery.

In 2016, total investment in agtech was $3.2 billion globally. The U.S. accounts for a large number of those deals, but of the top 10 non-U.S. deals, six were in China. The growing food tech startup scene in China is focused on food delivery, supply chain logistics, and alternative proteins. Singapore is also home to many new agtech ventures. Temasek Trust, the philanthropic arm of the city-state's sovereign wealth fund, has developed a new variety of high-yield rice that can withstanding extreme weather conditions using marker-assisted selection technology. Temasek Rice, as their product is called, is currently being grown in Indonesia. Garuda Robotics, a Singaporean startup, is using drone and sensor technology to map and capture more accurate data on Southeast Asian plantation farms so as to help these plantations tailor their land management plans to account for variations in weather, rainfall, soil quality, fertilizer, etc. (Yoshida 2016; Agfunder 2017).

There are many opportunities at the intersection of agriculture and big data. This trend is just starting in Asia and the prospects for "smart agriculture" in the region look bright given the ingenuity of local entrepreneurs and the exigencies of ensuring a steady food supply in the face of population increases and environmental degradation. To address the negative impact of climate change on agriculture, technological innovation is more important than ever.

In Summary

With the region's rising incomes and increasing populations, the outlook for Asian agribusiness is strong. In the coming years, the industry will be shaped by the trends discussed in the research note:

- Continued diffusion of supermarkets as the preferred method of food retail as more people emphasize convenience and time efficiency;
- Continued urbanization, which in conjunction with rising incomes means an increased demand for meat as people shift to diets with higher protein content;
- Increased intraregional trade provides opportunities for the region's producers to sell to neighboring countries;
- Climate change as a looming threat for the entire world that will require ever greater technological innovation;
- Increased consumer activity online due to greater internet connectivity and widespread adoption of mobile phone technology means fresh, new ideas for online customer engagement are needed.

The food and agriculture sector in Asia remains a dynamic and complex space. The overview of the trends and drivers for this industry provided above indicate that challenges and opportunities alike lie ahead for the region's agribusinesses.

References

Agfunder. 2017. *Agtech Funding Report: Year in Review 2016.* [Online]. San Franscisco: Agfunder. [Accessed 26 November 2017]. Available from: https://research.agfunder.com/2016/AgFunder-Agtech-Investing-Report-2016.pdf.

Asia Regional Integration Center. 2017. *Integration Indicators.* [Online]. [Accessed 26 November 2017]. Available from: https://aric.adb.org/integrationindicators.

Asian Development Bank. 2009. *Building Climate Resilience in the Agriculture Sector of Asia and the Pacific.* Mandaluyong City: Asian Development Bank.

Asian Development Bank. 2017. *A Region at Risk — The Human Dimensions of Climate Change in Asia and the Pacific.* Mandaluyong City: Asian Development Bank.

Brown, O. 2005. *Supermarket Buying Power, Global Commodity Chains and Smallholder Farmers in the Developing World.* New York City: UNDP Human Development Report Office.

Claxton, R. 2013. *Increasing Asian Meat Demand Creates Opportunities and is a Major Factor in Supporting Global Livestock Prices.* [Newsletter]. Paris: International Meat Secretariat.

De Silva, H. 2008. Using ICTs to Create Efficiencies in Agricultural Markets: Some Findings from Sri Lanka. Ottawa: International Development Research Center.

George, T. *et al.* 2011. *ICT in Agriculture: Connecting Smallholders to Knowledge, Networks, and Institutions.* [Online]. Washington, D.C.: World Bank. [Accessed 27 November 2017]. Available from: http://documents.worldbank.org/curated/en/455701468340165132/ICT-in-agriculture-connecting-smallholders-to-knowledge-networks-and-institutions.

GSMA Intelligence. 2015. *Mobile Internet Usage Challenges in Asia — Awareness, Literacy and Local Content.* [Online]. London: GSMA Intelligence. [Accessed 27 November 2017]. Available from: https://www.gsma.com/mobilefordevelopment/wp-content/uploads/2015/07/150709-asia-local-content-final.pdf.

GSMA Intelligence. 2016. *Global Mobile Trends.* [Online]. London: GSMA Intelligence. [Accessed 27 November 2017]. Available from: https://www.gsmaintelligence.com/research/2016/10/global-mobile-trends/580/.

Haggblade, S., Hazell, P. and Reardon, T. 2007. *Transforming the Rural Nonfarm Economy.* Baltimore: Johns Hopkins University Press.

Hu, D., Reardon, T., Rozelle, S., Timmer, P. and Wang, H. 2004. The Emergence of Supermarkets with Chinese Characteristics: Challenges and Opportunities for China's Agricultural Development. *Development Policy Review.* **22**(5). pp.557-586.

Huang, J., Wang, X. and Qui, H. 2012. *Small-scale Farmers in China in the Face of Modernization and Globalisation.* London/The Hague: IIED/HIVOS.

ITU Statshot. 2011. *From Billions to Trillions: Ubiquitous ICTs?* [Online]. [Accessed 27 November 2017]. Available from: http://www.itu.int/net/pressoffice/stats/2011/02/index.aspx#.VZoOEvlVikp.

LeClerc, R. and Tilney, M. 2015. AgTech is the New Queen of Green. 1 April. *TechCrunch.* [Online]. [Accessed 27 November 2017]. Available from: https://techcrunch.com/2015/04/01/the-new-queen-of-green/.

Moinuddin, M. 2013. Economic Integration and Trade Liberalization in South Asia. 27 August. *Asian Development Bank Institute.* [Online]. [Accessed 27 November 2017]. Available from: http://www.asiapathways-adbi.org/2013/08/economic-integration-and-trade-liberalization-in-south-asia/#sthash.i7y1vCd1.dpuf.

Nelson, G. C. *et al.* 2010. *Food Security, Farming, and Climate Change to 2050: Scenarios, Results, Policy Options.* Washington, D.C.: International Food Policy Research.

Nielsen. 2011. Surging Internet Usage in Southeast Asia Reshaping the Media Landscape. 10 November. *Nielsen Newswire.* [Online]. [Accessed 27 November 2017]. Available from: http://www.nielsen.com/us/en/insights/news/2011/surging-internet-usage-in-southeast-asia-reshaping-the-media-landscape.html.

OECD. 2017. *Meat Consumption.* [Online]. [Accessed 8 August 2017]. Available from: https://data.oecd.org/agroutput/meat-consumption.htm.

Pinstrup-Andersen, P. and Watson II, D.D. 2011. *Food Policy for Developing Countries: The Role of Government in Global, National, and Local Food Systems.* Ithaca: Cornell University Press.

Reardon, T., Timmer, C. P., Barrett, C. B. and Berdegué, J. 2003. The Rise of Supermarkets in Africa, Asia, and Latin America. *American Journal of Agricultural Economics.* **85**(5). pp.1140-6.

Reardon, T., Timmer, P. and Minten, B. 2012. Supermarket Revolution in Asia and Emerging Development Strategies to Include Small Farmers. *Proceedings of the National Academy of Sciences.* **109**(31). pp.12332-7.

Seifert, D. 2003. Efficient Consumer Response as the Origin of CPFR. In: Seifert, D. ed. *Collaborative Planning, Forecasting, and Replenishment: How to Create a Supply Chain Advantage.* New York: American Management Association, pp.1-26.

United Nations, Department of Economic and Social Affairs, Population Division. 2014. *World Urbanization Prospects: The 2014 Revision.* [Online]. Custom data acquired via website. https://esa.un.org/Unpd/Wup/.

United Nations, Department of Economic and Social Affairs, Population Division. 2015. World Urbanization Prospects: The 2014 Revision. New York City: United Nations.

Yoshida, T. 2016. Asia Digs Deep to Upgrade its Agriculture. Nikkei Asian Review. [Online]. 8 December. [Accessed 27 November 2017]. Available from: https://asia.nikkei.com/Business/Companies/Asia-digs-deep-to-upgrade-its-agriculture.

Chapter 2

Soyuz Foods International: Small Fruit, Big Dreams

Lin Fu,[1] Katherine Lyon,[1] Ran Kim,[1] Sen Cathy Chan,[1]
Chris Wien,[1] and Ralph D. Christy[1]

Introduction

After talking to yet another interested buyer, Helen del Rosario hung up the phone with a sigh. She had been fielding such calls from potential customers she had met at a trade show for a while now. The expressions of interest in her calamansi extract was the result of her marketing efforts at trade shows, but the volume the international buyers demanded was beyond the current manufacturing capacity of her company, Soyuz Foods International, Inc. ("Soyuz"). Expanding her processing facilities before a steady supply of fresh calamansi was available year round would be a risky move that could jeopardize her company financially—but how could she obtain customers before she had increased capacity?

As owner and general manager of Soyuz, a privately held calamansi processor operating in Manila and Davao City, Philippines, Helen had been promoting the company's calamansi extract at trade shows for the past few years. Her goal in participating in the trade shows was as much to advertise Soyuz as it was to promote the calamansi industry as a whole beyond the Philippines. Calamansi, a sour-tasting citrus fruit found throughout Southeast Asia, is particularly popular in the Philippines, but hardly known on the international market.

To promote calamansi internationally, Helen had combined forces with other Filipino calamansi processors and established the Philippines Calamansi Association Incorporated (PCAI).[2] Inspired by the story

---

[1]SMART Program, Cornell University.
[2]Originating from a calamansi interest group, the Philippine Calamansi Association Incorporated (PCAI) is an industry association with the mission "to elevate the Philippine Calamansi to a higher standard and promote it to the international market." While the members of PCAI refer to themselves as a "calamansi cluster," PCAI is truly an industry association. Membership is offered to interested businesses that commit to meeting the high quality standards set by PCAI. The main goals of PCAI are establishing international

of the New Zealand kiwifruit and its trajectory from the little-known "Chinese gooseberry" to a fruit found on supermarkets shelves around the world, Helen and the other calamansi processors hope to similarly "claim" calamansi for the Philippines. PCAI is ramping up efforts to put the "Philippine lemon" on the map by expanding overall marketing for calamansi-derived products and by increasing awareness of and support for the industry domestically, initiatives in which Helen is heavily involved. While Helen expects that these efforts will likely benefit Soyuz in the long term, she is also searching for the best short-term growth strategy to keep the company profitable. Soyuz currently exports high-quality calamansi extract to South Korea, and Helen would like to expand both the company's market reach and its product range. Her eyes searched the Manila skyline as she contemplated the possibilities for these moves and the inevitable challenges that each held for Soyuz.

Calamansi: The Philippine Lemon

Calamansi (*Citronella microcarpa*) is a fruit in the citrus family that is widely used in Filipino and other Southeast Asian cuisines. Other names for this fruit include cala-mondin, golden lime, and calaman-darin. Slightly smaller in size than a golf ball, calamansi has a thin, dark green peel that turns orange when fully ripened. Extremely sour in taste, with a flavor profile similar to a lime, it is commonly used in mari-nades, beverages, and as an additive in scented beauty and cleaning products in the Philippines.

Fig. 1: Calamansi fruit.

brand recognition, promoting increased quality and standards amongst Filipino calamansi processors, overcoming the supply side bottleneck, and promoting calamansi research needs among public research institutions.

Fig. 2: Calamansi tree.

While many in the Philippines claim that calamansi is indigenous to their country, the origin of the fruit is unclear. Nevertheless, calamansi is grown and consumed throughout the Philippines, although consumption statistics are difficult to come by as many families have one or two trees in their own backyard for personal use. The Philippines is not the only country, however, that grows and uses calamansi. Other Southeast Asian countries, such as Thailand, as well as China's Hainan Province also grow and consume it.

Commercially, calamansi is grown in orchards all over the Philippines. Farmers may grow the fruit as a single crop, more typical of large farms, or in smaller orchards that include other types of tree crops, for example, coconuts. In order to ensure that the trees can endure the monsoon season in the Philippines, calamansi is often grafted onto the rootstock of other native species, such as mandarin trees. Calamansi is harvested and sorted by hand. Once harvested, calamansi is sold either to the retail market as fresh fruit or to processors who make various commercial products from it.

The Philippine Context

The Philippines, an island nation in the Southeast Asia region, was the 44th largest economy in the world in 2011, with a GDP of US$224.8 billion. It is a lower middle income country according to World Bank classification — its 2011 GDP per capita was US$2,370 — and is middle of the pack in terms of economic performance within the Association of Southeast Asian Nations (ASEAN), the regional geopolitical and economic cooperation organization to which the country belongs.

The Philippines gained independence in 1946 after more than 300 years as a Spanish colony, followed by a short-lived republic, a period under American control, and occupation by the Japanese during World War II. Currently a presidential democracy, the country has seen its share of political turmoil. Since independence, there have been 11 presidents, numerous allegations of and investigations into corruption at all levels of government, several unsuccessful attempts at land reform, and a recently concluded secessionist movement. Income inequality remains a major source of social tension within the country.

In recent years, the Philippine government has had an annual target GDP growth rate of 5%. In 2011, the Philippine economy grew 3.7%, slower than expected due to weak public spending and weak demand from abroad. The economy is highly dependent on remittance-driven household consumption and the domestic services sector, including the fast-growing business process outsourcing (BPO) industry. In the first half of 2012, the economy posted a growth rate of 6.4%, the fastest since 2010. The country is outpacing its Southeast Asian neighbors and surpassing analyst forecasts (World Bank 2012; Office of the President of the Philippines 2012).

The business environment

On the World Bank's general Ease of Doing Business Index for 2013, the Philippines ranked 138th (out of 185 economies). This position puts the Philippines at a disadvantage when compared to ASEAN countries such as Thailand or Malaysia, which rank 18th and 12th, respectively. The trends in new firm creation also point to the relative difficulty small and medium enterprises (SMEs) encounter when navigating government rules and regulations. The 2009 World Bank Entrepreneurship Database cites the Philippines' business entry density rate (the number of newly registered corporations per 1,000 working-age people) at 0.19. This is among the lowest in the region, where Indonesia reports in at 0.27, Thailand at 0.59, and Malaysia at 2.42.

Despite the apparent challenge of starting a business, the Philippine government's stated policy toward SMEs is generally supportive. The National SME Development Agenda calls for greater communication between the different agencies that support SMEs as part of their mandate. This integrated strategy to foster SME growth offers government assistance in many areas such as technology, product development, finance, training, and marketing.

The agricultural sector of the Philippines

Agriculture ranks among the major economic activities in the Philippines. The contribution of agriculture to the country's 2011 GDP was 11.5%; moreover, the sector employs a third of the country's workforce (Navarro and Yap 2013). While agricultural exports have been important to the growth of the domestic agricultural sector and of the economy in general, its contribution to the Philippines' GDP in percentage terms is declining.[3] Still, the government hopes to improve the competitiveness of the country's agricultural commodities in the international market. The Philippines' share (8.3%) and value of agricultural products to total exports is the lowest among comparably-sized ASEAN countries — the Philippines counted US$3.2 billion in agricultural exports in 2009.

Within Philippine agriculture, fruits and vegetables represent a dynamic sub-sector, accounting for close to a third of total agricultural output by value. Many of the crops that the government has designated as high-value commercial crops (HVCC) are fruits and vegetables. Only one-tenth

---

[3]According to the Senate Economic Planning Office (SEPO), agricultural exports from the Philippines grew at an annual rate of 9.66% from 1980 to 2010, from approximately US$2.2 billion to US$4.1 billion. Agricultural exports as a share of GDP, however, has declined from 6.03% in 1980 to 2.05% in 2010 because non-traditional manufactured goods as well as the service and industrial sectors now represent a more important part of the Philippine economy.

of total agricultural area, however, is allotted to growing these products (Department of Agriculture, Philippines; SEPO 2012; Briones 2008). Fruit and vegetable crops are neglected in part because public investment in agriculture has mostly gone toward the rice sector. For example, while the rice sector received almost 60% of the agriculture budget in 2012, HVCC was allotted only 2.18%. Some argue that pursuit of the government's rice self-sufficiency objective is at the expense of the country's comparative advantage in high-value fruits and vegetables, rubber, oil palm, coffee, coconut, etc. Others contend that focusing on HVCC may reduce food production and lead to food insecurity (SEPO 2012).

Inside Soyuz

Vision, mission, and strategic direction

Soyuz's vision is "to export our native calamansi and other citrus fruits in single-strength concentrate and powdered form with quality that meets international standards." Soyuz's boldly-stated mission is "to forge partnerships with farmer groups and agricultural entrepreneurs through sustainable development initiatives, in order to improve their living conditions and minimize poverty in the farming sector." Soyuz did not start out in the calamansi business; in the early days, the company produced and sold various pureed fruit products before settling upon the idea of introducing the world to one of the Philippines' best loved culinary additives, calamansi. By pairing the company's socially conscious mission with promoting calamansi, Helen saw an opportunity to not only contribute to poverty alleviation in the Philippines, but also to introduce a new "super food" for consumers worldwide. Out of this combined vision Soyuz has grown into one of the most technologically advanced calamansi processors and exporters in the Philippines today. Incorporated in August 2003, Soyuz Foods currently processes calamansi into an extract on its own custom-fitted machinery in a rented facility in Davao City. The company also has an office in Manila, out of which Helen manages sales to her main customers in South Korea and actively advocates for the calamansi industry.

Consistent with its socially conscious mission, under Helen's leadership, Soyuz has been involved in contributing to poverty reduction and economic development in Mindanao, an area that has suffered tremendously from decades of fighting between the government and the local Islamic insurgency.[4] In Mindanao, the company has been working with Catholic Relief Services, an international NGO with a strong local presence in the Philippines, to establish direct supplier relationships with farmers in the region. In order to secure a steady supply of fresh calamansi to their nearby processing facility, Soyuz is willing to pay farmers a consistent price, above the local breakeven cost of production. Paying a consistent, elevated price should shield the farmers from the vicissitudes of the calamansi wholesale market and contribute to raising living standards. However, securing a steady supply of calamansi has been a challenge for Soyuz, in part because Mindanao, while an ideal location for a socially conscious business, is also the region where farmers have the least amount of training and access to extension and other support services. This illustrates a tension between the company's core business objective, to become a prominent calamansi producer and processor in the Philippines and internationally, and its socially-oriented objective to promote poverty alleviation in Mindanao.

Funding and organizational structure

To date, all company development and expansion has been funded by Helen and her husband, Arnie. Recently, several potential customers have reached out to Soyuz to discuss large orders, but these companies are un-willing to guarantee purchases until Soyuz can demonstrate greater pro-duction capacity. For their part, Arnie and Helen are hesitant to continue investing their own capital into the company without a guarantee of at least breaking even on the investment. While the two of them would ide-ally like to fund the expansion from the company's own sources, they are open to the idea of supply chain financing, in which their customers could co-invest in plant expansion. Not only would supply chain financing

---

[4]Mindanao is the second largest and easternmost island in the Philippines and is the eighth most populous island in the world. It is also one of the three island groups in the country, along with Luzon and Visayas. According to the National Statistics Coordination Board, Mindanao is the country's poorest region with a poverty rate of 40% compared to about 18% in Luzon. Six out of the country's ten poorest provinces are located in Mindanao.

provide funds for expansion, but it would also symbolize a strong commitment to a long-term business relationship by their customers. Until financial resources outside of the del Rosarios' personal savings are available to
Soyuz, expanding the company's production capacity remains a challenge.

Soyuz currently employs a total of 21 people, the majority of whom
are production workers. Arnie is the company president, while Helen is
the General Manager in charge of marketing. An important marketing
channel for Soyuz has been trade shows, which Helen has attended in
part using financial support from the Department of Trade and Industry
(DTI). Helen also directs product development, primarily by connecting
to outside research institutions such as the Department of Science and
Technology when the ideas for new products are beyond Soyuz's internal
research capacity.

According to Helen, a current challenge for Soyuz is that none of the
current employees have training in marketing, logistics, or accounting. As
Figure 3 illustrates, at present the company has several unfilled positions.
At present, Helen and Arnie do not think any of their employees are ready
to take on managerial responsibilities.

Product development

Using the calamansi extract the company already produces, Soyuz's food
scientists are developing a ready-to-drink (RTD) calamansi beverage and
calamansi concentrate. The calamansi concentrate is the least developed of
these new products: before developing this product further, Soyuz would
like to ensure that their process of making concentrate—involving water
extraction through low pressure, partial vacuum evaporation—does not
strip the resulting product of all its Vitamin C.

Producing the calamansi extract utilizes only 28% of the fresh fruit, so,
in order to reduce waste and utilize the remaining 72% of the fruit, Soyuz
is exploring potential new products. Through collaboration with research
institutes, Soyuz has found a way to utilize over 75% of the total calamansi
fruit by also producing essential oil and dietary fiber.

Soyuz strives to maintain the highest standards of product quality.
HACCP (Hazard Analysis & Critical Control Points) and halal-certified,
Soyuz aims to be a quality leader in the calamansi processing industry.

This commitment to quality has led Helen to forge new paths. In 2005, Soyuz initiated a research project with the Department of Science and Technology's Industrial Technology Development Institute to identify, test, and develop processes and packaging that would allow processed calamansi to be exported to other countries at a global quality standard.

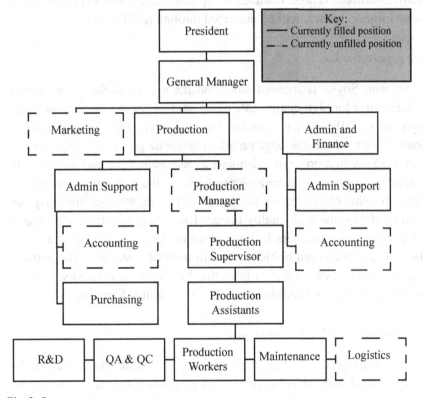

Fig. 3: Soyuz organogram.

Soyuz's marketing strategy

As stated in its vision statement, Soyuz wants to expand the reach of cala-mansi - and what they believe to be the fruit's health benefits[5] - beyond the borders of the Philippines. This passion underlies their strict adherence to

---

[5]Filipino folklore considers the calamansi fruit as a remedy for many ailments, including aging and sickness. To date, very little research has been done to scientifically validate the

exceptional quality standards. Soyuz's calamansi products have a guaranteed shelf life of at least one year at room temperature, without the need for freezing, refrigeration, or any artificial preservatives. With the exception of the ready-to-drink product currently under development, all new products are intended for commercial food and beverage customers. The ready-to-drink beverage, intended to replicate the calamansi juice made in many Filipino homes, will be marketed through retail channels.

The export market

At present, Soyuz is focused solely on the export market. The current opportunities for high quality calamansi products lie mainly in East Asian markets. In 2010, Helen attended her first international trade show in South Korea, where she began marketing Soyuz products. She successfully sold her first order of calamansi extract before the end of that year. Marketing promotions at trade shows focus on the nutritional content and health benefits of calamansi; the premium pricing strategy currently utilized reinforces the high quality image. The extract is currently packaged for commercial customers in large pouches, but it is displayed at trade shows in green-colored bottles for health-minded customers. The bottle is easy to grab and carry, with a label that highlights eco-friendly, healthy, on-the-go themes in addition to nutritional content information.

The domestic market for calamansi

The two most popular calamansi products on the domestic market are the ready-to-drink calamansi beverages and a calamansi-flavored sugar syrup (essentially, a calamansi lemonade concentrate). As Soyuz currently does not produce either of these products, it does not have a presence in the domestic market. If the company moves forward with plans to introduce a ready-to-drink calamansi beverage, it will face stiff competition from local and international food and beverage industry giants, such as Cenmaco, Coca Cola, Zest-O, and others.

---

wide range of health benefits, although Soyuz has commissioned a clinical trial, which is in its final stage. Once completed, the trial will clarify the hematological, antimicrobial, antioxidant, antiangiogenic, and dietary effects of calamansi consumption.

Domestically produced calamansi beverages and concentrate-syrups are currently competing with products backed by the sizeable marketing power of global food and beverage companies. In the retail setting, calamansi drinks compete for shelf space with all other beverages, including sodas, teas, and fruit juices.

Fig. 4: A selection of Soyuz products.

Due to this intense competition, the lifespan of a product may be very short. In order to maintain consumer interests and outpace competitors, beverage manufacturers are constantly introducing new products and attempting to differentiate their beverages. The most recent market trend is an appeal to health-conscious consumers. A few examples of new health-oriented products include Kraft Foods' Tang Pulpy, Bintang Toedjoe's Extra Joss Enerjuice, and United Laboratories' CarbTrim Ice Tea Mix (Euromonitor International 2017). With Helen's current efforts to research the health benefits of calamansi, there may be an entry for Soyuz into this market.

The export market for calamansi

While the export market for calamansi products is not as saturated as the domestic market, the competitive environment is no less intense. With its sights set on East Asia, Soyuz currently exports to South Korea and is cultivating interest among Japanese buyers. As Soyuz aims for additional foreign markets, it will not only be competing with other calamansi products, but with other citrus flavors as well. Calamansi may be the preferred citrus flavor domestically, but many substitutes are available outside of the Philippines. At the regional level, in East Asia, the Okinawa shikuwasa, a Japanese citrus fruit, is the main competitor for calamansi. Grown almost exclusively in Okinawa, Japan, the limited production volume and touted nutritional benefits have led to sales of shikuwasa at a high price point. Internationally, calamansi has yet to distinguish itself in the citrus market, historically led by lemons, limes, and oranges (USDA 2017). However, the use of lemons and limes is less common in the Southeast Asian region due to import tariffs on these agricultural goods (Spreen 2010), which may bode well for local products.

In the export market, Soyuz is targeting industrial buyers who will likely further process the calamansi extract into beverages. Therefore, fruit extracts and concentrates as well as ready-to-drink products are potential competitors for market share. As calamansi gains a greater following outside of the Philippines, more Filipino companies are competing for a share of the export market. For example, Southern Partners Fair Trade Corporation (SPFTC) and CEMS Food General Merchandise have started selling their calamansi extract through East Asia-based online distributors. SPFTC calamansi extract retails at US$5.25 per 1000 ml (in comparison, Soyuz sells its 500 ml pouch of extract for US$2.18). In addition to SPFTC and CEMS, other PCAI members have either already entered the export market or are actively pursuing East Asian customers. Both Greenchoice and Weambard already have distributors in East Asia, and Serramonte recently began contacting potential buyers in South Korea.

In the ready-to-drink segment of the market, Soyuz faces competition not just from multinational corporations like Coca Cola and Pepsi, but from established East Asian food and beverage distributors. These competitors include Wahaha and Vitasoy in the Greater China region, and

Lotte Chilsung and Dong A. Otsuka in South Korea. As larger regional food and beverage manufacturers and distributors pursue increased market share, many of them are aligning themselves with multinationals. Lotte Chilsung, a unit of South Korea's Lotte Group, recently became the largest shareholder in Pepsi-Cola Products Philippines, after acquiring 34.4% in the company (Bloomberg 2010).

Other Challenges Facing Soyuz

The challenges currently facing Soyuz can be grouped into two categories. Some emanate simply from being a part of a nascent industry, and therefore certain key structures, regulations, and practices are not yet in place. Other challenges are particular to Soyuz itself. Below are some of the key challenges, beginning with those affecting the entire industry.

Industry-level challenges

Insufficient supplies

Not having sufficient supplies of raw material is not only an issue for Soyuz but for the entire industry. The PCAI is confident that cooperation with government agencies and increased outreach to farmers will help them overcome the supply-side bottleneck. The Department of Agriculture has responded to their call by organizing forums with farmers in the Davao, Agusan, and Tarlac production regions and by supporting the first Calamansi Congress held in September 2013. In addition to farmer outreach, PCAI has also been in talks with public research institutions about addressing the gaps in agronomic and processing knowledge of calamansi.

Lack of a formal marketplace

In the long run, Helen would like to source all of the company's fresh calamansi directly from farmers; however, at present, Soyuz only gets about 25% of what it needs from farmers. This is not unlike other companies, who also source the bulk of their raw materials through middlemen. Middlemen are prominent players in the Philippine fresh produce industry, where no formal marketplace exists for many products, including calamansi. Middlemen thrive because, due to the geographic dispersion of farmers and poor transportation infrastructure, a centralized physical marketplace has not yet been established. Neither is there a virtual marketplace, as most farmers do not have ready access to internet. Since middlemen take a portion of the price paid by processors, at certain times of the year farmers receive very little for their produce. In short, in the absence of a formal market, both calamansi farmers and processors have trouble finding up-to-date, reliable information about pricing and availability.

Information gaps

Besides such hard-to-obtain market information, Soyuz Foods – and the calamansi industry as a whole – face additional information gaps. As the industry is in its infancy, very little research has been done on optimal production methods, processing, and packaging. Conducting such research is expensive and time-consuming and is generally undertaken in a partnership with government agencies and public research institutions. The Department of Agriculture does sponsor some of this research, but only 1.6% of their annual budget goes towards research (Gazmin 2013).

Since calamansi products for export must adhere to global food standards, another source of government support for SMEs is the Department of Science and Technology, which has sponsored (or co-sponsored) research into processing and packaging. Soyuz has partnered with the Department in the past, but, even with government support, such partnerships are too expensive to sustain at the company's current level of operation.

International Brand Recognition

After observing the failure of Filipino mango farmers to protect the "Manila Mango" brand on the international market, PCAI is determined to protect their products from imitators. Manila Mango is a proprietary name given to Atualfo mangoes, a variety which differs in size and color from the more common Haden and Tommy Atkins commercial mango varieties. When the Manila Mango was introduced to the international

Philippine Calamansi
Association, Inc.

Fig. 5: PCAI logo (received from Soyuz Foods).

market by Filipino farmers, it became immensely popular — but the name was not registered with the appropriate international intellectual property rights (IPR) authorities. Without geographic indication, a type of IPR protection, the Philippines did not have exclusive rights to use the Manila Mango label. In fact, most mangoes with this label in North America today come from Mexico, where businessmen took advantage of the booming market for this particular type of mango and its unprotected name. To avoid a similar situation, PCAI is currently pursuing geographic indication for calamansi from both regional and international IPR authorities to ensure that the calamansi name is associated strictly with the Philippines. In addition to the geographic indication efforts, PCAI has recently registered its own logo (Figure 5) for use as a quality and origin seal on calamansi products.

Quality and standardization

Currently, there are no content or production method requirements beyond those enforced by the Food and Drug Administration of the Philippines to ensure that calamansi products meet a uniform quality standard. As a result, the PCAI is pushing for increased product standardization within the industry. Regulation pertaining to content requirements, production methods, and quality are viewed as necessary steps for strengthening calamansi products on the international market. Not only will standardization increase consistency for customers, but regulations to control quality benchmarks are necessary in an industry where backyard processing operations dominate the rural domestic market.

Company-level challenges

Capacity and location

Helen's current labor force and equipment are sufficient to meet the needs of existing customers; however, the processing plant may need to expand if Soyuz begins to fill large commercial orders on a regular basis. But even with an expanded production capacity, the company will likely face the same critical bottleneck as many other Filipino calamansi processors: sourcing an adequate amount of raw fruit can be difficult.

A particular challenge for Soyuz is that, while an industry cluster has developed in Oriental Mindoro, where approximately 57% of the country's calamansi is grown, Soyuz is located in Davao, where Helen believes her company can have the greatest social impact. However, Davao currently produces only 5,080 metric tons (2.8%) of the country's total calamansi, and the per-hectare productivity is approximately 30% of that of farms in Mindoro. Productivity in Davao is hampered by suboptimal production methods, such as improper pest management and fertilizer regimes, as well as by frequent natural disasters such as typhoons.

Finding a steady supply of calamansi is also a challenge for Soyuz and the rest of the industry. While calamansi trees can produce up to three full crops per year and production can be increased by better agricultural practices such as fertilization and irrigation, a handful of more advanced, farmers have begun using these techniques to manipulate production timing. The large majority of farmers either choose not to alter the production cycle or do not have the technical knowledge required to do so. All this results in a highly seasonal fresh calamansi market, with the accompanying price variation. At present, price instability is the main barrier to convincing farmers to focus more exclusively on growing calamansi.

An obvious solution to the problem of raw material shortage would be to increase the land area under production. However, this also has its challenges as land can be difficult to acquire and retain in an ever-changing political climate. Currently, the average size of a calamansi farm is 0.85 hectares (Garganera 2008).

Implementation of current agronomic technology across the country is the only short-term solution for increasing and stabilizing supply, but may not provide large enough production increases to sustain the long-term industry demand from Soyuz and other processors. Moreover, increasing production off-season will require raw material prices to rise beyond the ability of processors to pay.

Underdeveloped international marketing channels

Having achieved the ability to export calamansi extract, Soyuz's biggest challenge has been finding cost-effective marketing methods and attracting international customers. The company's target market for calamansi extract is commercial processors and distributors in East Asia. Without an online marketplace for calamansi and its by-products, Soyuz must rely on its website, personal networking, and industry trade shows to establish customers. Even when Helen is able to establish contact with potential customers, language barriers and unfamiliarity with foreign market structures often result in difficult transactions.

Towards the Big Dream

As Helen sat in the Manila traffic, she asked her driver, Mang Tony, to turn down the music so she could phone her staff in Davao City to relay a change to an existing order. Keeping Soyuz's existing customers happy was an essential part of laying the groundwork for the company's expansion. Such growth, however, would require Soyuz to overcome a myriad of challenges. At the firm-level, Helen wondered how she could increase her processing volume. She was already working with Catholic Relief Services to source calamansi directly from farmers in Mindanao, but additional tonnage was still needed. In her role as president of PCAI, Helen hoped that the group's upcoming Calamansi Congress in Mindoro would be able to bolster public interest in promoting calamansi abroad. The Calamansi Congress would be co-sponsored by the governor of the province, but beyond that, it was uncertain how much help PCAI could realistically expect from the government. Given limited financial resources in both the public and private sector, prioritizing goals would be necessary, but PCAI was yet unsure about how to go about maximizing their collective potential growth. Moreover, it was unclear if and when the interests of PCAI and Soyuz might diverge. Such concerns percolated through Helen's mind as she worked toward increasing revenue and profits at Soyuz.

References

Bloomberg News. 2010. Lotte to Buy 34.4% Stake in Pepsi Philippines, Become Largest Investor. Bloomberg News. [Online]. 16 September. [Accessed 27 November 2017]. Available from: http://www.bloomberg.com/news/2010-09-16/lotte-to-buy-34-4-stake-in-pepsi-philippines-become-largest-investor.html.

Briones, M. R. 2008. Agricultural Diversification and The Fruits and Vegetables Subsector: Policy Issues and Development Constraints in the Philippines. Philippine Journal of Development. [Online]. 35(2). pp.77-102. [Accessed 27 November 2017]. Available from: http://dirp4.pids.gov.ph/ris/pjd/pidspjd08-2fruitsubsector.pdf.

Department of Science and Technology, Republic of the Philippines. [no date]. Calamansi Processing. Retrieved from: http://region6.dost.gov.ph/dost-livelihood-technologies/.

Euromonitor International. 2017. Soft Drinks in the Philippines. [Online]. London: Euromonitor International. [Accessed 27 November 2017]. Available from: http://www.euromonitor.com/soft-drinks-in-the-philippines/report.

Garganera, J. V. 2008. Value Chain Analysis of Calamansi. 30 June. First Regional Forum & Training Workshop Linking Small Farmers to Markets. [Online]. [Accessed 27 November 2027]. Available from: http://firstlsfmrtw.blogspot.com/2008/06/session-3-presentation-2-value-chain.html.

Gazmin, L. (Director of Department of Agriculture, Agribusiness Marketing and Assistance Services). 2013. Interview with (missing interviewer name). 8 January, Mandaue City.

Nations Online Project, Map of the Philippines. [Online]. [Accessed 27 November 2027]. Available from: http://www.nationsonline.org/oneworld/map/philippines-political-map.htm.

National Statistical Coordination Board. 2012. NSCB releases 2009 City and Municipal Level Poverty Estimate. [Online]. [Accessed 27 November 2027]. Available from: https://psa.gov.ph/content/nscb-releases-2009-city-and-municipal-level-poverty-estimate-0.

Navarro, A. M. and Yap, J. T. 2013. The Philippine economy in 2012 and prospects for 2013. [Online]. Makati City: Philippine Institute for Development Studies, Development Research News. [Accessed 27 November 2017]. Available from: https://dirp3.pids.gov.ph/ris/drn/pidsdrn13-1_rev5.pdf.

Garganera, J. V. 2008. Value Chain Analysis of Calamansi. [Online]. PhilDHRRA-LSFM Project. [Accessed 1 December 2017]. Retrieved from: http://firstlsfmrtw.blogspot.com/2008/06/session-3-presentation-2-value-chain.html.

Poquiz, J. 2012. Philippine Economy 5.9% Growth One of Highest in Asia. [Online]. Manila: Office of the President of the Philippines. [Accessed 27 November 2017]. Available from:http://www.competitive.org.ph/node/505.

Senate Economic Planning Office. 2012. Philippine Agricultural Exports at a Glance. [Online]. [Accessed 27 November 2017]. Available from: http://www.senate.gov.ph/ publications/AG%202012-02%20-%20Agricultural%20Exports.pdf.

Spreen, T. H. 2010. Projections of World Production and Consumption of Citrus to 2010. [Online]. [Accessed 27 November 2017]. Available from: http://www.fao.org/docrep/003/ x6732e/x6732e02.htm.

USDA, Foreign Agricultural Service. 2017. Citrus: World Markets and Trade. [Online]. [Accessed 27 November 2017]. Available from: http://www.fas.usda.gov/psdonline/ circulars/citrus.pdf.

World Bank. [no date]. Doing Business. [Online]. [Accessed 27 November 2017]. Available from: http://www.doingbusiness.org/.

World Bank. [no date]. Entrepreneurship. [Online]. [Accessed 27 November 2017]. Available from: http://www.doingbusiness.org/data/exploretopics/entrepreneurship.

World Bank. 2012. From Stability to Prosperity for All. [Online]. Manila: World Bank. [Accessed 27 November 2017]. Available from: http://documents.worldbank.org/curated/ en/763051468094148613/pdf/698330WP0P12740ch020120FINAL0051012.pdf.

Chapter 3

CEO Agrifood Limited: Growing Through Value-Addition

Faraz Haqqi,[1] Dora Heng,[1] Lindsey Joseph,[1] Kittikun Songsomboon,[1] Ralph D. Christy,[1] Kulapa Kudilok,[2] and Ravissa Suchato[2]

Introduction

Pita "Tim" Limjaroenrat returned his phone to his pocket and immediately set about locating his overnight bag. He had been asked to travel to Singburi, a city north of Bangkok, Thailand, where his brother Pasinn, the Director of Operations of CEO Agrifood Ltd., had called a meeting to discuss retooling the company's rice bran oil production facility. As the Managing Director, Tim alone had the authority to approve purchases, such as the needed updates to bring the most current technology available to the company.

As he gathered his belongings in preparation for the visit, he glanced out the window of his high-rise condominium in central Bangkok. The streets below were uncharacteristically deserted, as the city braced itself for another day of anti-government protests. In the early months of 2014, the protests had become a central part of life in Bangkok, and Tim worried about their impact on Thailand's economy and on his company.

With a background in both the private and public sectors, Tim could appreciate both sides of the current political debate, which had its origins in a redistributive agricultural subsidy program. Although unsure of how the situation would be resolved, he was certain that a company like CEO, which produces value added products from the country's staple, rice, could help alleviate rural poverty, an issue at the heart of the problem.

Tim was passionate about both rice bran and value addition. His goal was to become an expert in all things related to rice bran and continue to add value to the main agricultural crop of his homeland. However, at present, CEO's production process was limiting its growth, with 100 metric tons of crude wax and gum by-products generated each month.

[1]SMART Program, Cornell University.
[2]Department of Agriculture and Resource Economics, Kasetsart University.

These by-products were driving up the cost of operations. Faced with these challenges, CEO Agrifood needed to consider other sources of revenue. Furthermore, competition was intensifying as other companies (both domestic and international) were moving up the value chain into the consumer market by developing products from rice bran and other by-products.

Tim knew his business could not afford to carry on as usual and that changes had to be made. He knew that the business needed to be scaled up; however, he was not quite sure how.

Thailand: The Macro-Environment

In 2013, Thailand seemed to be on the verge of becoming a Southeast Asian success story. Spurred by strong economic growth over the previous decade, the country had made great strides in addressing a number of social issues and was expected to meet most of the United Nations' Millennium Development Goals by 2015. Unemployment rates in 2013 were less than half of what they had been in 2005, while average incomes had increased from US$6,800 to more than US$10,000 (EIU 2014). Thailand had been especially successful at reducing poverty rates, which had fallen from 43% to 13% between 2000 and 2011, leading the World Bank to reclassify Thailand as an upper-middle income country in 2011 (World Bank 2014).

Although it had experienced rapid modernization, the Thai economy remains largely agricultural. In 2012, 40% of the workforce was employed in agriculture and cultivation, as estimated by the World Bank, and value-added agricultural products accounted for an estimated 12% of its total GDP (World Bank 2013). Rice is the country's most important agricultural product. In addition to being an important export, it serves as an important food product, and an integral part of the Thai culture.

Rice production in Thailand

The growing of rice is intricately intertwined with Thai identity, putting rice production at the forefront of Thailand's economy and politics (Figure 1). In 2013, the country produced more than thirty-one million

Fig. 1: Rice production is an integral part of the Thai economy; seen here, harvesting rice in Thailand.

tons of rice, with particularly high yields in the fertile delta of the Chao Praya River (Prasertsri 2013). Rice from Thailand is in high demand, both in international and domestic markets. Rice is a staple of the national diet, although increasing urbanization and the growing popularity of Western foods suggest that Thailand's traditional enthusiasm for rice is waning. In fact, per capita rice consumption fell by 16% between 1990 and 2011, from 119 to 100 kg per year (Institute of Nutrition Mahidol University 2011). Although it had cut back on its exports in recent years, Thailand remains one of the world's leading exporters of rice. In 2013, the country exported eight million tons of rice, which comprised approximately 25% of its total production, and generated $5.7 billion in export revenues for the country (Pratruangkrai 2013).

The rice subsidy scheme

Although the country as a whole has grown more prosperous, the economic and social gains were not distributed equitably among the Thai population. Nearly 90% of Thailand's 70 million people reside in rural areas that have not adequately benefited from commercial activities in urban economic centers like Bangkok (World Bank 2014). Attempting to compensate for their exclusion, the Thai government instituted a number of redistributive policies in 2011, including some controversial agricultural subsidies.

The government's rice subsidy scheme guaranteed farmers higher-than-market prices for rice. The government intended to hold the rice in warehouses, limiting exports in an attempt to drive up global prices. Having done so, the government intended to gradually release its stockpiles into the market at premium prices. In practice, however, when Thailand reduced its rice exports, other major exporters like India and Vietnam very quickly made up the shortage. Global prices for rice remained stable, and Thailand's government was unable to recoup the costs of the subsidy, leading to billions of dollars in losses. In spite of these setbacks, the government did not repeal its subsidy.

The rice subsidy's failure sparked an investigation by the country's anti-corruption commission into the already-embattled government. Critics accused the government of pursuing populist policies to shore up support in the country's agricultural northern region. In early 2014, a number of large anti-government demonstrations were staged in Bangkok, prompting the government to agree to special elections in February 2014. With the support of the rural poor, the government seemed assured of another victory at the polls; however, some analysts had raised the possibility of military or judicial coups to remove the government from power.

The possibility of such political maneuvers left the future shrouded in uncertainty. A change in government could potentially lead to a drastic reshaping of Thai agricultural policies, which would have far reaching effects on the viability of agribusinesses in Thailand. For CEO, fluctuations in rice production would lead to the reduced availability and increasing cost of its primary input, rice bran. As the protests wore on, Tim and his brothers closely followed the political developments.

Value addition in rice production

The changing economic and social environment held additional impli-cations for Thai businesses, beyond its impact on government policies. The combination of factors such as rising wages and an aging population suggested that the labor intensive business models employed by many local industries might not be sustainable. According to the Asian Development Bank, further development of the Thai economy would require the adoption of strategies that emphasized "skills development, innovation, productivity growth, and environmental sustainability" (Asian Development Bank 2013).

One way to achieve this goal was for Thai agribusinesses to create new value-added products that would move them higher up the value chain. For example, through additional industrial processes, crude rice bran can be refined into a commercial-grade cooking oil. Tim had been exploring options in this area, and saw CEO's experiment with the joint venture T.R.B.O.[3] as an opportunity to learn more about the consumer market for rice bran oil and its related products.

Rice bran oil markets

In 2013, interest in rice bran was growing globally, as evidenced by the establishment of the International Council of rice bran oil at the first Thailand Conference on Fats and Oils (Bhosale 2013). With a burgeoning middle class in Thailand, there was growing interest in healthy living and, as part of it, increasing demand for rice bran oil (Euromonitor International 2013). Rice bran oil has been touted for its nutritional value (Figure 2); the fully refined oil is rich in Gamma Oryzanol, Omega 6 and 9 fatty acids, and Vitamin E, which may help reduce cholesterol levels. Additionally, its high smoke point makes it particularly appealing to Asian consumers, as deep frying is common in Asian cuisines. Besides household use, rice bran oil is also increasingly in demand by the prepared foods industry, particularly in upscale restaurants and by snack food manufacturers. This is due to certain favorable characteristics such as stability, high cooking temperatures, and aromatic flavor (de Guzman 2003).

As an established rice bran oil market, Thailand currently produces around 60,000 tons of rice bran oil per year, and is the third largest producer after India and Japan, which produce 900,000 and 70,000 tons, respectively

---

[3]"The Rice Brain Oil Company," a consumer goods branch of CEO business (to be discussed in more detail later).

(Sohini, 2014). The oils and fats industry has recorded a healthy Constant Average Growth Rate (CAGR) of 8% in recent years, and within the oils and fats industry, the vegetable and seed oil sector in particular is expected to record an even faster value growth of 10% (Euromonitor International 2013). Average unit prices for oils and fats as a whole are forecasted to grow by 3% in 2012, partly attributed to the increase in demand for healthy offerings in the vegetable and seed oil sector. In most other oil categories, average unit prices either decline or remain constant due to increasing competition. To meet rising demand, Thailand and Japan are both considering

Fig. 2: Nutritious rice bran oil.

importing rice bran oil from India to meet their domestic consumption (Ghosal 2013). If CEO Agrifood can further supply the market with fully refined rice bran oil, the demand of the market will easily absorb their production.

Outside of Thailand, Japan has developed its rice bran oil market to claim a 3% market share, despite its limited access to paddy production. Globally, consumption of rice bran oil is growing stronger to meet the increasing demand for natural, value-added healthy food products. The popularity of rice bran oil has also been growing in other countries including Korea, China, Indonesia, and recently, the United States. All of these countries represent potential new markets for CEO.

CEO Agrifood Limited

CEO Agrifood Ltd. was founded by Tim's father, Pongsak Limjaroenrat, in November 2005. When his father abruptly passed away just three months into the venture, Tim, the eldest son, assumed responsibility for the company. At the time, Tim was working towards master's degrees in business administration and public policy at the Massachusetts Institute of Technology and Harvard University in the United States. After his father's death, Tim suspended his studies and returned to Thailand. When he took over, the small family-operated business had recently been incorporated with 100 million baht (US$3.1 million) and was 27% owned by Japanese stakeholders.

Fig. 3: The CEO factory (image courtesy of CEO website).

Together with his brothers and cousins, Tim re-oriented the company to produce and sell an expanded line of rice bran oil products. His family management team included a factory manager, a quality control director, an operations director, a business development director, a sales and trading specialist, and an accountant, all located in Bangkok. Together they formulated plans to build a rice bran oil factory (Figure 3), to procure raw materials, and to form partnerships with buyers.

CEO's strategy centered on purchasing rice bran from independent mills and employing an additional value-adding process to remove wax and gum from the bran in order to extract its 12% crude oil content. The company would produce crude rice brain oil, which would then be further refined for commercial use by a partner with more advanced facilities. Further, the defatted rice bran, a by-product of the original process, was to be sold as animal feed.

To realize this plan, the team's first responsibility was to build relationships with Thai farmers, focusing primarily in the rice-growing regions of Singburi province. By setting up such long-term relationships, CEO's goal was ensure a steady supply of rice bran. After many rounds of negotiations, Tim secured a daily delivery of more than 400 metric tons of rice bran for 9.20 baht (US$.29) per kilo.

Next, the scientists on the team began designing a plant using the 20 million baht (US$625,000) the company had left of its capital. They chose to locate the plant in Singburi due to its close proximity to hundreds of rice paddies in the area. This allowed raw materials to be transported to the factory as quickly and cheaply as possible. Additionally, because the technology needed to set up a rice bran oil production facility was not available in Thailand, Tim contracted Indian, German, and Brazilian technicians to recommend and set up machinery for high quality production. Once the production facilities were completed, CEO's Japanese shareholders inspected the factory and were satisfied with the quality, and production began.

Since crude rice bran oil could not be sold directly to consumers without further refinement, Tim set out to develop key buyer relationships with his two Japanese stakeholders, the Sojitz Corporation and the Boso Oil & Fat Company. These strategic vertical partnerships in the rice value chain meant that CEO had a market for its crude bran oil and, in the process, it gained access to the lucrative Japanese market. To sell the defatted rice bran, CEO sought contracts with various animal feed companies in Thailand.

As manufacturing capacity increased, CEO hired more workers, created partnerships with snack manufacturers, and produced hundreds of metric tons of crude oil and defatted rice bran per day.

The road to profitability

CEO's increased productivity coincided with the global spike in food prices in 2008, when global markets were experiencing shortages due to droughts, oil price increases, and a general escalation in the agriculture industry's production costs. The price of rice bran oil followed the general trends of other value-added agricultural products, which meant significantly higher profit margins for CEO, enabling the company to pay off large amounts of its debt, and becoming profitable for the first time.

Within two years of assuming control of the company, Tim and his brothers had a successful plant, with over 100 employees between its corporate headquarters in Bangkok and its factory in Singburi. They had developed relationships with other rice bran oil producers around the world, and had forged strong partnerships with their two Japanese stakeholders to whom they sold crude oil. They also contracted with several animal feed companies, who purchased the defatted rice bran product.

By 2008, CEO Agrifood Ltd. was producing over 80 metric tons of crude rice bran oil and 320 metric tons of defatted rice bran per day, which it sold to its partners for further refinement. By 2012, the company had become the third largest producer of rice bran oil in Thailand, with 1.03 billion baht (US\$32,187,500) in revenue and 51 million baht (US\$1,593,750) in capital. The company's products had met several international standards, including the GMP (Good Manufacturing Practice), HACCP (Hazard Analysis and Critical Control Points), and various ISO (International Organization for Standardization) standards. CEO was also making progress towards its goal of using meaningful innovations in rice bran oil production to improve consumer health.

Production and innovation: new avenues, new challenges

His company's success notwithstanding, Tim had an even greater vision for the business. Understanding the importance of constant innovation, Tim overcame the limited technical expertise within his staff by partnering with leading research institutions to pursue development initiatives. Tim's goal was to turn CEO Agrifood into a top international rice bran company, recognized as an expert on rice bran in all of its product forms. The next frontier would be developing consumer products bottled under their own brand.

Fig. 4: Refined rice bran oil (image courtesy of CEO website).

To achieve this, CEO underwent several significant changes in 2012. First, the company invested in a refining plant that was able to produce semi-refined rice bran oil (Figure 4). While this intermediate product continued to be sold for industrial use to their Japanese partners, it was a step in the right direction – CEO was on its way to creating its own brand. If they could obtain the capital needed to produce and brand fully refined oil, they would be on par with their rice bran oil competitors in Thailand.

Though the process of refining was expensive and required many new machines and a considerable amount of time, Tim felt that creating his own product was a crucial step to making CEO self-sufficient and a way to eliminate CEO's reliance on the Japanese market.

Unfortunately, the addition of the new refinery came with a new set of problems. The plant was not running nearly as efficiently as they had planned, producing more than 3.2 tons of unused by-products every day. The two by-products, wax and gum, contained 55% and 38% of crude oil, respectively. Without further extraction, this crude oil was lost, and the revenue remained unrealized. Tim knew he had to find a way to extract this oil to increase efficiency and profit, in part because CEO would either have to store the waste products or dispose of them properly, and either option would hurt its profits.

Tim knew that the wax and gum could be turned into useful products, such as a substitute for soybean wax and gum products, as soybean was becoming a recognized allergen. The wax could be used in products including supplements, cosmetics, food coating, candles and automobile waxes, while the gum could be added to emulsifiers, supplements, and even acid oil used for biodiesel. The industrial uses were endless, but the by-products would have to be refined for their use, with each product requiring different refinement processes. He knew that his Indian and Japanese counterparts were utilizing this gum and wax, but the technology was not readily available in Thailand and designing a new refinery would be costly and time intensive. In the long term, however, the investment could save his business.

In addition to further refining the company's main product into semi-refined oil, Tim was looking ahead to entering the consumer market directly, by creating "The Rice Brain Oil Company," more popularly referred to as T.R.B.O™, a consumer goods branch of the business. Founded in 2012, T.R.B.O.'s mission was to expose Thai consumers to CEO's goal of being the expert on all things rice bran. Using the highest grade rice bran available, the company began producing high quality, health-conscious snacks and supplements. Through a partnership with CAL Intertrade Co., Ltd. and CDIP (Thailand) Co., Ltd. CEO was able refine its crude bran oil into snacks and vitamins.

Due to these strategic partnerships and sizeable investments in marketing, the T.R.B.O™ brand flourished. But expanding their set of products required significant research and development and did not happen overnight. For example, the company launched a line of rice bran oil cosmetics but stopped production to do further research and redefine the line. New product development was tedious and time-consuming – but, Tim felt, it would help CEO reach its goal of becoming a foremost producer of rice bran oil products. If the company could strategically launch more consumer products – including body oils, lotions, waxes, and food products – it could make a sizeable return and grow the business in a new direction.

Looking Towards the Future

CEO's future presents both challenges and opportunities for growth in the midst of uncertainty. Thailand continues to experience waves of political and economic unrest, which have the potential to unleash far-reaching shocks on the country's economy, especially its agricultural sector. Tim is unsure of how these factors would impact his business in the coming years. He recognizes the importance of carefully considering a variety of growth areas to maintain competitive advantage while still adding value to the Thai economy.

CEO Agrifood is at a crossroads with several possible avenues for expansion. It can continue to refine its rice bran oil to a purified rice bran oil bottled by the company, potentially allowing CEO Agrifood and T.R.B.O. to become household names. This option would narrow CEO's focus on rice bran oil, competing with the other top two producers. This move would require a significant investment in costly technology, and would possibly cut the road to diversification.

CEO could also diversify its product line by creating new value-added products from the wax and gum by-products. This seems to be almost a necessity given that the by-products come with the production process, but turning them into value-added products requires a sizeable investment up-front. Can CEO afford this investment now?

Alternatively, CEO could invest further into its T.R.B.O. brand and produce more consumer products. But would it make sense to do this alongside the other developments, or should CEO focus more exclusively on this path for growth?

Just as important as deciding about the right products, CEO also needs to consider which markets to sell in. Should the company limit itself to the domestic Thai market, at least for now? Or should it try to enter other markets such as China and India, perhaps through international partnerships? If CEO decides to enter other markets, which products should it take to those markets?

As he is preparing to leave for the meeting, Tim Limjaroenrat does not know the correct answer to these questions. But he knows that successful companies innovate, change, and seize opportunities. He knows that the time for CEO is now.

References

Asian Development Bank. 2013. Thailand: Overview. [Online]. [Accessed 21 November 2017]. Available from: http://www.adb.org/countries/thailand/main.

Bhosale, J. 2013. International Council of Rice Bran Oil Formed at Bangkok. The Economic Times. [Online]. 3 October. [Accessed 21 November 2017]. Available from: https://economictimes.indiatimes.com/markets/commodities/international-council-of-rice-bran-oil-formed-at-bangkok/articleshow/23466564.cms.

de Guzman, D. 2003. Health benefits strengthen rice bran oil use. Chemical Market Reporter.

EIU (Economist Intelligence Unit). 2014. Thailand: Country Data. [Online]. [Accessed 21 November 2017]. Available from: http://country.eiu.com/thailand.

Euromonitor International. 2013. Oils and Fats in Thailand. London: Euromonitor International.

Ghosal, S. 2013. Japan may import rice bran oil from India, to improve fiscal numbers. The Economic Times. [Online]. 17 October. [Accessed 21 November 2017]. Available from: https://economictimes.indiatimes.com/news/economy/foreign-trade/japan-may-import-rice-bran-oil-from-india-to-improve-fiscal-numbers/articleshow/24276480.cms.

Institute of Nutrition Mahidol University. 2011. Rice Consumption per capita of Thais. [Online]. [Accessed 21 November 2017]. Available from: http://www.inmu.mahidol.ac.th/th/.

Prasertsri, P. 2013. Thailand: Grain and Feed Update. [Online]. Bangkok: United States Department of Agriculture Foreign Agricultural Service. [Accessed 21 November 2017]. Available from: http://gain.fas.usda.gov/Recent%20GAIN%20Publications/Grain%20and%20Feed%20Update_Bangkok_Thailand_12-2-2013.pdf.

Pratruangkrai, P. 2013. Commerce Forecasts This Year's Rice Export Total at 8.5m Tonnes. The Nation. 38(53876). p.2B.

Sohini, D. 2014. Thailand Interested in Importing Rice-bran Oil from India. Business Standard. [Online]. 12 February. [Accessed 21 November 2017]. Available from: http://www.business-standard.com/article/markets/thailand-interested-in-importing-rice-bran-oil-from-india-114020501078_1.html.

World Bank. 2013. World Development Indicators. [Online]. [Accessed 21 November 2017]. Available from: https://data.worldbank.org/data-catalog/world-development-indicators.

World Bank. 2014. Thailand Overview: Context. [Online]. [Accessed 21 November 2017]. Available from: http://www.worldbank.org/en/country/thailand/overview.

Chapter 4

Maharashtra Hybrid Seeds Company: Evolution of an Agribusiness Success Story

Benjamin R. Zehr[1]

Introduction

Having built Maharashtra Hybrid Seeds Company Private Limited (Mahyco) from a small operation on his own small farm into one of India's largest and most diversified seed companies, Dr. Barwale had reason to reflect on his company's success. "It was the national task; at the time, there was a need to organize the seed industry to produce superior seeds for the farmer," Dr. Badrinarayan Barwale said as he gazed out the window of Mahyco's head office in Dawalwadi, Maharashtra. At nearly 86 years of age, and having been awarded the World Food Prize (1998), an honorary Ph.D. from Tamil Nadu University, and the Padma Bhushan (2001)— India's highest civic honor—Dr. Barwale had been at the forefront of the development of the Indian seed industry since his youth. In the years following British departure from the country, he participated in the independence movement against the Nizam of Hyderabad, which landed him time in prison as a teenager. Barely into his 30s, Dr. Barwale had helped create a number of farmer organizations and was an active participant in local government, all the while building his own private seed company, Mahyco.

In the 50 years since its founding, Mahyco has seen India through its most transformative years post-independence. Through tumultuous periods of war, sweeping economic reforms, and ongoing social change, the importance of agriculture has remained constant. Dr. Barwale helped Mahyco navigate difficult times by emphasizing the company's mission and creating a corporate culture centered on empirical research and a focus on the farmer's needs. Arguably standing at an important juncture in its life as a company, Mahyco has implicitly followed a number of growth strategies relevant to various emerging market contexts worldwide.

[1]SMART Program, Cornell University.

53

Initially a small operation in rural Maharashtra, the company started by selling its core set of hybrid row crops, initially in its home region and then expanding to nearby states. As it expanded its reach, Mahyco began investing more in product development and R&D, offering a successful series of vegetable and cash crops to supplement its core staple seed business. Following a period of consolidation during the Indian economic crisis in the late 1980s and 1990s, Mahyco used licensed technology from a multinational corporation to diversify into biotechnology and genetically modified varieties of cotton—a move that saw the company grow rapidly in the 2000s. In the time since, Mahyco has expanded internationally, acquiring complementary businesses in Africa and Southeast Asia to grow their customer base and to diversify against regulatory risk in India. Today the company stands as a representation of India itself, with a tumultuous, informative past and an uncertain, yet exciting, future in a changing world.

India - A Sleeping Giant

Today the world's third largest economy in purchasing power parity terms, India rose to the fore of the emerging economies in the early 1990s following policy reforms heralded by the Congress Party. The liberalization of the economy spurred massive private and international investment in the country's plentiful natural resources and huge labor pool. Table 1 and Figure 1 below illustrate India's own economic picture in recent years and GDP growth relative to other major economies. Though not to the same degree as countries like Brazil, India has experienced lopsided growth – metropolitan areas espouse higher standards of living and per capita GDP, while the northeast of the country has remained largely agrarian and "destitute" (Fan 2008:17).

India's Prime Minister, Narendra Modi, was swept into office in 2014 on a wave of frustration with economic stagnation, corruption, and a strong desire for change in the face of a modernizing world. The former tea-seller's success in revving up private-sector growth as Chief Minister of Gujarat provided the mandate he needed to expand his policies into a national platform, emphasizing growth, job creation, cheap energy, and integration with the global economy. Under Modi, analysts worldwide expected the nation to outpace China by 2016 and begin to put in place reforms that would increase its competitiveness and reduce the stymieing corruption that has plagued the country for decades (Bhupta 2014).

Table 1: India's Macroeconomy 2016.

Indicators	2009	2010	2011	2012	2013	2014
Population (millions)	1,214	1,230	1,247	1,263	1,279	1,295
Population Growth (%)	1.4	1.4	1.3	1.3	1.3	1.2
GDP Growth (%)	8.5	10.3	6.6	5.1	6.9	7.3
Inflation, GDP deflator	6.1	9	6.4	7.6	6.2	3
GNI per capita (USD)	1150	1260	1410	1500	1530	1570
FDI Inflows (Billion USD)	35.58	27.39	36.49	23.99	28.15	33.87
Agriculture Value Added (% GDP)	17.7	18.2	19	18.7	18.6	17.8
Agricultural Land (% land area)	60.6	60.4	60.4	60.4	60.6	-
Urban Population (%)	30.6	30.9	31.3	31.6	32	32.4

Source: The World Bank

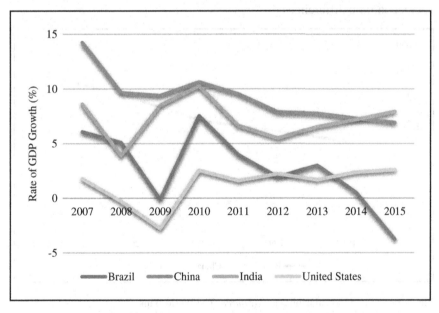

Fig. 1: GDP Recent Growth of Major Economies (*Source*: The World Bank 2012).

After two years in office, Modi retained the image of the hard-working, incorruptible, pragmatic statesman—he has consistently made efforts to clean up the largesse of the country's infamous bureaucracy, streamline government agencies, promote more foreign investment in railways, defense, and manufacturing, and establish stronger ties with the rest of the world (Bellman 2015). Since 2014, India's growth has picked up, reaching 7.4% in 2015, its fastest in five years.

With growth, however, comes the need to improve the productivity of India's arable land. With the largest land bank in the world at 195.25 million hectares, India still lags behind China and Brazil in its food supply per capita. Figure 2 below illustrates India's inability to keep pace with its peers, largely due to its high population growth rate (Figure 2, FAOSTAT). Although it currently produces enough food to feed everyone in the country, primary production statistics do not take into account spoilage, other food waste, and unequal distribution of calories due to socioeconomic differences.

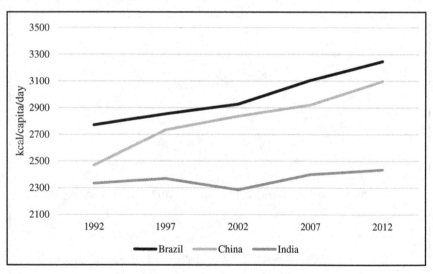

Fig. 2. Food Supply (kcal/capita/day) (*Source*: The World Bank, 2012).

The government sees the potential to make India both a food sovereign nation as well as an exporter of global commodities such as cane sugar, cotton, and tea. Given its historical strength in agriculture and underdeveloped infrastructure, the country can realistically achieve this goal in the coming decades. Considering both population and wealth trends in the subcontinent, however, some estimates suggest that India may face a food shortage of nearly 50 million tons by 2020 if it fails to promote a holistic reassessment of agricultural priorities, chief among which will be intervention from the private sector in both the pre- and post-harvest value chain.

The government sees the potential to make India both a food sovereign nation as well as an exporter of global commodities such as cane sugar, cotton, and tea. Given its historical strength in agriculture and underdeveloped infrastructure, the country can realistically achieve this goal in the coming decades. Considering both population and wealth trends in the subcontinent, however, some estimates suggest that India may face a food shortage of nearly 50 million tons by 2020 if it fails to promote a holistic reassessment of agricultural priorities, chief among which will be intervention from the private sector in both the pre- and post-harvest value chain.

Agriculture at a Glance

Agriculture has been a key component of the nation's identity since the Classical Age of Indian history, contributing to the potency of its culture, the strength of its traditions, and the resilience of its many peoples. In more modern times — fueled in part by British colonial rule — agriculture became the driving force behind India's importance in the global economy as well as a source of enormous wealth, albeit not for farmers themselves. Since independence, Indian agriculture has gone through a series of structural changes that have had lasting economic, social, and environmental impacts on the country.

Traditionally, Indian farmers grew a diversity of well-adapted crops on small plots of land, primarily for subsistence consumption or local distribution. During colonial rule, however, the British pushed for more extensive production of cash crops such as tea, cotton, and spices for export, fueling industrial growth in Britain while leading to disenfranchisement of farmers and famine as imperial interests took precedence over sustainable domestic production (Corner House 2002). The Great Bengal Famine of 1943, the last famine of its kind in the country, resulted in the deaths of between 1.5 and 4 million Indians, and has been attributed to the British focus on the export production of cash crops while neglecting domestic food needs.

The Green Revolution

Intended to be a solution to the food sovereignty issue created by the colonial era, the Green Revolution (GR) introduced a suite of technologies designed to increase yields for basic cereals. Semi-dwarf high yielding varieties (HYVs) of rice and wheat, produced and proliferated through international public sector research, resulted in a production boom for staple grains throughout Asia. Those HYVs were sensitive to fertilizers, whose application increased yields considerably. Widespread use of synthetic pesticides became the norm with the adoption of these hybrid varieties as well. With recent memories of widespread famine, India quickly adopted the agricultural technologies introduced by the international seed centers and distributed them with the help of a burgeoning private sector. An illustration of the success of such input-focused interventions was an overall increase in wheat production of 168% during the three decades from 1961-1991.

Instrumental in this transformation, India's agribusiness sector accounted for 17.8% of GDP and supported the largest share of the workforce (49.7%) in 2014, in comparison to manufacturing, which generated 17.05% (The World Bank 2015). Although services and other areas of the economy contribute more to the sheer economic activity in the country, agricultural production remains important because it supports a large part of the population, many of whom are food insecure.

According to the 2011 census, 25.7% of India's population lived in rural areas and below the official poverty line. The corresponding statistic in urban areas is 13.7% (The World Bank 2012). Increased access to improved seeds, synthetic fertilizers and pesticides and other Green Revolution technologies helped farmers dramatically raise cereal yields. While they constitute a major expense for farming households, manufactured inputs are an important option for raising yields and incomes (Iyer and Singhi 2012).

While most domestic companies that make up these industries have historically been government-run to some degree, the passage of recent laws and relaxation of foreign direct investment (FDI) restrictions—as well as the anticipation of further loosening under the new administration— are continuing to draw international players. In 2006, FDI limits, or the maximum percentage of a domestic firm that foreign MNCs were permitted to own, were increased to 51% in retail businesses. Eight years on, in 2014, 100% FDI, or full foreign ownership, has been permitted in industries ranging from renewable energy to food processing under the government's 'Make in India' campaign (Government of India no date).

At the heart of the input sector lies the seed industry. The choice of which crop to grow is the precursor to all other on-farm decisions during a planting season. While in the past, a farmer's choice was mainly between local seed and seed from the public sector, the result of earlier research efforts has seen a number of private companies enter the space. Since the 1990's, the distribution of research spending on seed in India has flipped, with the private sector investing the most in the development of improved seed.

The Seed Industry

The research, production, and distribution of seed in the decades after independence was controlled by a combination of a government-backed organization, the National Seeds Corporation (NSC), as well as state seed corporations (SSCs) run independently by their respective states. While seed production and marketing are undertaken by the public sector, still accounting for the majority of seed distribution today, the sector now consists of hundreds of companies of various sizes and specialties.

The old system of NSC and SSCs was established in the 1960s to meet latent demand for new seed varieties created by the Green Revolution. Accompanying these public sector entities came restrictions on private involvement, with commercial imports of inputs being banned and private vegetable seeds requiring special government clearance. However, as part of an economy-wide liberalization process in the 1980s and following the Indian economic crisis in the 1990s, the seed industry was stripped of a number of controls it had in place prior to independence. Inclusion of seeds as a "core industry" in 1986 allowed private seed companies to exceed Rs. 1 billion in assets for the first time (Pray and Ramaswami 2001: 409).

The New Seed Industry Development Policy of 1988 and economy-wide liberalization in 1991 reduced regulations on technology transfer, inputs, and foreign investment for the industry. As a result, private research expenditure increased by Rs. 113.2 million in seven years between 1987 and 1995. In the same time period, the number of research-oriented seed companies increased from 17 to 38 as well, with 50-60% of seed value sold by the private sector, indicative of a structural shift (Pray and Ramaswami 2001: 408). The industry has continued to mature in recent decades, along with the larger input sector of India, driven by numerous domestic players developing a wide swath of new, high quality seed varieties for the farmer to choose from.

The Indian seed industry today is the sixth largest in the world, providing over 3 million tons of seed to farmers in 2010, and constituting a USD$2 billion industry today. A key contributor to this growth over the past decade has been hybrid and certified seed produced by hundreds of small to medium sized private enterprises - a prime example of their success is the jump in cotton productivity, a yield increase of 144% since the introduction of transgenic Bt cotton in 2002. While hybrid seeds have seen substantial success, poor transportation infrastructure and the relative isolation of rural farmers have kept market penetration low, at around 25% of the seed market as of 2012 (Iyer and Singhi, 2002: 59). However, within this disadvantage lies an opportunity, as it represents a potential market of 110 million farmers (Salve 2014).

Despite the ubiquity of seed companies today, access to quality seed, backed by privately funded research, is a relatively new phenomenon. One of the first companies to embrace hybrid technology, Mahyco — led by Dr. Badrinarayan Barwale — was a leader in the industry. Dr. Barwale and Mahyco contributed substantially to the Green Revolution's impact on Indian productivity, being the first Indian company to ever produce hybrid sorghum, millet, and cotton seeds.

Dr. Badrinarayan Barwale

Born in 1930 to a family of farmers and part-time workers—and as a teenager adopted to be the breadwinner for distant relatives following the death of an uncle—Badrinarayan Barwale spent his childhood in rural Maharashtra. The shift from his paternal family to a new home placed significant pressure on the young Badrinarayan to earn an income to support his aunt and two female cousins. With only a primary education, he worked odd jobs and tended to the farm, experimenting on his own crops to select the hardiest plants to replant the next season. In the process, Barwale developed a keen interest in plant breeding and began selling his seed to neighbors — the first steps in what would become his life's work (Barwale 2008).

When Barwale was coming of age, lack of public seed research, limited farmer extension programs, and undeveloped connective infrastructure limited smallholder exposure to new technologies. In this context, the primary means of acquiring seed was either to save seed from a previous season, or to use a neighbor's seed in exchange for monetary or in-kind payment. Farming was a subsistence activity first, and a commercial one once all the needs of the household were met. Before the advent of the Green Revolution, yields were low and highly variable, with the prospect of food shortages a constant threat.

Thus, the impetus to produce improved seeds for Maharashtrian farmers was a desire to help smallholders better their standards of living during a time when the majority of India's agricultural households lived near or below the poverty line — a reality Barwale himself had experienced. If he could strive to perfect the most critical aspect of the agricultural equation, he reasoned, he would be able to have an impact on not only millions of Indian farmers, but the newly independent Indian nation. After the Land Ceiling Act of 1961, the land held by Barwale's family was reduced to a mere five acres, with the remaining land being acquired by the government. This proved to be a major obstacle for Barwale, and provided the push needed to formalize the idea as a corporation rather than a one-man operation. With some success producing and selling his first hybrid varieties of okra, a widely consumed vegetable crop, Barwale brought together some prominent local figures to set up a collaborative company they named the Maharashtra Hybrid Seeds Company (Figure 3).

Maharashtra Hybrid Seeds Company Pvt. Ltd.

Early days and technology acquisition (1964-1980)

From its outset, the goal of the company was to improve the welfare and quality of life of the Indian farmer through superior quality seeds. With this goal in mind, Barwale sought to use Mahyco as a means to employ traditional breeding, hybrid technology, and an expansive network of distributors to spread awareness about the importance of high quality seed for the improvement of Maharashtrian agriculture. Building a brand and a company culture would be important steps on the road to establishing a strong company. Barwale

Fig. 3: Mahyco logo.

traveled tirelessly to government distribution centers, farmer cooperatives, and formed relationships with other seed producers during Mahyco's first decade.

At first, progress was slow. Access to few financing options limited early growth and was dependent on voluntary donations from partners alongside their small revenue base. At the time, agricultural technology in the country was in its infancy, and Barwale had to rely on traditional, manual breeding to conduct research on the farm. Those methods included the selection of specific, desirable traits over generations, re-planting those hardy seeds, and continuously selecting for better performers each season. For example, harvesting and replanting seeds whose parents performed better in drought conditions would result in the development of a reliably drought tolerant variety over time. This variety could then be labeled and sold in the market. On the other hand, these varieties were not protected by intellectual property legislation and could be retained and replanted. Thus, traditional breeding resulted in one-time revenue for Mahyco.

The breakthrough step for Barwale was the use of publicly available varieties of vegetables such as okra, first sold by Mahyco in 1968, which he bred to be more productive through hybrid breeding techniques. In contrast to traditional breeding, hybridization takes two genetically distinct parents and crosses them to produce hardy offspring that benefit from hybrid vigor—an ideal combination of genes that results in higher yields and better overall performance that fades over successive generations as genes disperse. The Rockefeller Foundation provided technological support to Mahyco during this phase that would be key to its long term success.

"In those years, the Rockefeller Foundation had signed an agreement with the Indian Council of Agricultural Research to help them produce high yielding varieties of maize and other staple crops," Barwale said, recalling the early days of the company. As part of the Rockefeller Foundation's involvement in India, they partnered with Dr. Barwale and his new company, providing technical help and advising on seed production, processing, and labeling. Thus, with the assistance of Foundation representative Dr. Wayne Freeman, Mahyco began regular production of sorghum and pearl millet, along with vegetable crops, that soon gained traction in local and regional markets.

Having instilled his employees and partners with his personal belief that farmers should inform every company decision, Barwale was working to create a culture of accountability and responsibility within Mahyco. His vision for the company revolved around developing products tailored to farmer needs rather than a one-size-fits-all approach to seed varieties. Painstakingly collecting input from local farmers each season, he worked to develop varieties of seeds that suited the local growing conditions. "Farmer First" became the company's motto.

Barwale also made efforts to work with local government officials. Recounting these interactions, Barwale noted how "the Chief Minister — who visited local sorghum fields after hearing about the success of our hybrid sorghum — immediately turned around and asked me how many packets of the seed he could order to Delhi immediately." As Dr. Barwale tells it, the combination of farmer testimonials, in-person visits, and active relationship-building helped Mahyco gain the support of the state government at a time when the private seed industry was tightly controlled and competing directly with the government. With the blessing

of high profile public figures, Mahyco was able to continue its research
and develop a reliable brand.

Growth and expansion to new markets (1981-1990)

Having built a base of government support and a strong brand in Maharashtra, Mahyco began to expand its partnerships, acreage under contract,
and infrastructure. Setting up a corporate office in Mumbai was an important step as it allowed the company to tap into Mumbai's government
and corporate network to bring Mahyco to the rest of the nation. The company continued to sell dozens of hybrids developed at its research center
in Jalna - including crops such as hybrid wheat, millet, sorghum, eggplant,
gourds, tomatoes, cauliflower, and cabbage.

Mr. Barwale saw an opportunity to develop new markets across the
country. Perhaps one of the most pivotal periods for the company came
with the transition of management from Dr. Barwale to his son, Mr. Raju
Barwale, who had joined the company in 1976. A graduate of the G.B.
Pant University of Agriculture and Technology in Pantnagar, India's first
agriculture university, Mr. Barwale was keen to help transition Mahyco
towards what he called a "family business, professionally run." He
determined that the core strengths of the company were its purpose, values,
and culture; the improvement of farmer livelihoods and the focus on
customer service and satisfaction drove employees and management alike
to continue to innovate and grow its customer base with rare discipline.
Mr. Kishor Pande, the administrator of Mahyco's Head Office, cites the
company's culture as a key advantage: "The interaction with an owner
or a director, one-on-one communication, especially for the junior staff,
is one of the key areas of focus when it comes to retaining the employee.
If someone is considering leaving the company, they will think twice,
because Mahyco feels like a family."

With a renewed perspective and purpose, Mahyco began to devote
more of its resources to infrastructure. During the years 1981-1990, the
company invested significantly in automation, computerization, and
processing infrastructure in key cities across the country. In addition, it
devoted a large percentage of its funds to research and development. The
introduction of three new hybrids, Jowar MSH 51, Bajra MBH 110, and

Cotton MECH 1 sparked a boom in sales for Mahyco, increasing seed revenue from Rs. 5 crores to over Rs. 45 crores annually.

Sustained growth across India gave the company a strong platform for the introduction of new hybrids and varieties at regular intervals, and continued financial success buoyed the spirits of the company's employees and executives. The coming years would prove to be challenging, however, as Mahyco faced unexpected crises and opportunities that it would have to navigate in order to fully establish itself as India's premier seed company.

Mahyco (India) in Transition (1991-2000)

Challenges

India faced a multifaceted crisis in the 1980's that culminated in political upheaval and a perilous debt situation in the 1990s. Ethnic insurgencies in Punjab, Jammu and Kashmir, and Sri Lanka had spilled over into the country, indirectly resulting in the assassinations of two consecutive Prime Ministers, Indira Gandhi and her son, Rajiv Gandhi. The end of the Gandhi dynasty, which had administered India for all but five of the 44 years since independence, threw the country into political and economic turmoil (BBC 1991). Moreover, the collapse of the Soviet Union, a major trading partner, had left India with nowhere to turn but the International Monetary Fund. For the first time since its independence, the country was on the brink of defaulting on loan payments to creditors in 1991 (Weintraub 1991).

In the 1990s, Mahyco began to experience growing pains. The success of the company's core hybrid varieties across the country had created complacency and inefficiency in the company's middle level management, and a growing labor force had proven difficult to handle, particularly given India's very restrictive labor laws. Additionally, the company was attempting to stay abreast of the economy, which was projected to perform poorly in the short term.

The thriving research program at Mahyco, led by Director of Research Dr. Rajendra Mishra, suffered a tragic setback on April 26th, 1993. During a routine trip between the Aurangabad and Mumbai offices, the Air India flight on which the Director of Research was traveling crashed during takeoff from the Aurangabad airport, killing 55 of its 112 passengers, including Dr. Mishra. The loss of Mahyco's Director of Research compounded the issues the company was already facing. This led Mr. Barwale to reshuffle its management structure, improve operational efficiency, reach an agreement with its labor unions, and develop a new future strategy.

Cost cutting and re-framing

In the years between 1991-2000, Mahyco underwent a series of changes that would ultimately shape its long term strategy as a science company. The first order of business was to "rationalize" its resources, shutting down 25% of its processing plants, 20% of its sales offices, 35% of its production centers, and laying off nearly 30% of Mahyco employees in order to become more focused. Mr. Barwale also narrowed the number of products on offer from 444 to 182 during this period, choosing crops that represented the most value per research rupee spent.

"This period represented a transition from a family business to a professional business, a maturing process," said Mr. Barwale, reflecting on the time of change. Along with the cost-cutting, Mr. Barwale was intent on being first to the table when it came to the newest technology and using it to advance the company's position in India. The recent success of MNCs in the field of genetic engineering was of particular interest to Mr. Barwale as he considered future options for Mahyco. At the same time, he needed to find new R&D leadership that would take on ambitious projects. It was clear that in order for Mahyco to continue to provide its wide variety of hybrid seeds to farmers across the country, it needed a more lucrative source of revenue. He saw genetic engineering as a way for Mahyco to stay at the cutting edge of the maturing seed industry, but he did not have the funds or germplasm available to finance new research infrastructure immediately.

With the future of the company uncertain, Mr. Barwale contacted his sister, Dr. Usha Barwale Zehr, a biotechnologist who had recently completed her Ph.D. at the University of Illinois at Urbana-Champaign (UIUC). Her husband, Brent Zehr, had also received a Ph.D. in Agronomy from UIUC, and had taken a faculty position at Purdue University at the time. Seeing the need for new research leadership in the company, Mr. Barwale persuaded both Dr. Usha and her husband, Dr. Brent, to join the company as Co-Directors of Research in 1996. Simultaneously, Mr. Barwale began searching for new technologies that could be applied to the Indian context.

India's first biotech company - involvement with Monsanto

On a mission to enhance their seed offerings, Mahyco entered talks with Monsanto. One of the world's largest chemical and biotechnology companies, Monsanto had discovered and patented a gene from the *Bacillus thuringiensis* bacterium that made host plants resistant to a key pest, the fruit and shoot borer insect. Protection of the harvest from this one pest had the potential to increase output twofold in India, a country whose cotton-growing climate was especially favorable to the insect. At first, Mahyco licensed the Bt technology from Monsanto and began a long process of research, trials, and regulatory approvals to produce local varieties of Bt Cotton. Forming Mahyco-Monsanto Biotech shortly after with 50/50 ownership, they began a sub-licensing scheme in order to disseminate the technology to hundreds of smaller seed companies and earn revenue while anticipating commercial release of the crop. It soon became clear, however, that Mahyco did not have the research capacity to develop a broad pipeline of Bt products. Mr. Barwale was faced with a decision in the late 1990s: on one hand, he could sell equity in the family business in exchange for the technology. Surrendering a significant chunk of the family's autonomy in the business strategy was a heavy tradeoff that he had to weigh against the benefits of rapid development of new varieties and cash for investment in new research facilities. On the other hand, Mahyco could continue to license the technology and use its small research facility in Jalna for the foreseeable future, until they had the resources to grow internally. A key factor in the decision was whether or not Mahyco would be able to stay competitive within an increasingly populated seed industry.

After weighing the pros and cons of an equity purchase, Mr. Barwale determined that a relatively small portion of the company's equity was an acceptable tradeoff for a dominant position in the Indian seed industry. In 1998, Mahyco negotiated a purchase of the "Bt gene" from Monsanto in exchange for 26% equity in the company. This sale both gave Mahyco one of the most important pest control technologies in the world and a valuation of Rs. 700 crore, or $106 million (US$2016). The board was confident that this technology, as well as the family's partial loss of autonomy in the short term, would yield huge dividends some years down the line. Moreover, the use of this new technology would allow Mahyco to innovate beyond cash crops like cotton. Mustard, chickpea, brinjal, and rice were hugely important staple crops that the company saw as furthering their "Farmer First" mission down the line.

Faced with the development of Bt Cotton and taking no chances on a controversial technology, the Indian government established one of the most rigorous genetic testing and approvals processes in the world. While there were some voices in opposition to GM crops, it was largely considered by government and industry leaders that the extensive commercialization process would put concerns at ease. Thus, GM crops were expected to be released in a controlled, orderly fashion with strict price controls and regular testing.

In response to confidence in the technology's future and with cash in hand, Mr. Barwale led the construction of a brand new research facility and corporate campus near his father's home village of Mandwa, near Jalna. Built in the village of Dawalwadi, in the heart of India's cotton growing region, this campus was to be one of the largest biotech research facilities in Asia, the engine of Mahyco's research activities for the foreseeable future. The Dawalwadi campus was designed to host over 100,000 sq ft of laboratories and over 160,000 sq ft of fully equipped greenhouses, in addition to space for field trials, a variety of corporate activities, as well as a small on-campus residential colony for scientists and their families, all located on 110 acres of land.

Genetic modification - past and present

Much of the distinction between conventional breeding and genetic modi-fication involves the integration of genes from a different species into the host plant. Called "plant transformation", this process was pioneered by researchers at Cornell University in the 1980s. Using what was named the "gene gun", scientists were able to use ballistics to insert marker genes into plant cells and use the modified cells to grow plants to seed, thus speeding up the breeding process substantially as compared to conventional selection. Though the gene gun has become an outdated technology, it opened the door to large scale adoption of the process, as well as further innovation.

Today breeders use more elegant means to integrate their genes of interest into the plant genome. The discovery of a naturally occurring bacterium, *Agrobacterium*, whose means of survival involve modifying the genome of its host plant, gave researchers the opportunity to take advantage of a natural process to achieve their goals. With *Agrobacterium* as a vehicle, they are able to edit the plant genome precisely and with minimal energy.

The resulting undifferentiated plant cells can then be grown out to seed, tested in the field, and sold for their new traits. Thus, Mahyco utilized the Bt gene licensed from Monsanto to create dozens of locally adapted varieties of pest-resistant cotton to sell to the Indian market. However, the regulatory process for GMOs in India, one of the world's strictest and most time-intensive, would take a great deal of patience to deal with.

The Bt Era (2001-2010)

"Even if your base hybrid is ready to be modified, developing a transgenic crop, getting permits from state and central governments, and doing all the tests involves a minimum of around 8-10 years from farmer input through to commercial release," said Dr. Ritesh Mishra, the scientist in charge of regulatory affairs for Mahyco. Environment safety, food safety, agronomic safety are three aspects that must be cleared by the Genetic Engineering Approval Committee (GEAC) for a crop to be considered as safe as conventional crops and released for commercial cultivation. Despite politically driven slowdowns in the approvals process, Bt Cotton was officially released in 2002.

The development of Bt Cotton marked a turning point for Mahyco. Due to exponentially growing rates of adoption, as well as the creation of a sub-licensing program that made the technology available to hundreds of smaller seed companies, 90%+ of cotton grown in India was transgenic in 2015, and the country was able to increase production from 1.5 million tons in 2002 to over 6 million in 2013. Today, India is the world's largest exporter of cotton and its second largest producer. At the same time, pesticide use has been halved and productivity per unit of land area has doubled.

This success has translated into tremendous growth for the company. Revenues increased by Rs. 10 billion between 2001-2011, with over 6.5 million farmers being affected by its new technology. Secondary impacts of this marked reduction in pesticide use have been an uptick in field biodiversity, lower costs of cultivation, and an additional annual income of over Rs. 210 billion for Indian farmers as a whole.

The R&D budget of the company subsequently increased as well, growing in tandem with sales. Over the 2010-2015 period alone, the R&D budget grew by 130.31% with an annualized growth rate of 10.18%. Funded by Mahyco's newfound profits, Rs. 600 million was spent on the expansion of the Dawalwadi Research Center to make space for a broader swath of projects and research activities. After a decade of challenges, Mahyco had found a compelling, impactful answer to its uncertainties, and a new path forward. Table 2 shows the changing structure of the company over the past 30 years.

Bt brinjal and the regulatory shake-up

The success of Bt Cotton in India was an encouraging sign for Mahyco research. Seeing the widespread adoption of the technology and its impact on farmer incomes, the company invested heavily in a new pipeline of GMOs. One such crop was a "Bt" variety of eggplant, or brinjal, as it is called in India. Brinjal is grown on 550,000 hectares in the country and is especially susceptible to pest damage, requiring dozens of pesticide applications per season to yield marketable fruit. For Mahyco, it appeared to be an ideal crop on which to demonstrate the viability of GM food crops.

A collaborative project between Mahyco and Indian universities, including the University of Agricultural Sciences, Dharwad, and Tamil Nadu Agricultural University in Coimbatore, Bt Brinjal was intended to be commercially released in 2010 and made available, free of cost to farmers, in a number of locally adapted varieties. Field trials conducted during development had predicted a potential pesticide reduction of 42% and doubling of yield as a result of the new gene. Also, net economic benefits were predicted to be over $100 million in direct and indirect savings. Brinjal production in India accounts for 27% of global production and is widely considered to be the common man's food. With infestation rates of up to 95% in bad years, pest damage in this crop disproportionately affects the food insecure and cash poor. From Mahyco's perspective, Bt Brinjal would be a contributor to food security and a precedent for safe GM food crops.

Table 2: Mahyco's Performance Over Three Decades (Figures in Million Rupees).

Mahyco	1981	1991	2001	2011	2015
Total Group Revenue	50	550	1,770	14,360	21,530
Seeds & Biotech	50	450	1,610	11,500	18,010
Investments	-	100	160	540	260
Engineering	-	-	-	2,270	2,860
Group Assets	10	210	2,000	4,950	8,780
Seeds & Biotech Assets	10	160	1,830	3,530	6,510
Investments	-	50	110	240	40
Engineering	-	-	60	1,160	2,210
Number of Employees	-	-	1,585	1,150	1,974
Other Legal Entities	2	5	10	13	14
R&D Spend Growth (5-yr avg)	-	-	-	10.67%	9.78%

Although Mahyco had no direct financial stake in the cultivation of Bt Brinjal at the time, the crop remained critical to its future pipeline of GM food crops. Despite the success of Bt Cotton and the widespread use of cotton oil in processed foods and animal feed, there were no commercially approved GM "food crops" (as defined by the government) on the market yet. The hope of the industry and the fear of opponents to the technology was that one commercial approval would open the floodgates for dozens of GM seed varieties to be sown in Indian soil.

After three years of mandated field trials, biosafety studies, and full approval from the GEAC, Bt Brinjal was given commercial approval on 14th October, 2009. Prior to the release, however, the then-Environment Minister Jairam Ramesh declared an indefinite moratorium on the cultivation of the crop, citing "broad public concerns" over the release of a GM food crop and lack of an "overriding urgency" to introduce the crop. Even as further tests were conducted and the government failed to provide tangible next steps on the path to commercialization, the moratorium was never lifted and remains a point of contention at the time of this writing. Neighboring Bangladesh, on the other hand, approved Bt Brinjal for cultivation in 2013, with positive results thus far: farmers in the country have reported a near-complete halt in pesticide use.

It remains to be seen if the newly elected BJP government will shift its stance on GMOs. While Prime Minister Narendra Modi has been verbally supportive of the role of biotechnology in agricultural development, substantive action is not forthcoming. For the time being, the issue remains politically volatile. Mahyco, undeterred by these roadblocks, has continued to develop its product pipeline and examine alternative courses of action in the interim.

Change in the Air - Going International (2011-2020)

Diversification

Mahyco has recently set its sights beyond the borders of India, both to diversify and to supplement its current business activities. Since 2000, the Mahyco Group of companies has been pursuing various domestic and international acquisitions, both in and out of the seed industry. Moreover, it has continued to develop crop varieties suited to its international pursuits as a means of expansion and risk reduction given the uncertain Indian regulatory environment.

The Group today consists of 14 legal entities, as compared to the two in 1981. Recent moves have included the opening of Mahyco offices in Vietnam, Singapore, Mauritius, and Bangladesh, and the acquisition of fresh produce companies, a Zimbabwean cotton company, a European engineering company, as well as a handful of other Indian seed companies. Embracing a mindset of complementarity, Mahyco has used these moves to augment its strength in research and establish itself in new Asian and African markets in particular, all of which are projected to grow rapidly over the next two decades.

"We have to think about a situation where only non-food-crops are allowed in the country", said Dr. Bharat Char, the lead biotechnologist at Mahyco, when asked about the regulations in India itself. "For the government, it is a safe decision that would avoid the controversies of GM food crops. Given that situation, we have to adapt." While the Indian pipeline for the company has continued to build — including crops such as Bt Rice, virus resistant Bt Okra, herbicide tolerant Bt Cotton, and a pest resistant Bt Chickpea — the future of domestic GM releases remains uncertain. This is problematic for the company as R&D remains capital intensive, accounting for over 10% of company revenues in 2015. With no revenue streams apparent in the near future, the company will need to determine how best to recoup its investment in these crop varieties.

Dr. Usha Zehr, now the Chief Technology Officer of Mahyco, echoes the need for company's recent moves abroad: "One of the key elements that we have learned from the GM experience is that we need to make sure that our risks in terms of research portfolio are diversified and that we create a balance to ensure that Mahyco as a company, for the next 50 years, is going to be in a strong position to continue to deliver products that bring value to the farmers we serve."

Future challenges

A far cry from its humble beginnings, Mahyco now operates in nearly all of India's 29 states, as well as five other countries in Asia and Africa, with a portfolio of 167 different seed varieties across 30 row and vegetable crops. The company now faces new realities as it continues to grow in size and scope. For one, it must compete with new entrants, many of whom are multinational corporations with larger budgets and economies of scale. Coinciding with looser FDI restrictions, companies such as Pioneer, DuPont, Monsanto, and Syngenta have established themselves as major players in their specialized segments. At the same time, numerous domestic companies have entered the marketplace since 2000. Seed companies in Maharashtra alone number in the hundreds, each operating in their local areas with a brand-loyal base.

Despite MNCs establishing a foothold in India through their core crops such as corn and rice, Mahyco's research team is confident they can continue to stay competitive. Although farmers can now choose from a number of local brands as well, Dr. Char emphasizes that "Mahyco is unique in that we work across many of the major crops. If you look at cotton there is a core subset of competitors, whereas if you look at rice, you find a different set of companies. It depends on the crop. Among the Indian players, many companies tend to focus on one crop or a few crops, while we have a very robust research program, which is definitely not the industry standard."

Climate change represents a much broader challenge. As global climate patterns are projected to continue to become more erratic, nations such as India will be forced to adapt. Given the importance of climate, specifically a reliable monsoon season, for food production in India, Mahyco has been exploring a wide range of crops and complementary products as tools for climate adaptation. According to Dr. Char, "the fact is that we are faced with a crisis, whether it is water use, temperatures, soil changes, or monsoon patterns, there is no getting around it. When your climate has changed and your environment has changed, there's really nowhere to run. It would be difficult in the short term to breed crops that would be resilient in this time frame, which creates an opportunity for biotech traits to be useful and accepted."

Mahyco's leadership, led by Mr. Barwale, remains optimistic about the industry, citing a substantial need for improved seed and competitiveness with neighboring economies. "Government policies are a big factor, and we have to engage actively with the government to ensure that the policies are ones we can live with," said Mr. Barwale. Despite decades of development, it seems the Indian farmer's basic needs have not changed: the need for seed is a constant and evolving challenge that Mahyco seeks to overcome in the decades ahead. It is also clear that Mahyco's leadership sees the company's broad focus on R&D tailored to meet ground realities as its competitive advantage.

Mr. Barwale can also rest assured that succession within the family is secure for the time being. His eldest son, Shirish Barwale, joined the company in the mid-2000s to manage its vegetable seed business. With a B.Sc. in Applied Economics from Cornell University and an MBA from INSEAD, Shirish is in charge of international expansion and broader strategy for the company. Mr. Barwale's younger son, Aashish, a Cornell alumnus holding an MBA from Harvard Business School, recently joined to head some of the company's newest auxiliary businesses. With both sons deeply involved in the direction of Mahyco, the company is unlikely to face a crisis of succession in the foreseeable future.

Walking with the Indian Farmer

The company's history exemplifies key moments of transition for the industry and the successful evolution of a business from a small family operation to a professionally run corporation. Through changing economic, political, and social environments, Mahyco has tried to remain true to its grounding philosophy that the primary directive of the company comes from the farmer's needs. The Indian farmer dictates the direction of the company, and it is the desire to help the farmer that drives Mahyco forward.

Sitting in his well-worn office chair, deep in recollection of decades gone by, Dr. Badrinarayan Barwale spoke about the earliest challenges the company faced—problems of seed certification, transportation, and government intervention in the fledgling seed industry. Forever a farmer at heart, Dr. Barwale described, at length, various anecdotal encounters with fellow farmers, important policymakers, and the intricate details of producing the first hybrids by hand with a telling fondness. Despite the ever-present difficulties of building a business in an unpredictable environment, he remained confident in the future of a company he first imagined in 1964. "There have always been challenges," he recalled with a smile, "but the farmer always wanted good seed—subsidies and technicalities were all political issues—at the end of the day, the farmer always wanted good seed, so they always bought ours."

References

Barwale, B. 2008. *My Journey with Seeds and the Development of the Indian Seed Industry.* Mumbai: Indian Merchant's Chamber.

BBC. 1991. *1991: Bomb Kills India's Former Leader Rajiv Gandhi.* [Online]. [Accessed 25 November 2017]. Available from: http://news.bbc.co.uk/onthisday/hi/dates/stories/may/21/newsid_2504000/2504739.stm.

Bellman, E. 2015. The Top 10 Successes of Narendra Modi's First Year. *The Wall Street Journal*. [Online]. 26 May. [Accessed 25 November 2017]. Available from: http://blogs.wsj.com/indiarealtime/2015/05/26/the-top-10-successes-of-narendra-modis-first-year/.

Bhupta, M. 2014. India's GDP Growth Will Overtake China's over 2016-18: Goldman Sachs. *Business Standard India*. [Online]. 5 December. [Accesssed 25 November 2017]. Available from: http://www.business-standard.com/article/economy-policy/india-s-economic-growth-will-overtake-china-s-over-2016-18-goldman-sachs-114120400588_1.html.

Carl, P. and Bharat, R. 2001. Liberalization's Impact on the Indian Seed Industry: Competition, Research, and Impact on Farmers. *International Food and Agribusiness Management Review*. **2**(3/4). p.409.

Corner House. 2002. *The Origins of the Third World: Markets, States and Climate*. [Online]. Sturminster Newyon: The Corner House. [Accessed 25 November 2017]. Available from: http://www.thecornerhouse.org.uk/sites/thecornerhouse.org.uk/files/27origins.pdf.

FAOSTAT. 2016. *Data*. [Online]. [Accessed 25 November 2017]. Available from: http://www.fao.org/faostat/en/#data.

Fan, Q. 2008. *The Investment Climate in Brazil, India, and South Africa: A Comparison of Approaches for Sustaining Economic Growth in Emerging Economies*. Washington, D.C.: World Bank.

Government of India. [no date]. *Food Processing*. [Online]. [Accessed 25 November 2017]. Available from: http://www.makeinindia.com/sector/food-processing/.

Iyer, A. and Abheek, S. 2012. *Indian Agribusiness: Cultivating Future Opportunities*. [Online]. Mumbai: The Boston Consulting Group. [Accessed 25 November 2017]. Available from: http://media-publications.bcg.com/Indian-Agribusiness.pdf.

Lazzaro, J. 2013. Bengal Famine Of 1943 - A Man-Made Holocaust. *International Business Times*. [Online]. 22 February. [Accessed 25 November 2017]. Available from: http://www.ibtimes.com/bengal-famine-1943-man-made-holocaust-1100525.

Salve, P. 2014. How Many Farmers Does India Really Have? *Hindustan Times*. [Online]. 7 August. [Accessed 25 November 2017]. Available from: http://www.hindustantimes.com/india/how-many-farmers-does-india-really-have/story-431phtct5O9xZSjEr6HODJ.html.

Tamil Nadu Agricultural University. 2016. *List of Seed Industries in India*. [Online]. [Accessed 25 November 2017]. Available from: http://agritech.tnau.ac.in/agricultural_marketing/pdf/Seed_Industries_India.pdf.

World Bank. 2012. *GDP Growth (annual %)*. [Online]. [Accessed 25 November 2017]. Available from: http://data.worldbank.org/indicator/NY.GDP.MKTP.KD.ZG.

World Bank. 2015. *Manufacturing, value added (% of GDP)*. [Online]. [Accessed 25 November 2017]. Available from: http://data.worldbank.org/indicator/NV.IND.MANF.ZS.

World Bank. [no date]. *India.* [Online]. [Accessed 25 November 2017]. Available from: http://data.worldbank.org/country/india.

Weinraub, B. 1991. Economic Crisis Forcing Once Self-Reliant India to Seek Aid. The New York Times. [Online]. 29 June. [Accessed 25 November 2017]. Available from: http://www.nytimes.com/1991/06/29/world/economic-crisis-forcing-once-self-reliant-india-to-seek-aid.html.

Chapter 5

Metro Kang Jian: Marketing Strategies in a Competitive Health Supplements Industry

Lin Fu,[1] Parth Detroja,[1] Saebyul Kim,[1] Di Wang,[1] and Hanqing Yang[1]

Introduction

It was January 2016, and the streets of Taipei were bustling with people preparing for the upcoming Lunar New Year festivities. 2016 would be the year of the monkey, a creature of tremendous intelligence and innovativeness according to traditional Taiwanese culture. As Jack Ho gathered his staff in the Riviera Hotel in downtown Taipei, he was hoping to borrow some of that ingenuity in guiding his new venture, Metro Kang Jian (MKJ), as it prepared to enter the highly-competitive Taiwanese health supplement industry.

A lifelong entrepreneur, Jack runs several successful companies in his native Taiwan, including the aforementioned Riviera Hotel. Several years ago, as Jack was searching for promising business ideas, he stumbled upon a fascinating medicinal mushroom known in Chinese as *niuzhangzhi*. Used for centuries by the aboriginal Taiwanese as a treatment for a host of ailments ranging from liver disease to cancer, *niuzhangzhi* is colloquially referred to as the "Ruby of the Forest." Jack saw a growing demand for health supplement products in Taiwan, driven by a rapidly-aging population. To take advantage of this enticing opportunity, he co-founded MKJ in 2014 with his cousin, Alex Ho, to market and distribute *niuzhangzhi* and other medicinal mushroom products.

In just over a year, Jack was ready to lead this fledgling company into its next stage. After many long hours in the laboratory, MKJ had developed its own product line consisting of seven mushroom-based products which would be sold under its own BALANSTART brand. However, Jack understood that breaking into the crowded Taiwanese health supplement market would not be a walk in the park. A great many competitors ranging from well-known multi-national corporations to other small startups like

---

[1]SMART Program, Cornell University.

MKJ (and several "snake oil" merchants as well) were already competing for the pocketbooks of Taiwanese consumers.

At the same time, Jack knew he needed to develop a long-term growth strategy for MKJ. Although the Taiwanese market was the company's primary focus, Jack expected that there would likely be demand for Metro Kang Jian's products in countries such as China, Japan, and the United States. Entering these other markets would allow the company to achieve sustained revenue growth that would not be possible in the smaller Taiwanese market alone. However, market conditions and regulatory environments vary greatly throughout the world and choosing which market to enter would be a difficult yet crucial decision. All of these questions made for an exciting atmosphere at the Riviera Hotel, as Jack and his staff understood that the manner in which MKJ tackled these challenges would likely dictate the long-term fortunes of the company.

Taiwan: An Overview

Officially known as the Republic of China (ROC), Taiwan has a population of 23.4 million people. Han Chinese make up 95% of the population, and Mandarin is the official language. However, despite its shared culture with mainland China, Taiwan's contentious historical relationship with the People's Republic of China (PRC) has resulted in unresolved political and economic issues and an ambiguous international status (Winkler 2011).

Considered one of the four "Asian Tigers" due to its rapid industrialization in the past half century, Taiwan has developed into an advanced market economy, facilitated by liberal economic policies encouraging free trade and foreign investment. As a largely export-oriented economy, Taiwan is particularly sensitive to fluctuations in global demand. Beginning in the 1970s, the Taiwanese economy transitioned from agriculture and labor-intensive manufacturing to services and capital-intensive manufacturing. Today, the largest industries include information technology, electronics, telecommunications, chemicals, metallurgy and machinery (Liu and Shih 2013; BartelsmannStiftung 2017).

Although Taiwan is home to several leading multi-national corporations such as Taiwan Semiconductor Manufacturing Company (TSMC) and High Tech Computer Corporation (HTC), the economy is dominated by small and medium enterprises (SMEs). In 2014, the number of SMEs in Taiwan surpassed 1.3 million and accounted for over 97% of all Taiwanese enterprises. In the same year, the number of people employed by SMEs reached 8.6 million, representing 78% of all employed persons (Ministry of Economic Affairs, Taiwan 2015). Most Taiwanese SMEs rely heavily on the original equipment manufacturing (OEM) model and often lack internal R&D capabilities (Lee 2010).

Taiwanese Health Supplement Market

The Taiwanese health supplement market registered a robust growth rate of 4.7% from 2009 to 2014, and is expected to grow at a slightly lower rate for the foreseeable future as the market continues to mature (Euromonitor International 2016b). Growth is largely driven by the rapidly-aging population, which is currently one of Taiwan's greatest challenges. Taiwan has the highest rate of aging in the world and, according to the projections by the country's National Development Council, the number of people over the age of 65 is projected to increase from 12% in 2014 to 20% by 2025 (Ministry of the Interior, Taiwan 2015).

The health supplement market in Taiwan is highly competitive and market share is distributed among a diverse set of companies ranging from multi-national corporations (e.g., Amway, Herbalife, GNC) to large Taiwanese corporations (e.g., Grape King), and a number of Taiwanese SMEs. The most popular sales channels are direct sales and brick and mortar stores, although e-commerce is becoming increasingly prominent. The majority of brick and mortar establishments are small drugstores, which are not always staffed by licensed pharmacists. This can result in sales staff pushing products which earn them the highest commissions instead of the products that best meet the consumers' needs.

Health supplements in Taiwan are governed by the Health Food Control Act, which was passed by the Taiwan Food and Drug Administration (TFDA) in 1999 (Hobbs *et al.* 2014). Under this act, health supplements may not be marketed with health claims unless they obtain "health food" certification through the TFDA. Prospective products applying for certification must undergo third-party testing for safety, efficacy, and stability to ensure that the product is not harmful to human health and is able to deliver the intended functional benefits. There are currently four levels of testing which may be required based on the nature of the product (see Table 1). Products may apply for a specific function from a list of 13 (see Table 2). The application process takes 1-2 years, and certified products may display a TFDA-approved stamp on their packaging (Liu and Lee 2000; Wu 2015). Certified products have a significant advantage in the eyes of Taiwanese consumers, as they are perceived to be safe and effective.

Table 1: Four categories of health supplements outlined by the TFDA. Each requires a different level of testing.

Category	Description
1	Conventional food in commonly processed form
2	Conventional food in uncommonly processed form
3	Unconventional foods
4	Foods with carcinogenic risks

Table 2: Thirteen functional claims for which a product may apply.

Functional Claim	
1	Blood lipid modulation
2	Gastrointestinal function improvement
3	Immunoregulation
4	Bone health promotion
5	Dental health promotion
6	Liver protection
7	Anti-fatigue
8	Anti-aging
9	Blood sugar modulation
10	Reduction in body fat formation
11	Blood pressure modulation
12	Iron absorption promotion
13	Allergy modulation

Medicinal Mushrooms: *Lingzhi* **and** *Niuzhangzhi*

Ganoderma lucidum, commonly known as *lingzhi* in Chinese, is a medicinal mushroom that has been used in traditional Chinese medicine for over 2000 years. Recent scientific studies have shown that the major bioactive compounds in *lingzhi* are β-D-glucan polysaccharides and over 130 types of triterpenoids. β-D-glucan molecules bind to membrane receptors on immune effector cells, leading to improved immune system function. Triterpenoids isolated from *lingzhi* have shown anti-tumor, immunoregulation, hepatoprotection, and anti-oxidative properties (Konopski *et al.* 1994; Mueller *et al.* 1996, 2000; Wang 1997).

Antrodia cinnamomea, commonly known as *niuzhangzhi* in Chinese, is a medicinal mushroom native to Taiwan. *Niuzhangzhi* is found naturally in the rotten inner cavity of the *Cinnamomum kanehirae* tree, and has been used by Taiwanese aboriginals for hundreds of years for detoxification after bouts of heavy alcohol consumption. Due to extensive logging in Taiwan from 1920 to 1970, wild *Cinnamomum kanehirae* trees are increasingly rare and, as a result, artificial methods have been developed for *niuzhangzhi* cultivation (Wu *et al.* 2011). Currently four cultivation methods are practiced, with the two most popular being solid state cultivation and submerged cultivation. Solid state cultivation takes up to 6 months and is costlier. However, it results in higher quality mushrooms and can be used to cultivate both fruiting bodies and mycelia. Submerged cultivation is less costly and only takes 15-30 days, but can only be used to cultivate mycelia, which are of lower quality. Like *lingzhi*, *niuzhangzhi* also contains β-D-glucan polysaccharides, but has a higher concentration of triterpenoids. In addition, *niuzhangzhi* contains benzenoids, lignans, benzoquinones, and maleic/succinic acid derivatives, which have been shown to provide functional health benefits (Madamanchi and Tzeng 2011). *Niuzhangzhi* is considered to be a higher-value medicinal mushroom and is typically priced higher than *lingzhi*.

Traditionally, *lingzhi* and *niuzhangzhi* were dried and consumed as part of a broth, along with other medicinal herbs. Those dried whole mushrooms can still be found on the market, but the most popular product forms nowadays are capsules, powders, and liquid extracts. *Lingzhi* and *niuzhangzhi* are advertised as general health supplements, although *niuzhangzhi* is also specifically advertised as an anti-fatigue and liver-protection supplement.

Lingzhi and Niuzhangzhi Markets

The market sizes for *niuzhangzhi* and *lingzhi* in Taiwan are 18 billion TWD (approx. $550 million USD) and 15 billion TWD (approx. $416 million USD), respectively. Although there are around 200 *niuzhangzhi* distributors and 300 *lingzhi* distributors, only seven *niuzhangzhi* products and ten *lingzhi* products have TFDA-approved "health food" certification. The markets are dominated by several large companies including Grape King, Quaker, Guo Ding, and Li De. These companies have established brands which are trusted by consumers, and their products can be found in nearly every drugstore. *Lingzhi* and *niuzhangzhi* must also compete with substitute products that advertise similar benefits such as multivitamins, vitamin B, chicken essence and clam essence, some of which are significantly cheaper than *lingzhi* or *niuzhangzhi*.

Several years ago, an article was published highlighting potential negative side effects of *niuzhangzhi* (Appledaily 2013). This article was quickly discredited due to its questionable testing protocol, but the *niuzhangzhi* market briefly took a hit due to the negative press. Although the market has since recovered, consumers are more sensitive to safety issues surrounding *niuzhangzhi* and thus may rely even more on the "health food" certification to distinguish safe and effective products.

Metro Kang Jian: Company Overview

Metro Kang Jian (MKJ) is a Taipei-based health supplements distribution company co-founded in 2014 by cousins Jack and Alex Ho. MKJ officially launched in the second half of 2016. It currently sells one of its planned seven products through its online platform (http://balanstart.com. tw/). The company has eight employees organized into four departments (marketing, research & development, human resources, and finance) under a general manager who reports directly to Jack and Alex Ho (see Figure 1). The company has also hired the services of an outside consultant, Dr. Lv.

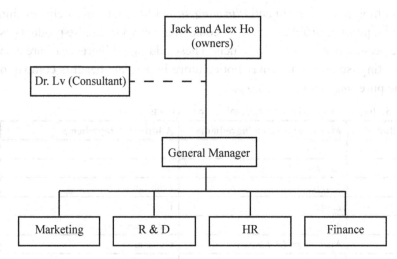

Fig. 1: Organizational chart of Metro Kang Jian.

MKJ is a joint venture by Metro, a company owned by the Ho family that has 70% equity, and Kang Jian Biotech, an OEM medicinal mushroom supplier owned by Dr. Minnan Lai, which owns the remaining 30% equity. Dr. Lai, known in Taiwan as the "Father of *Niuzhangzhi*," is an expert in medicinal mushroom cultivation and was the first to develop an artificial method for cultivating *niuzhangzhi* in 1989. He subsequently founded his own company, Kang Jian Biotech (KJB), which supplies a variety of mushroom-based products to Taiwanese health supplement companies, including several of MKJ's competitors. Besides being financially invested in MKJ, KJB will also be MKJ's sole supplier of mushroom-based products. KJB's current production capacity is 100 tons per year, which may be increased, if needed.

Metro Kang Jian Product Line

Working in conjunction with KJB's product development team, MKJ has developed a product line consisting of seven unique products, all of which contain either *lingzhi* or *niuzhangzhi* (see Table 3). Although two of the seven products are pure *lingzhi* and *niuzhangzhi*, the remaining five contain additional functional ingredients. These "combination" products are uncommon in the *lingzhi* and *niuzhangzhi* market, but MKJ believes this can be a point of differentiation, as consumers may view these products as more personalized lifestyle products. These additional ingredients are also fast-acting, so consumers may notice more immediate benefits compared to the pure *lingzhi* and *niuzhangzhi*.

Table 3: Ingredients in Metro Kang Jian's seven products.

Product no.	Mushroom-based ingredients	Additional ingredients
1	*Lingzhi*	-
2	*Niuzhangzhi*	-
3	*Lingzhi*	Probiotics
4	*Lingzhi*	Enzymes
5	*Niuzhangzhi*	Monascus Purpureus
6	*Niuzhangzhi* + *Lingzhi*	Ginseng
7	*Niuzhangzhi*	Turmeric Curcumins

Marketing Strategy: Taiwan

The most prominent challenge for MKJ is developing an effective marketing strategy to break into the crowded Taiwanese health supplements market. As discussed previously, competition within this space is intense, with many established companies and brands, some of which have annual advertising budgets in the 50-100 million NTD range (approx. $1.5-3 million USD), according to MKJ's estimates. To survive and thrive in this environment, MKJ must differentiate its product offering in the minds of consumers and begin to establish brand recognition.

Branding

From the outset, Jack has recognized the critical importance of branding in this consumer-oriented industry. Thus, he hired a consulting company to assist in developing MKJ's brand identity and a corresponding logo (see Fig. 2. for the MKJ logo). The result was BALANSTART. The Chinese characters in the company logo call upon the idea of a person reaching a state of inner balance and peace. MKJ would like to push BALANSTART as a "lifestyle brand." Instead of simply selling a product with certain functional benefits, MKJ wants to market a means to achieving a balanced and healthy lifestyle. In addition, MKJ believes that the BALANSTART logo projects the ideas of quality, trust, and modernity through its simple design, lively colors, and bold character styling.

Fig. 2: MKJ's logo (*Source*: MKJ website).

Product differentiation

As discussed previously, MKJ will differentiate its offerings by creating "combination" products which combine *lingzhi* and *niuzhangzhi* with other functional ingredients to create a more personalized experience. In addition, MKJ's products are highly potent, as they are produced using KJB's proprietary solid cultivation technique. As a result, consumers only need to take two capsules per day, as compared to an average of 4-6 capsules daily for most competing products.

The average price point for *lingzhi* and *niuzhangzhi* products is between 1200 and 2000 NTD per month (approx. $35-65 USD). MKJ plans on pricing its products on the higher end of this range, as consumers will associate a higher price with higher quality.

Packaging is another potential point of differentiation for MKJ. Although the packaging design has not been finalized, MKJ would like the packaging to reflect the same themes of quality and modernity. Most *lingzhi* and *niuzhangzhi* products on the market use mushroom images on their packaging, but MKJ has decided against this, as they believe the images seem old-fashioned and may detract from the modern feel of the packaging.

The final piece of the product differentiation puzzle is the TFDA "health food" certification. MKJ is applying for dual certification for its pure *lingzhi* (immunoregulation and anti-aging certifications) and *niuzhangzhi* products (liver protection and anti-fatigue certifications). There is currently only one other mushroom-based product on the market with dual certification. As discussed previously, consumers place great emphasis on the TFDA "health food" stamp, as it signifies safety and efficacy, especially in light of recent scandals. (See Figure 3 for a photo of MKJ's products.)

Sales channels

MKJ has decided to sell exclusively through e-commerce for the time being, due to budget and staffing limitations. Customers will be able to purchase all seven products online through MKJ's official website. In the future, MKJ plans to expand its sales channels to include other e-commerce platforms such as Momo, Yahoo, and PChome, and eventually move into brick-and-mortar drugstores as well. In addition, MKJ plans to take advantage of Jack's existing corporate relationships through the Riviera Hotel by hosting promotional events with corporate partners where employees can learn about and purchase MKJ's products.

Fig. 3: All of Metro Kang Jian's products are sold as capsules (*Source*: Authors).

Promotional channels

MKJ's primary promotional channels will include its official website as well as its social media pages (Facebook, YouTube, LINE@), which will directly link back to the official website so that customers can easily purchase products. The official website will reflect the brand image with a clean, modern style and will contain background information on MKJ's products and on Dr. Lai. Endorsements by medical professionals can be extremely influential in the Taiwanese health supplement market, as consumers tend to put their trust in these experts. Thus, an endorsement from the "Father of *Niuzhangzhi*" could aid in convincing consumers to make a purchase.

Exploring New Markets

Although penetrating the Taiwanese health supplement market is MKJ's primary objective, Jack has a global vision for the company and is interested in exploring potential new markets outside of Taiwan, which will allow MKJ to achieve sustained revenue growth. Jack believes there might be demand for MKJ's products in China, Japan, and the United States. In deciding which of these markets to enter, the key factors MKJ must consider include demand for its products, existing competition, and government regulations.

United States

In 2015, the US health supplements industry generated revenues of $27 billion. From 2010 to 2015, the industry registered an annual growth rate of 4.7%, and revenues are expected to continue growing at a rate of 3-5% through 2020. The industry is extremely competitive and highly fragmented, as no company has more than a 5% market share (Euromonitor International 2016c). Growth in the industry has been driven by stabilizing household incomes, rising healthcare costs, and increasing interest in healthy living. However, some consumers are reducing their supplement use and are instead turning to functional foods as a more natural way to receive the proper nutrition. Additionally, although overall revenues for the industry are projected to increase steadily, individual products or brands may experience revenue volatility as health fads come and go (Yucel 2017).

US consumers value quality, safety, and efficacy when choosing from the large variety of health supplement products on the market. In fact, consumers cite compelling scientific research as the single most important factor when making purchasing decisions. Price is also an important factor due to the discretionary nature of health supplement products. Lower priced products appeal to a larger consumer base, but can also signify lower quality, whereas premium pricing and branding signify high quality and can sometimes lead to increased demand (Yucel 2017).

Differences in consumer preferences are largely age-related. Older consumers are primarily concerned with long-term health benefits, and are attracted to products that address age-related problems, such as digestive health, heart health, and joint health. Younger consumers gravitate toward products that fulfill specific needs such as improving sleep, delivering energy, or boosting athletic performance (Euromonitor International 2016c; Yucel 2017).

In the US, health supplements are regulated under the Dietary Supplement Health and Education Act of 1994 (DSHEA). The general regulatory environment is relatively lax, as dietary supplements are considered to be foods and thus do not require formal FDA testing, as would be the case for drugs. However, the FDA does require a 75-day premarket notification for any products containing a "New Dietary Ingredient (NDI)." *Niuzhangzhi* and *lingzhi* would fall under the NDI category. These notifications should present sufficient evidence to demonstrate a "reasonable expectation of safety." Alarmingly, about 75% of these notifications fail to satisfy this requirement. A company may still market their product despite the FDA's safety concerns, although this is not recommended (Ullman 2014). Recent scandals involving adulterated dietary supplement products have prompted legislators to push for increased oversight of the industry (US FDA 2011).

The sub-category of herbal supplements generated revenues of $3.5 billion in 2015. Although revenues for this sub-category have grown at an annual rate of 3.8% from 2010 to 2015, the growth rate has lagged behind that of the overall health supplements industry (Euromonitor International 2016c). This is likely due to several regulatory scandals involving herbal supplement manufacturers since 2010, which have resulted in product recalls and scrutiny from the media and the FDA. However, as these companies producing low-quality products improve their formulations and manufacturing practices, or remove their products from the market, herbal supplements are expected to experience increased demand, as consumers generally hold herbal supplements in high regard due to their natural healing potential (Yucel 2017).

A number of existing *lingzhi* products are on the US market—the majority of which come in capsule, powder, or liquid extract form. *Lingzhi* products in the US are labeled as "*Ganoderma lucidum*," "Ganoderma," or its Japanese name, "Reishi." There are a number of domestic products, but imported products are available as well. Currently no US companies are producing *niuzhangzhi* products. The only products available on the US market are imported from Taiwan or Japan. These products are very expensive compared to other health supplement products. In addition, they are not well known brands, so it is difficult for consumers to evaluate and investigate product quality.

Japan

The Japanese health supplements industry generated revenues of ¥1.1 trillion (approx. $9.9 billion USD) in 2015, representing a 1% increase from 2014 (Euromonitor International 2016a). The single most important trend in the Japanese health supplement industry is the strong preference for Japanese products. The majority of Japanese consumers (70%) spend less than $26 USD per month on health supplements, and Japanese consumers tend to prefer products with easy-to-understand labels and ingredients, which make them feel empowered (Food and Development 2014).

In 2013, non-store retailing (door-to-door sales and digital sales) accounted for 74.3% of sales, while in-store retailing accounted for 25.7% of sales. Door-to-door sales generated $2.14 USD billion, representing a 2.1% decrease from the previous year, while digital sales, including over-the-phone sales, TV show commerce, and e-commerce, generated $250 million USD in sales, representing a 40% increase from 2012. Door-to-door sales are expected to continue decreasing while digital sales are projected to continue increasing rapidly (Ministry of Economic Affairs, Taiwan 2015; Cabinet Office of Japan 2013).

Food for Specified Health Uses (FOSHU) refers to foods containing functional ingredients that have been officially-approved to claim physiological effects on the human body (Ministry of Health, Labour, and Welfare, Japan no date). A typical approval process takes 2 to 3 years and costs $1-1.5 million USD. In addition, the procedure for importing health supplements is not straightforward and can be time-consuming (Won 2010).

A new regulation on health supplement labelling in Japan came into effect in April 2015, which introduced a new category, "Foods with Functional Claims (FFC)." This new law is expected to result in increased sales for manufacturers as they no longer need to seek government approval before launching their products with health claims. Instead, they now only need to notify the Consumer Affairs Agency before launching and marketing their product. This new law has the potential to drive faster growth in the Japanese market (Euromonitor International 2016a). However, as Japan has an established, unique health care culture where consumers have a strong preference for Japanese products, the growth rate will likely be moderate.

China

Although China possesses a long history of traditional herbal medicine use, it has only been in the last 25 years that China's health supplement market has taken off. In 2014, China's health supplement market generated revenues of 100 billion Chinese Yuan (approx. $15.3 billion USD), with an annual growth rate of 10% to 15% (CHYXX 2015).

Despite the rapid growth of China's health supplement market, it has one of the world's strictest regulatory environments regarding health supplements. No product in capsule or tablet form can be sold as food in China. Rather, products must be registered as either a health food or drugs with the China Food and Drug Administration (CFDA) and can only be sold after being approved by the CFDA. Health foods have a blue stamp on their packaging, commonly known as a "blue hat" due to the image. There are two types of health foods: nutritional supplements such as vitamins and calcium tablets, and functional health foods such as fish oil and ginseng tablets. Both types need to be tested on toxicology, hygiene, stability, and active ingredients. Additional animal and/or human studies may be required for functional health foods depending on the functions that the product is applying for. There are a total of 27 functions approved by the CFDA (US-China Health Products Association 2014).

The CFDA registration process requires an enormous investment of both time and money. A typical registration can take two to three years to complete and costs over $50,000 per product. If a product contains an ingredient that is new to the market, it can take as long as five years and can cost over $100,000 (US-China Health Products Association 2014). In 2013, there were 668 dietary supplement products approved by the CFDA, but only nine of them were imported products. Since it is extremely costly and time-consuming to import health supplement products into China, cross-border e-commerce has become the primary distribution channel for foreign companies in the health supplement industry.

Currently, direct sales and conference sales are the most profitable sales channels in China. Amway and Avon are the only two health supplement companies that have been granted a direct sales license in China. Domestic brands are less competitive compared to major foreign brands. Amway's total sales reached 30 billion Yuan (approx. $4.5 million USD) in 2013. In 2010, the cumulative total sales of the five largest domestic health supplement companies were still lower than that of Amway (CHYXX 2015).

New rules governing the health food market, the Administrative Measures on Health Food Registration and Filing, took effect in July 2016 (Ip *et al.* 2016). Under the new regulations, China has adopted dual systems (registration and notification) for health food regulation instead of only using the existing registration system. Domestic companies that are using new ingredients not listed in the Health Food Function Claim Catalog and Ingredient Catalog are required to go through the registration process. Companies not using a new ingredient can enter the market after merely completing the notification procedure. The notification system also applies to imported goods that are considered nutritional supplements such as vitamins and minerals. However, imported health supplements that do not belong in this category still need to register with the CFDA. The new regulations also stipulate that the labels on health supplements may not include disease prevention claims and must contain the statement "this product cannot replace medication" (National People's Congress 2015)."

The Future

Back at the Riviera Hotel, the meeting was underway, and the entire staff was engaged in a lively discussion. How will Metro Kang Jian differenti-ate its products and establish its brand in the crowded Taiwanese health supplement market? Which international market looks most attractive? Despite the challenges ahead, this was an exciting time at Metro Kang Jian. The critical decisions MKJ will make in the following months would likely determine the company's long-term fortunes. Will Metro Kang Jian rise to the top of the Taiwanese health supplement industry as Jack had envisioned, or will it slowly fade into anonymity, drowning in a sea of competition?

References

Appledaily. 2013. Píngguǒ diàochá jīngjì bù yǐnmán niúzhāngzhī hán dú chī duō shāng shèn. *Appledaily*. [Online]. 22 May. [Accessed 21 November 2017]. Available from: http://www.appledaily.com.tw/appledaily/article/headline/20130522/35033635/.

BartelsmannStiftung. 2017. *Taiwan*. [Online]. [Accessed 21 November 2017]. Available from: http://bti2003.bertelsmann-transformation-index.de/1 31.0.html?&L=1.

Cabinet Office of Japan. 2013. *Kenkō shokuhin' no hyōji-tō no arikata ni kansuru chōsa hōkoku.* [Online]. [Accessed 21 November 2017]. Available from: http://www.cao.go.jp/consumer/iinkaikouhyou/2013/houkoku/201301_kenkoshokuhin_houkoku.html.

Cabinet Office of Japan. 2014. *Shokuhin hyōji bukai kaku chōsa-kai no shingi kekka torimatome.* [Online]. [Accessed 21 November 2017]. Available from: http://www.cao. go.jp/consumer/iinkaikouhyou/2014/houkoku/1407_syokuhin_houkoku.html.

China Industry Information (CHYXX). 2015. *2015 Nián zhōngguó bǎojiàn pǐn hángyè fāzhǎn xiànzhuàng jí shìchǎng fēnxī yùcè [tú].* [Online]. [Accessed 21 November 2017]. Available from: http://www.chyxx.com/industry/201510/352040.html.

Euromonitor International. 2016a. *Vitamins and Dietary Supplements in Japan.* [Online]. [Accessed 21 November 2017]. Available from: http://www.euromonitor.com/vitamins-and-dietary-supplements-in-japan/report.

Euromonitor International. 2016b. *Vitamins and Dietary Supplements in Taiwan.* [Online]. [Accessed 21 November 2017]. Available from: http://www.euromonitor.com/vitamins-and-dietary-supplements-in-taiwan/report.

Euromonitor International. 2016b. *Vitamins and Dietary Supplements in the US.* [Online]. [Accessed 21 November 2017]. Available from: http://www.euromonitor.com/vitamins-and-dietary-supplements-in-the-us/report.

Food and Development. 2014. Trends in the Market for Dietary Supplement, Health Ingredients and Production Technology. Available at: http://www.kenko-media.com/food_devlp/skpdf/1403-sd-01.pdf.2014 (in Japanese).

Hobbs, J. E., Malla, S., Soga, E. K. and Yeung, M. T. 2014. *Regulating Health Foods: Policy Challenges and Consumer Conundrums.* Cheltenham: Edward Elgar Publishing.

International Business Publication. 2015. *Taiwan Investment and Business Guide Volume 1 Strategic and Practical Information.* Washington, D.C.: International Business Publications.

Ip, K., Lau, N. and Gong, J. 2016. *China Revamps Health Food Regulatory Regime.* [Online]. [Accessed 21 November 2017]. Available from: http://documents.lexology. com/9c96f345-6e59-4352-8e88-9bc5a9c640b8.pdf.

Konopski, Z., Smedsrod, B., Seljelid, R. and Eskeland, T. 1994. A Novel Immmunomodulator Soluble Aminated-1, 3-D-Glugan: Binding Characteristics to Mouse Peritoneal Macrophages. *Biochimica et Biophysica Acta.* **1221**(1). pp.61-65.

Lai, T., Gao, Y. and Zhou, S. 2004. Global Marketing of Medicinal Ling Zhi Mushroom *Ganoderma lucidum* (W. Curt.: Fr.) Lloyd (Aphyllophoromycetideae) Products and Safety Concerns. *International Journal of Medicinal Mushrooms*. 6(3). pp.219-230.

Lee, W. C. 2010. *Taiwan's Politics in the 21st Century: Changes and Challenges*. Hackensack: World Scientific Publishing.

Liu, E. and Lee, V. 2010. *Regulation of Health Food in Taiwan*. Hong Kong: Research and Library Services Division Legislative Council Secretariat.

Liu, D. N. and Shih, H. T. 2013. *The Transformation of Taiwan's Status Within the Production and Supply Chain in Asia*. Washington, D.C.: Brookings Institution.

Madamanchi G. and Tzeng, Y. M. 2011. Review of Pharmacological Effects of Antrodia camphorate and Its Bioactive Compounds. *Evidence-Based Complementary and Alternative Medicine*. **2011**.

Ministry of the Interior, Republic of China (Taiwan). 2015. 210,000 births registered in 2014, the second highest in the past decade. 2 February. *Ministry of the Interior, Republic of China (Taiwan)*. [Online]. [Accessed 21 November 2017]. Available from: http://www.moi.gov.tw/english/english_moi_note/e_moi_note_detail.aspx?sn=74.

Mueller A., Raptis J., Rice P. J., Kalbfleisch J. H., Stout R. D., Ensley H. E., Browder W. and Williams D. L. 2000. The Influence of Glucan Polymer Structure and Solution Conformation on Binding to $(1\rightarrow3)$- Beta-D-Glucan Receptors in a Human Monocytelike cell line.*Glycobiology*. **10**(4). pp.339-346.

Mueller A., Rice P. J., Ensley H., Coogan P. S., Kalbfleisch T., Kelley J. L., Love E. J., Portera C. A., Ha T. Z., Browder I. W. and Williams D. L. 1996. Receptor Binding and Internalization of a Water-soluble $(1\rightarrow3)$-Beta-D-Glucan Biologic Response Modifier in Two Monocyte Macrophage Cell Lines. *Journal of Immunology*. **156**(9). pp.3418-3425.

Ministry for Health, Labour and Welfare, Japan. [no date]. *Food for Specified Health Uses (FOSHU)*. [Online]. [Accessed 21 November 2017]. Available from: http://www. mhlw.go.jp/english/topics/foodsafety/fhc/02.html.

National People's Congress. 2015. *Zhōnghuá rénmín gònghéguó shípǐn ānquán fǎ*. [Online]. [Accessed 21 November 2017]. Available from: http://www.npc.gov.cn/npc/cwhhy/12jcwh/2015-04/25/content_1934591.htm.

Small and Medium Enterprise Administration, Ministry of Economic Affairs. 2015. *White Paper on Small and Medium Enterprises in Taiwan 2015*. [Online]. Taiwan: Small and Medium Enterprise Administration, Ministry of Economic Affairs . [Accessed 21 November 2017]. Available from: http://book.moeasmea.gov.tw/book/doc_detail. jsp?pub_SerialNo=2015A01241&click=2015A01241.

Ullman, M. 2014. *Negotiating the New Dietary Ingredient Notification Process*. London: Natural Products Insider.

U.S.–China Health Products Association. 2014. *China's Dietary Supplement Sector and Key Issues*. [Online]. Delaware: U.S.–China Health Products Association. [Accessed 21 November 2017]. Available from: http://uschinahpa.org/wp-content/uploads/2012/01/China%E2%80%99s-Dietary-Supplement-Sector-and-Key-Issues-2014.pdf.

U.S. Food and Drug Administration. 2011. *Draft Guidance for Industry: Dietary Supplements: New Dietary Ingredient Notifications and Related Issues*. Silver Spring: U.S. Food and Drug Administration.

Wang, S. Y., Hsu, M. L., Hsu, H. C., Lee, S. S., Shiao, M. S. and Ho, C.K. 1997. The Anti-Tumor Effect of *Ganoderma lucidum* is Mediated by Cytokines Released from Activated Macrophages and T Lymphocytes. *International Journal of Cancer.* **70**(6). pp.699-705.

Winkler, S. 2011. *Biding Time: The Challenge of Taiwan's International Status*. Washington, D.C.: Brookings Institution.

Wu M. F., Peng F. C., Chen Y. L., Lee C. S., Yang Y. Y., Yeh M. Y., Liu C. M., Chang J. B., Wu R. S., Yu C. C., Lu H. F. and Chung J. G. 2011. Evaluation of Genotoxicity of *Antrodia cinnamomea* in the Ames Test and the In-Vitro Chromosomal Aberration Test. *In Vivo.* **25**(3). pp.419-423.

Wu, P .W. 2015. A review on the analysis of ingredients with health care effects in health food in Taiwan. *Journal of Food and Drug Analysis.* **23**(3). pp.343-350.

Yano Keizai Institute. 2015. *Kenkō shokuhin ichiba ni kansuru chōsa kekka 2014*. [Online]. [Accessed 21 November 2017]. Available from: https://www.yano.co.jp/press/press.php/001361.

Yucel, I. 2017. *Vitamin & Supplement Manufacturing in the US*. [Online]. [Accessed 21 November 2017]. Available from: http://clients1.ibisworld.com/reports/us/industry/default.aspx?entid=490.

Won, H. S. 2010. *Preparation for Export Guideline of Health Functional Food*. [Online]. South Korea: Ewha Womans University. [Accessed 21 November 2017]. Available from: http://www.ndsl.kr/ndsl/search/detail/report/reportSearchResultDetail.do?cn=TRKO201100000756.

Chapter 6

Kirirom Food Production:
Cambodia's Flagship Dried Fruit Company

Martha Anderson,[1] Juliana Batista,[1] Amruta Byatnal,[1]
Elif Senvardarli,[1] and Margaret van Wassenaer[1]

Introduction

The warm summer sun was just setting over Phnom Penh when Chhorn Dalis, Kirirom Food Production's (KFP) Managing Director, got off the phone with a distributor from Canada who was interested in bringing KFP dried fruit products to the North American market. Though a large contract would secure much needed revenue for the fifteen-month-old company, it would require a vast improvement in its production capacity. This task would not be easy in Cambodia's challenging business climate. Being a new company still in the process of fine-tuning its product line and improving its factory facilities, it would not be easy for KFP to fill this large order from the Canadian distributor. Moreover, the competition in the international dried fruit market would be intense as supermarket shelves were already filled by a couple of well-established brands and many smaller, certified organic and fair trade, boutique brands. Although aware of the challenges, Dalis also was excited about upcoming opportunities and the chance to make KFP stand out in the crowd. Her past experiences of managing successful businesses in Cambodia made her a perfect candidate for the task.

Background

Kirirom Food Production (KFP) was born out of the love Dalis' parents had for mangoes. In 2002, Dalis' father planted a few trees on a small plot of land in the Kirirom region of southern Cambodia. The Kirirom region is known for its mangoes and produces about half of Cambodia's total

---

[1]SMART Program, Cornell University.

mango harvest. Over time, as his small orchard grew to 500 hectares, Mr. Chhorn witnessed a chronic oversupply of mangoes during peak seasons. When the markets could not absorb the influx of fresh fruits, the prices would plummet, leading to a waste of mangoes and reduced incomes for farmers in the region. Seeing a potential opportunity, Mr. and Mrs. Chhorn, in consultation with their daughter Dalis, decided to build what would become Cambodia's first dried fruit factory. The KFP facility, completed in October 2014, was built to absorb the oversupply of mangoes and produce high quality dried fruit products.

At present KFP is producing three different types of dried mangoes and has expanded to dried pineapples and dried papayas. It is also in the process of building an additional facility to produce frozen mangoes. Its largest export clients are in South Korea, China, and Japan. As KFP continues to expand across product lines, it continues to seek new markets.

The Cambodian Context

The Kingdom of Cambodia is located in Southeast Asia and is bordered by Thailand, Laos, and Vietnam. Covering nearly 70,000 square miles, it has a population of around 15.6 million, of whom 80% live in rural areas. The country's population is young: 65.3% of its people are under the age of 30. With its large and young work force, the country is in a demographic bonus period (UNDP 2017).

Cambodia's recent history is characterized by significant turmoil. Following independence from France in 1953 the country experienced political unrest as the Vietnam War progressed and conflict spilled over into Cambodia. Soon after the monarch was ousted in a military coup, the Communist Party of Kampuchea, better known as the Khmer Rouge, gained power under the leadership of Pol Pot, whose reign resulted in the Cambodian Genocide that killed over 2 million people, a fifth of the population at the time. Educated citizens were the primary target of the genocide and executions took place in killing fields throughout the country. Families that managed to escape execution were relocated, imprisoned, and battled starvation and disease. Landmines from past conflicts still riddle the countryside, leading to a disproportionately high number of amputees (CMAC 2010). Landmines pose a significant risk to the 80%

of Cambodians who rely on agriculture for their livelihood. The effects of past conflicts are still evident as the people of Cambodia strive to develop their economy and recover from the past. Pol Pot's regime had a direct effect on the Chhorn family: the newly married Mr. and Mrs. Chhorn and their one-year-old daughter Dalis were separated and forced to migrate across the country. At times, Mrs. Chhorn had to walk for miles carrying baby Dalis.

The brutal past has slowed Cambodia's economic growth. The country's GDP per capita is only $1,094, similar to that of Bangladesh. In 2011, 20.5% of the Cambodian population lived below the poverty line (World Bank 2014). The economy is still heavily agrarian: 40% of Cambodia's GDP is attributable to agriculture (FAOSTAT 2016). The informal sector plays a large role in Cambodia's economy; it accounts for 62% of GDP and 85% of employment. The informal economy includes small-scale producers and distributors of goods and services. They typically operate independently, either self-employed or family laborers, and operate with little to no capital or access to financing (EIC 2006a, 2006b). Though the official currency is the Cambodian Riel, many shops prefer to use U.S. dollars for consumer purchases. Cambodia's weak financial standing is a disadvantage for a company trying to expand internationally; at the same time, the country's poverty limits KFP's domestic market options.

Poor infrastructure remains a pressing challenge for Cambodia. The country's infrastructure is far less developed than its neighboring countries. Only half of its national roads and around 15% of provincial roads are paved. Since the railway system is underdeveloped, it is also underutilized. Access to electricity is limited and expensive (Heng 2014). The majority of the population relies on biomass for cooking and heating and uses car batteries and kerosene for other minor electrical needs. The KFP facility runs on biomass energy because Dalis is reluctant to connect to the power grid due to fluctuations in service and the high cost.

Mango Markets

Many barriers impede the growth of the mango industry in Cambodia. Poor overall infrastructure is a major impediment. The country also lacks much of the data to appropriately track the flow of goods. Further, many foreign markets have higher standards for packaging and labeling than are currently required in the domestic market. The Cambodian Ministry of Agriculture, Forestry, and Fisheries has been encouraging the growth of the Cambodian mango market and has promoted the Kirirom region as a sustainable locale to cultivate and harvest mangoes. The Sales and Marketing Director of KFP, and Dalis' sister, Chhorn Vimol, hopes that as a result of this promotion, the Kirirom region will one day be associated with mangoes similar to the way champagne is associated with the Champagne region of France. This association would benefit producers of mango and mango-based products, like KFP, to brand and market their products more successfully.

Although KFP targets both domestic and international markets, the company has found greater traction internationally. As of December 2015, only 24% of KFP's total production was sold domestically. The remaining 76% was exported. The products sold domestically are branded with KFP packaging and labeling, whereas those sold internationally are in wholesale form and therefore are not labeled. For this reason, domestic and international sales have their unique set of marketing requirements and challenges.

International markets

Scope

Cambodia is relatively new to the international mango market but has the potential to become a large exporter in the region. Although its first official fresh mango exports began in early 2014, the country has 65,000 hectares of fertile mango plantations currently under cultivation that yields nearly 2.6 million tons of fresh mangoes harvested per year on a biennial harvest (Kang 2015). This level of production is comparable to that of Thailand, the third largest fresh mango producing country in the world after India and China (Mitra 2016). The favorable Cambodian climate means that mangoes may be harvested twice a year, a fact that has drawn positive attention from international companies and distributors. At the moment, the main importers of Cambodian mangoes are China, France, Malaysia,

Singapore, Thailand, and Vietnam in order of volume. In the past few years, fresh mango exports from Cambodia have increased in the range of 30-50% per year as the country continues to gain traction (Un 2015). The opening of the export markets spells good news for mango-related businesses.

As for dried mangoes, Cambodian products must compete with well-established brands as well as smaller niche players. The Philippines and Thailand are both major exporters of dried mangoes. Brands like 7D Mangoes, Cebu Brand, and Philippine Brand (all three are from the Philippines and the latter two are owned by the same parent company) can already be found on North American supermarket shelves, in retailers like Walmart and Costco. Smaller specialty brands specializing in dried fruit, including dried mango, also abound. Mavuno Harvest, started by a U.S. Peace Corps volunteer, produces organic and fair trade dried fruit sourced from family farms in sub-Saharan Africa. Nature's All Foods, owned by Natierra, offers organic and fair trade freeze-dried fruits and vegetables.

Challenges

The international markets where KFP distributes and sells its products include South Korea, China, and Japan. In the future, KFP hopes to expand to the North American, European, and Australian markets. Consumers in each of these market have differing preferences. Chinese consumers prefer sweet and sticky dried mangoes that are chewy, while South Korean and Japanese consumers tend to gravitate toward less sweet tastes. After KFP learned about these different consumers preferences from its distributors, the company has tried to tailor its products to match the varying consumer preferences.

Unfortunately, KFP cannot use its brand name "Kirirom Food Production Co." in China because another company has already secured the trademark rights to the name. Coupled with the fact that KFP products are sold wholesale, this means that KFP does not have name recognition abroad. As the company grows, KFP hopes to transition to selling only branded products abroad.

To reconcile differences in labeling and certification requirements in international markets, KFP is seeking certifications with the International Organization for Standardization (ISO) and Hazard Analysis Critical Control Points (HACCP). KFP is committed to operating at the highest international standards and Dalis is confident that the company meets these standards. However, the certification processes may take up to a year for approval. Once KFP obtains these certifications it will be easier to market its products internationally and to expand into more markets. In addition to ISO and HACCP, KFP is considering various other accreditations including certified organic, fair trade, and women-owned to further appeal to foreign markets and increase their visibility.

Domestic market

Scope

For most Cambodians dried fruit products are a novelty, especially dried mangoes, KFP's flagship product. Before KFP, dried mangoes were only produced as a small-scale, artisanal product. Traditionally the only similar product is called 'stir mango', which is a smoky fruit leather made at home by slow cooking ripe mangoes over the fire until they are dry. Introducing KFP's dried fruit products to Cambodian consumers is a challenge because it means introducing a whole new flavor that competes with traditional foods.

KFP began supplying to local markets only in November 2015. Retail outlets in the Cambodian domestic market are of two main types: supermarkets and local markets. The two differ in consumer demographics, products range, and price. Fresh mangoes in local markets generally retail for US$0.25, while KFP's dried fruit products retail for US$1.20 per pack, making the product a luxury item in comparison. KFP aims to market its products to a variety of consumers, including locals, expats, and tourists of all income levels alike. The company plans to conduct in-depth market surveys soon in order to learn more about consumer preferences and strategically place its products based on these findings.

Competitors

As KFP built the first Cambodian dried fruit factory, at the moment its direct competition are a few artisanal domestic producers. Cambodian Harvest is the biggest domestic competitor to KFP, operating as an NGO and supported by Australian Mercy. The proceeds of Cambodian Harvest benefit those disabled as a result of landmine injuries. Their dried mango products are different from KFP's products because they have higher sugar and water content, while the KFP products are drier—appealing to different consumer preferences. Cambodian Harvest also uses a larger package size per stock keeping unit (SKU[2]) but on a per gram basis is priced lower.

KFP faces much tougher competition against imported dried mango products. At present, KFP's main competitor is the Philippines' 7D Mangoes, which is one of the largest dried mango suppliers in the world. 7D Mangoes has a wide product range, including dried mangoes, mango puree, and mango juice. The company has many online marketing channels and is able to ship its own products.

Papaya and Pineapple Markets in Cambodia

Similar to dried mango, dried papaya and dried pineapple products are most commonly imported to Cambodia. KFP decided to expand into these fruit products because many domestic smallholder farmers, especially those in the Kirirom area, grow papayas and pineapples. Papaya has become popular with farmers due to its fast growth, high yield, long fruiting period, and high nutritional value. Those fruits also reach maturity at different times of the year, allowing the factory to remain open during the mango off-season.

Since the varieties of pineapple and papaya that grow naturally in Cambodia are not ideal for drying, KFP has imported different varieties of trees from neighboring countries and is expanding the mango orchard to include other types of fruit trees.

---

[2]A SKU is a store's or catalog's product and service identification code, often portrayed as a machine-readable bar code that helps the item to be tracked for inventory.

Company Profile

The Chhorn family has run various successful enterprises over the past decade, so when they decided to build a factory to produce dried mangoes, they were able to leverage the financial success of their existing businesses to launch KFP (See Table 1, Timeline of events). While a significant amount of initial investment was needed, the family is confident that the company can become profitable in its second year of operations.

KFP aims to develop a trusted, world-class, socially responsible brand that uses sustainable and organic farming techniques. The company was founded with three values in mind:

1. To produce a quality product with integrity;
2. To "do the right thing," ensuring all relevant stakeholders along the supply chain are happy and satisfied;
3. To produce a healthy product.

KFP plans to employ local farmers, utilize local mangoes as much as possible, and commit to international standards in labor and production.

Table 1. Timeline of events.

Date	Event
2001	Mr. and Mrs. Chhorn start to buy land for their farm
2012	KFP starts construction of a dried fruit factory
Oct 2014	The construction of the dried fruit factory is completed
Feb 2015	Management transferred to Dalis; Sales & Marketing Department to Vimol.
Apr 2015	Dalis hires a new consultant that specializes in production techniques.
June 2015	KFP establishes partnership with a distributor in Siem Reap, Cambodia
Oct 2015	KFP begins the production of dried pineapple and papaya
Nov 2015	KFP begins sales at local retailers

Building the Factory and Overcoming Challenges

Once the Chhorn family decided to build the factory, Dalis and her friend Sok Ly, who would eventually take the lead on international marketing for KFP, conducted a market analysis and identified Lucky Construction, a foreign-based company, to build the factory. After a week of discussions, KFP and Lucky established a joint venture (JV). In exchange for building the fruit drying facility and teaching KFP the operational know-how, KFP would supply all their products to Lucky exclusively. KFP broke ground on the 500 m^2 manufacturing plant in 2013 and construction was completed in October 2014.

During construction, it became apparent that Lucky was not as knowledgeable about the fruit drying process as KFP was led to believe. The technology Lucky provided was not sufficient to build an efficient, state-of-the-art operation. "During construction, they would ask us how it should work," Dalis said incredulously. In addition, after construction was completed, "it turned out that the dryers were not very efficient. A 12-hour drying job took 36 hours." After only a few months of operation, KFP realized that the inefficiency of the dryers created a major bottleneck in the production process.

The relationship with Lucky quickly soured. When Lucky failed to purchase the initial dried mangoes KFP produced, this breach of contract was the final straw for KFP and they dissolved the JV. "It seems like they just wanted to sell their equipment to us and they were not the real experts they claimed to be," concluded Dalis.

In 2015, just four months after the completion of the factory, Dalis became Managing Director. She saw great potential in the company's future and wanted to see Cambodian products both in local and international markets.

Organizational Structure

Upon becoming Manager Director, Dalis immediately put together a management team. She knew she needed a team she could rely upon during what promised to be a challenging time for the company. She first looked to trusted family and friends. To head the sales and marketing departments, Dalis recruited her sister Vimol, who was working with the French Embassy Commercial Attaché at the time. Reporting to Vimol would be Dalis' friends, Svay Nakry and Sok Ly, as Export Director and international marketing lead, respectively. The company's five key personnel (Factory Manager, Marketing and Sales Manager, Procurement Manager, Human Resources and Admin Manager, and Accounting Manager) would all report to the General Manager, Dalis. (See Figure 1 for the Organizational Chart.)

Although the factory is located next to the family farm two hours south of Phnom Penh, KFP decided to house its administrative and management offices in the capital so as to be closer to key distribution channels and to have better access to commerce. Senior management, marketing and sales, as well as human resources and management functions were moved to the capital. Factory management, procurement, and accounting departments remained on-site in Kirirom. To maintain the close working relationship between the two offices, there is constant travel between the two locations. The HR/Admin Manager visits the farm and the Farm Manager visits Phnom Penh on a weekly basis.

Upgrades

With the factory operating at a suboptimal level owing to the failure of the JV with Lucky, KFP started searching for ways to upgrade its production system and sought technical assistance from international experts.

Fig. 1: KFP organogram.

After another round of intensive market analysis, Dalis identified another foreign-based company, Lilly Consulting, which was more experienced in processing dried fruits. KFP hired Lilly to identify KFP's weaknesses and to suggest improvements to its production system. KFP decided to go ahead with a purchase agreement to upgrade its seven existing dryers. If KFP secured a buyer contract before the upgrades were installed, it would purchase two additional dryers to further increase production capacity.

As discussions for the upgrades continued with Lilly, KFP received news that Lucky had broken ground on a new dried fruit facility. Within the next couple of months it would be operational and would become KFP's first domestic competitor. When asked if she was worried, Dalis responded, "I don't worry about competition because when we looked at the quality, it's not as good....We have our own market."

Supply Chain

Once the factory's capacity surpassed the production of the family mango orchard, a procurement strategy had to be established to purchase additional mangoes and other local fruits to keep the factory operating at full capacity. To ensure that the mangoes purchased meet certain quality specifications, KFP employed a mango broker (referred to as a caretaker) who was to work with the KFP farm manager to procure mangoes. Together, the two visit farmers in the Kirirom region to look at their early crops; if the grower looks like a potential KFP supplier, the caretaker returns 60 days before the mangoes are ready for harvest. At this point, the mango broker offers the farmer a 5% deposit in order to ensure first access to harvesting. (See Figure 2 for dried mango value chain.)

Fig. 2: Dried mango value chain for KFP.

As the harvest approaches, the mango broker returns to the farms with his own harvesting team, who are trained in picking mangoes that meet KFP's specifications. The team harvests any mangoes that are at the desired ripeness and may return multiple times in order to give each fruit the time needed to mature. The caretaker pays the farmer for all the fruits harvested. Although it is more expensive to have harvesters return to farms on multiple occasions, this process allows KFP to get the best quality fruit from which to produce dried mangoes. Furthermore, the use of a mango broker limits KFP's risk because the broker is the one taking possession of the fruits at the farm level.

Once the dried mangoes are packaged, KFP sells them to distributors both internationally and domestically, who in turn, sell to retailers. KFP works with three domestic distributors. LSH, the primary distributor, supplies around 2,000 retail outlets, 200 of them in Phnom Penh. LSH is the distributor for over 4,000 international products; KFP is the only domestic company that LSH works with. "They [KFP] are not the market leader yet," says LSH, so "we need to take the lead on increasing brand awareness and pushing the brand. The price is competitive."

Products

Dried fruits: mangoes

KFP's factory is located amidst 39,000 hectares of mango farms in the Kirirom region. While international firms have to pick mangoes before they are ripe so that they can be shipped over long distances without spoilage, KFP can start processing ripened mangoes the day they are harvested. The entire production process, from the arrival of fresh mangoes at the factory to the final packaged product ready for sale, takes about 7-10 days, making KFP's dried mangoes some of the freshest in the market.

When a mango is picked affects the taste of the resulting dried mango products. Table 2 gives an overview of Kirirom's products. Dried mangoes made from fully ripened fruits have a naturally sweet flavor and can be processed by only adding preservatives and a light sugar coating. KFP's "Extra Low Sugar" dried mango product is made from fully ripened mangoes. No sugar is added to the product and so, it tastes less sweet than other dried mangoes in the market. This "Extra Low Sugar" product is also sometimes referred to as "Normal."

KFP also processes mangoes that have either skin impurities or cracked skins. Mangoes with visual imperfections, which cannot be sold at market prices, can be processed into dried mangoes. Since such mangoes would naturally spoil if left on the branches, they are processed before they are fully ripened. Sugar must be added to these mangoes in order to maintain taste consistency when processes into dried mango. The "Low Sugar Dried Mango" product contains some added sugar, but still tastes much tangier due to the use of unripe mangoes. KFP's third product line is the "All Natural Dried Mango." This product does not contain added sugars or preservatives. The preservative-free product has a much shorter shelf life (six months), so product turnover must be higher.

Currently, KFP sells its three types of dried mangoes in bulk to international wholesalers. The "Extra Low Sugar" product sells for USD $7000/ton, the "Low Sugar" sells for USD $6,000/ton, and "Natural" sells for USD $8,000/ton. Domestically, only the "Extra Low Sugar" product is available for sale. KFP uses two different types of packaging for its "Extra Low Sugar" product: a 70 gram pouch with hang holes and a 60 gram paper box. Packaging costs for the paper box ($0.07 per piece) is 2.5 times that of the plastic pouch ($0.028 per piece), but the paper box packaging can be placed on supermarket shelves, making it is easier for the consumer to spot.

As of December 2015, only 24% of KFP products were sold under its own brand. As KFP finalizes more contracts, the company hopes

Table 2. Characteristics of KFP dried mangoes.

Product	Characteristics		Price/Ton	Shelf Life
Extra Low Sugar (Normal)	☑	Preservatives	$7000	1 year
	☐	Sugar Added		
	15%	Natural Sugar		
	☐	Coloring Agents		
Low Sugar	☑	Preservatives	$6000	1 year
	☑	Sugar Added		
	☐	Natural Sugar		
	☐	Coloring Agents		
Natural	☐	Preservatives	$8000	6 months
	☐	Sugar Added		
	☐	Natural Sugar		
	☐	Coloring Agents		

to eventually sell all its products under its own label. As the company expands, it will need to develop more detailed branding and marketing plans and test different types of packaging.

Other dried fruits: papaya and pineapple

To utilize its factory at full capacity, KFP started drying fruits like papayas and pineapples that would ripen during the mango off-season (August to October). In October 2014, KFP bought some papayas and pineapples from nearby farms and experimented with drying. By October 2015, KFP started selling packaged dried papaya and pineapple products.

KFP realized that if the company were to continue with this line of production, it would need to grow vertically and plant its own trees. When dried, locally grown papayas do not taste as good as varieties grown elsewhere. In 2016, KFP purchased 4,000 papaya trees to add to its farm and ensure a consistent supply of papaya for the factory. That same year, KFP also planted 40,000 pineapple plants.

Since papayas and pineapples are processed only in the mango off-season, the volume of production is much lower than that of mangoes. KFP does not sell its dried papaya and dried pineapple products wholesale; rather, the company packages them in the paper boxes to be sold in the tourist market at a premium price.

Future plans for dried fruit products

KFP has also tested drying jackfruit, ginger, coconut, and banana. Based on internal testing and initial market analysis, only jackfruit seems to be a promising product addition. While KFP currently has the formulas ready for the product, it does not have the needed production capability.

Innovative products: frozen mango

KFP sometimes receives product development ideas from its buyers. A South Korean company recently expressed interest in importing frozen mango products from Cambodia, or as KFP calls it "ice mango." To accommodate the new demand, KFP is adding a freezing facility where frozen mangoes can be processed separately. Mangoes will still need to be peeled and cut, but instead of being soaked and treated with preservatives, KFP will place the mango on a popsicle stick for deep freezing. The frozen mangoes will sell under the KFP brand in South Korea.

The new freezing facility will be built by the South Korean company. In exchange, KFP committed to working exclusively with that South Korean company for five years. KFP will also make a payment in the form of the first two containers of ice mango. Recalling their previous failed JV experience, Dalis remarks "The most important thing is that they [the South Korean company] bring the right equipment in exchange for the right product." As of January 2016, construction of the freezing facility was halfway complete.

Other mango products

While the pineapple and papaya products allow for the operation of the company year round, Dalis reaffirms that "we are first and foremost a mango company." As the company grows, KFP hopes to diversify its line of mango products and continue to use as much of each mango as possible. In an effort to reduce waste, KFP composts all mango by-products like skins and seeds. In the future, the company hopes to make jams or mango preserves out of the fruit left on the seeds after the peeling and cutting processes. "I even heard that it is possible to make gluten free flour out of the heart of the seeds but I am not sure if that's even possible," says Dalis.

Conclusion

As Dalis reflects on how far KFP had come just in the past few months, she feels proud of the company's progress. There are many challenges ahead and many decisions to be made. The opportunity to export to North America would be an exciting step forward for the young company, but Dalis wonders if expanding into new international markets is the best move right now since KFP is still trying to build brand equity at home. Choosing the right partners and distributors for further expansion would be critical. Now that the company has started to take off, Dalis expects KFP to stop operating in the red and start breaking even and generating profits. Many options are available to achieve these goals, and Dalis is looking forward to experiencing KFP's continuing evolution.

References

Cambodian Mine Action Centre (CMAC). 2010. CMAC Annual Report 2010. [Online]. Phnom Penh: Cambodian Mine Action Centre (CMAC). [Accessed 21 November 2017]. Available from: http://cmac.gov.kh/userfiles/file/Annual%20Report%202010.pdf.

Economic Institute of Cambodia (EIC). 2006a. Decent Work in the Informal Economy in Cambodia: A Literature Review. [Online]. Bangkok: International Labour Office. [Accessed 21 November 2017]. Available from: http://www.ilo.org/wcmsp5/groups/public/---asia/---ro-bangkok/documents/publication/wcms_bk_pb_132_en.pdf.

Economic Institute of Cambodia (EIC). 2006b. Handbook on Decent Work in the Informal Economy in Cambodia. [Online]. Bangkok: International Labour Office. [Accessed 21 November 2017]. Available from: http://www.ilo.org/wcmsp5/groups/public/---asia/---ro-bangkok/documents/publication/wcms_bk_pb_126_en.pdf.

FAOSTAT. 2016. Cambodia. [Online]. [Accessed 21 November 2017]. Available from: http://www.fao.org/faostat/en/#country/115.

Heng, P. 2014. Three keys to unlocking Cambodia's growth. East Asia Forum. [Online]. 13 November. [Accessed 21 November 2017]. Available from: http://www.eastasiaforum.org/2014/11/13/three-keys-to-unlocking-cambodias-growth/.

Kang, S. 2015. Gov't Signs Deal to Export Mangoes to S Korea. The Cambodia Daily. [Online]. 9 Dec. [Accessed 21 November 2017]. Available from: https://www.cambodiadaily.com/news/govt-signs-deal-to-export-mangoes-to-s-korea-102475/.

Mitra, S. K. 2016. Mango production in the world – present situation and future prospect. Acta Horticulturae. [Online]. 1111(41). pp.287-296. [Accessed 21 November 2017]. Available from: https://doi.org/10.17660/ActaHortic.2016.1111.41.

Un, R. 2015. Mango Exports Looking Sweeter. Khmer Times. [Online]. 21 July. [Accessed 21 November 2017]. Available from: http://www.khmertimeskh.com/news/13529/mango-exports-looking-sweeter/.

United Nations Development Program (UNDP). 2017. About Cambodia. [Online]. [Accessed 21 November 2017]. Available from: http://www.kh..org/content/cambodia/en/home/countryinfo.html.

World Bank. 2014. Poverty has fallen, yet many Cambodians are still at risk of slipping back into poverty, new report finds. World Bank. [Online]. 20 February. [Accessed 21 November 2017]. Available from: http://www.worldbank.org/en/news/press-release/2014/02/20/poverty-has-fallen-yet-many-cambodians-are-still-at-risk-of-slipping-back-into-poverty.

Chapter 7

CDIP: Introducing Crocodile Oil to ASEAN+3

Amanda Peçanha Hickey,[1] Charley Du,[1] Xue Jiang,[1] Gabriel Polsky,[1]
Maritza Rodriguez,[1] Kulapa Kuldilok,[2] and Ravissa Suchato[2]

Introduction

It was an early morning on what promised to be a hot summer's day in Bangkok. Pissanu Daengprasert, the CEO of "Conceptual Development Intellectual Property" (CDIP), was sitting at his desk deep in thought. CDIP is a Research and Development (R&D) and manufacturing firm that creates unique products for clients in the skin care and dietary supplements industries. Additionally, Pissanu considers himself a connector of people, and his company is a first choice for businesses in his network looking to develop a new product. A week ago, Pissanu received a phone call from an old friend, the Managing Director of Sriracha Crocodile Farms (SCF), the largest Siamese crocodile farm in Thailand. Sriracha currently sells crocodile skin to luxury apparel brands in Europe. The company had concerns regarding the costly disposal of crocodile fat, a by-product. SCF wanted to refine the oil and develop a line of skin care products, and approached CDIP for help because CDIP has similar products on the international market and R&D experience using unique ingredients in skin care products. After some deliberation, SFC offered CDIP a deal to become the exclusive purchaser of SFC's crocodile fat, ensuring supply of a possibly lucrative input and possibly handing them a competitive advantage in a growing Asian skin care market. Pissanu was excited about the opportunity; however, CDIP had never marketed products directly to consumers given that their expertise is in business-to-business (B2B) sales channels. As a result, this opportunity to grow would require treading into unknown territory for CDIP.

---

[1]SMART Program, Cornell University.
[2]Department of Agriculture and Resource Economics, Kasetsart University.

Pissanu's Task

Upon hanging up his phone, Pissanu realized he had to focus his energy on deciding which markets would be the most receptive to the new crocodile oil-based products, and the strategies needed to enter them. He narrowed his geographic options down to the ASEAN+3 countries[3] due to their proximity, both geographically and culturally, to Thailand. CDIP could enter those markets as either a supplier of crocodile oil in the B2B market, a supplier of skin care products for the business-to-consumer (B2C) market, or both. Each combination of possible markets would entail a unique set of risks. Although CDIP has limited experience selling under its own brand, the B2C markets in those countries are large. To decide how to move forward, Pissanu needed to carefully consider the interactions between the target countries' environments and his firm's competencies.

CDIP's Competencies

CDIP was founded in 2010 by the Daengprasert twins, Pissanu and Sittichai. Both brothers are very well educated. Pissanu received his MBA from a top Thai university, and Sittichai has an extensive background in Chemistry. Additionally, The Daengprasert family has a history in the pharmaceutical industry spanning the past three generations. Currently, CDIP has 30 employees, all of whom have received advanced degrees in science and business from some of Thailand's best universities. The company is located on the grounds of Thailand's "Science Park" (TSP) near Thammasat University.[4] CDIP takes advantage of the Thai government's

---

[3]ASEAN+3 includes the 10 members of the Association of Southeast Asian Nations (ASEAN) which includes: Brunei Darussalam, Cambodia, Indonesia, Lao People's Democratic Republic, Malaysia, Myanmar, the Philippines, Singapore, Thailand, and Vietnam plus the People's Republic of China, Japan, and Korea.

[4]Thailand Science Park (TSP) was set up in 2002 and managed by the National Science and Technology Development Agency (NSTDA). TSP is an important part of the Thai government's efforts to increase Thailand's capabilities in research and development by promoting R&D activities in the private sector. Located next to Thammasat University, TSP has tenants that collaborate amongst themselves and use the resources, faculties and facilities of Thammasat. After successfully applying to be a tenant at TSP, a company enjoys privileges and benefits including import tax exemption on research machinery,

generous funding, aimed at encouraging the formation of new Thai companies to diversify and improve the country's technology sector. Their location within Thammasat University allows CDIP to benefit from research conducted by professors there, helping them take advantage of consumer demand for new innovation in the pharmaceutical industry.

In describing his company, Sittichai says that he "acts like a middleman, and makes sure that everyone gains in his arrangements." In practice, this is exactly what CDIP does: it buys patents produced in university labs and uses them to manufacture products for pharmaceutical and supplement companies, who then sell the innovative end-product to their respective consumers. CDIP offers a variety of services that range from formulation, registration, and research to product training and artwork design. Clients can pick and choose any or all of the services that CDIP provides. For example, CDIP helped a client formulate an instant coffee product with ginseng that is marketed as a male performance enhancing supplement. Another company approached them to find a way of packaging fish oil that would make it more appetizing to consumers — CDIP developed the technology to encapsulate the oil which improves its taste. Similarly, it can help its clients create packaging and product messaging and guide them through the process of inspection conducted by Thailand's Federal Drug Administration (FDA).

In the past three years, CDIP's revenue has increased from around $0.56M to $2.78M. With the goal of pursuing an Initial Public Offering (IPO) on the Thai Stock Exchange by 2017, CDIP has focused on growing their services for current clients. Now, Pissanu sees the crocodile oil venture as a way to further expand CDIP's revenue streams. Nevertheless, CDIP is still inexperienced in selling directly to consumers. As Pissanu mentioned in an interview, "The expertise of CDIP lies in Original Equipment Manufacturing (OEM) and not marketing or branding." Pissanu considers marketing and branding the essential puzzles that need to be solved in order to sell directly to consumers, both within Thailand and abroad. Moreover, CDIP only has expertise within Thailand and they have

corporate income tax exemption of up to 8 years, up to 300% tax deduction for R&D expense and work permit for foreign researchers and scientists.

struggled to find international B2B clients who can provide a substantial part of their revenue.

As a result, CDIP's B2B channels will continue to be the priority and the pillar of its core business. However, it realizes that it needs to expand into other areas where it can grow its presence and create additional revenue opportunities, including diversifying to markets outside of Thailand and creating new and successful products it can sell directly to consumers.

The Product: Crocodile Oil

To respond to the proposal made by the SFC, Pissanu has begun considering the potential products that CDIP can create from crocodile fat. Researchers have observed that, although crocodiles live in contaminated water and often incur wounds, they do not suffer from infections. Further research, dating from the early 1990s, revealed that crocodile fat has antimicrobial, antifungal, and collagen stimulating qualities that help reduce scars and infections (Li et al. 2012). However, the scientific rationale behind its use on human skin is not completely understood, and the long-term side effects of this product remain unknown (Li et al. 2012). Nonetheless, it is well established that crocodile oil can be used on human skin for burns, wounds, sunburns, and even eczema due to its Omega-3, -6, -9 composition that is similar to human oils.

The Thai crocodile farming industry is currently the largest in the world (Fernquest 2011), and CDIP has the capability to convert crocodile fat to a marketable oil. CDIP's manufacturing and R&D experience will allow them to produce oil that is of higher quality and purer than that of potential competitors. They can either sell the oil to other manufacturers who will use it as an ingredient in their own products, or CDIP can use it in their own line of consumer-facing products, which could include ointments, essential oils, soaps, creams, and balms. To make their own products, CDIP will need to draw on their product development expertise to incorporate crocodile oil with other ingredients that might appeal to different consumers. One possible ingredient is tea tree oil, which has anti-acne functions. CDIP can include both crocodile oil and tea tree oil in a product to create an innovative anti-acne treatment. CDIP can also experiment with star grass extract, a natural product with whitening capabilities.

Furthermore, CDIP can capitalize on "a first-mover advantage" since no other natural ingredient with the same benefits as crocodile oil is on the market. Even though Asian skin care products already use animal ingredients such as snail slime, emu oil, and horse oil, these products are not direct substitutes for crocodile oil since they lack antimicrobial and antifungal properties.

Nevertheless, Pissanu is still worried about using crocodile oil as an ingredient for skin care products since he is unsure about consumer reception to such an exotic ingredient. In addition, the Siamese crocodile is an endangered species. Although products made from endangered species can be legally traded after getting a certification from the Convention on International Trade in Endangered Species of Wild Fauna and Flora (CITES), which ensures that international trade of endangered animals or its by-products does not threaten the animal's survival, using by-products of these species could impact CDIP's brand image. Pissanu's worries about selling crocodile oil-based products were somewhat assuaged after learning that the SFC is already "a licensed international trader, caretaker and breeder of crocodiles authorized by CITES" (Sriracha Farm 2015). Even though Pissanu is concerned about the complexities of launching this type of product, he thinks expanding CDIP's product offering might be more important. In order to do that, Pissanu needs to understand important factors about the ASEAN+3 markets. How are the markets different and similar to each other in terms of purchasing power, consumer attitudes, and regulations? What does the competitive landscape look like across these diverse markets?

Skin Care Products in ASEAN+3 Markets

The Asia Pacific region, and more specifically ASEAN+3 countries, has become the biggest market for skin care products and an inspiration for many products made by American and European companies. In 2009, the Asia Pacific region accounted for 44% of global skin care sales, and is expected to exceed 50% by 2015 (Euromonitor International). Asian skin care companies usually have a different focus as compared to their American and

European counterparts when selecting ingredients due to consumer preferences, such as demand for whitening products (Issuu 2014).

As depicted in Table 1, in 2014, the skin care market in the Asia Pacific region was $53.7B. It is expected to grow to $69.7B in 2019 at a rate between 4% and 6% year-over-year. As a point of comparison, the US market for skin care in 2014 was $13.7B with growth not expected to exceed 2.3% until 2019 (Euromonitor International). Consumer preferences for skin care products differ in Asia. On average, East Asian women's beauty regimen has 10 steps, as compared to about 3-4 for an American woman (Chu 2015).

Table 1: Overview of the skin care industry in selected Asian countries.

	Skin care market (BB USD)	Skin care growth	Supply	Demand	Regulation
Thailand	1.81	2.9%	Medium local supply	Whitening and acne	Low regulation
China	23.11	8.7%	No local supply	Whitening/ moisturizer	Medium regulation
Japan	15.46	0.2%	No local supply	Local brands	High regulation
South Korea	5.01	2.8%	No local supply	Local brands	High regulation
Indonesia	1.46	14.2%	Limited local supply	Herban oils and medicines	Large Muslim population
Philippines	0.75	2.6%	Limited local supply	Whitening and acne	Low regulation

Though several broad trends encompass the East Asian beauty markets as a whole, the deeper challenge is for CDIP to understand the factors that differentiate the markets. Some consumers emphasize the use of plant-based products, while others experiment with animal-based products.

For instance, South Korean and Thai consumers have a positive attitude towards animal-based products, while Chinese consumers rely mostly on plant-based products, even though they are receptive to animal-based products as well.

Since a variety of factors, such as consumer purchasing power, trends in cosmetic uses, and domestic competition, can help inform Pissanu's decision, he needs to understand the interplay amongst these factors. For example, when one country's cosmetics industry is large and competitive, while another country's cosmetics industry is small and receptive to animal-based products, which one is more attractive?

To understand the trade-offs between those factors, Pissanu first came up with a shortlist of six ASEAN+3 countries that he thinks have the most potential, based on Gross Domestic Product (GDP) and the size of the skin care markets. These countries are: Thailand, South Korea, China, Indonesia, Japan, and the Philippines.

Skin Care Products in Thailand

The skin care market in Thailand is worth 1.81B USD, and its 2014-2019 CAGR, Compound Annual Growth Rate, is projected at 2.9% (Euromonitor International. Skin Care). Male consumers are a strong presence in the Thai skin care market, accounting for 30.42% of total consumption (Manager 360° Magazine). This percentage is higher than in other countries; for example, in Japan, which is one of the largest skin care markets in the world, male consumers only account for 4.9% of the market (Yano Research Institute 2015). Additionally, Thai citizens' purchasing power is relatively high, since the country's GDP per capita is on the higher end for Southeast Asia at $5,426 (The World Bank 2010).

Multinational firms, such as Unilever and P&G dominate the mass market and they tend to have local manufacturing operations (Euromonitor International 2011g), while domestic firms are more competitive in the high-end market. Competition on the production side of the crocodile oil market is very limited. CDIP has an exclusive agreement with the largest crocodile farm in Thailand for their highest quality fat. CDIP could sell raw crocodile oil to either high-end or mass-market firms. The high-end domestic market is valued at $56.4M, and the high-end multinational segment is valued at $144M. Additionally, the mass segments see $188.9M and $482.3M in sales for domestic and multinational firms respectively (Euromonitor International 2011g).

Consumers in Thailand are open to experimental products and animal products, due to a deeply rooted cultural and historical relationship with traditional medicine. A resurgence of traditional medicine in Thailand began in 1978, when the World Health Organization (WHO) urged member countries to work to integrate traditional forms of medicine into their national health systems (WHO 2013). Since then, the Thai government has taken action to increase the prevalence of traditional medicine through investment, as well as the creation of the Institute of Traditional Thai Medicine in 1993 (WHO 2013). The purpose of Thai medicine, which is based on Buddhist principles, is to keep the four elements, Earth, Wind, Fire, and Water, in balance within the body. In 2009, the traditional Thai medicine market was worth over $7.6M (WHO 2013). Via discussions with industry insiders, Pissanu has learned that animal and natural products are in demand in the local market. While these trends do not specifically apply to crocodile oil, the potential is there (Teeranachaideekul 2016).

The skin care and cosmetics industry has little regulation, making it easy to introduce new products and new ingredients (Teeranachaideekul 2016). Skin care products and cosmetics in Thailand are regulated based on ingredients, which are broken into three categories: specially controlled substances, controlled substances, and allowable substances (Thailand Law Forum 2011). The only products that need approval from the Thai FDA are products that include specially controlled substances. As a result, new products can easily enter the skin care market due to low regulation and a multitude of manufacturers that will work on a contract basis. Brand loyalty, however, is very high. It can be difficult to capture a competitive amount of the market.

Skin Care Products in South Korea

South Korea is well known for setting cosmetic trends that spread all over Asia, making it a valuable market to enter. South Korea's skin care industry has a CAGR of 2.8% as of 2014-2015, representing only a small percentage growth compared to the growth rates of the industry in China or Indonesia. However, South Korea ranks number four in its retail value of $5.01B in total skin care sales, or $99.7 per capita spending, just behind China, Japan, and USA; thus representing a lucrative market for skin care products (Euromonitor International, South Korea). Furthermore, Korea's skin care industry is appealing not only to women, but also to men, who represent a high growth segment and 20% of the market (Euromonitor International 2011c). LG Household and Health Care (LG H&H) and AmorePacific are two Korean companies that were ranked first and second, respectively, for their value share worldwide (Euromonitor International 2011c). In fact, these two companies have more than 50% of the market share in Korea (Euromonitor International, South Korea). Koreans are loyal to local brands and tend to trust local skin care manufacturers. At the same time, while these Korean companies are considered domestic brands, most of their raw materials are imported from abroad. For example, ginseng is sourced from China (Amore Pacific, no date). In addition, these conglomerates focus on producing plant-based products. LG H&H even claims that animal-derived ingredients can irritate the skin (LG Household & Health Care 2014).

Moreover, South Korea has developed a strong market for premium products, which represents more than 59% of the market share since 2009 (Euromonitor International 2011f). AmorePacific, LG H&H, and other conglomerates offer both premium and mass products.[5] Small manufacturers specialize in premium products and differentiate themselves from the competitive conglomerate environment by selling animal-based products instead of plant-based ones.

For example, Genno Lab, a skin care manufacturer established in 2013, imports raw alligator oil from Australia to produce its own alligator-based products. It first launched alligator oil products in 2015 after acquiring a patent for its product and production methods (Genno Lab no date a). Genno Lab was able to expand the market for alligator oil products by advertising the anti-aging and skin nourishing capabilities. In May 2015, Genno Lab exported alligator-oil based products to the United States. The company is likely to grow fast given that it has penetrated international

---

[5]Mass products refer to products targeted at general consumer market. They tend to be cheaper, of lower quality and made in higher quantities than premium products.

markets in less than a year and has obtained the Korean government's support (Genno Lab no date b).

Small manufacturers specializing in premium products include Mizon, whose products are made from snail slime (Mizon no date a) has an in-house R&D business unit that holds 16 technology patent certificates (Mizon no date b). In addition, it manufactures its own products and sells to end-consumers in Asia, Europe and the United States.

Products from conglomerates and small manufacturers share similar purposes: anti-aging, moisturizing, and whitening. As crocodile oil has other unique properties, it could be tailored for different types of consumers (Euromonitor International 2011f). Yet, there are high barriers for entering the Korean market since knowing the language and having a strong local network are requirements for doing business in South Korea (Export.gov no date). At the same time, two conglomerates dominate the Korean skin care industry and competing against them requires a large investment and products that cannot be easily imitated. On a more positive note, CDIP can take advantage of the Korean Ministry of Trade's agreement for tax-free animal fat imports from ASEAN countries (Malaysia Ministry of International Trade and Industry 2015).

Skin Care Products in China

With the rapid growth of skin care and cosmetics consumption during the last decade, China has become the world's second largest cosmetics consumer market (Reportlinker 2015). Furthermore, only 10% of the population uses cosmetics regularly, suggesting there is still plenty of room for China's skin care market to continue growing (Fung Business Intelligent Center 2015). Sales in the skin care industry reached $2.1B in 2014 and are set to reach $3.3B by 2019 (Euromonitor International 2011d). Consumers between the ages of 20 and 30 have been the driving force of the rapid growth of China's skin care market (Fung Business Intelligent Center 2015).

International brands continue to dominate the skin care market in China, with eight out of top 10 players being foreign companies. The largest companies are Procter & Gamble (P&G), L'Oreal and Shiseido. The domestic players, such as Jala Group, Shanghai Jahwa, Shanghai

Inoherb and Proya Cosmetics, have gained a solid foothold with their herb-centric products. Products with whitening functions are popular across all categories of skin care, including cleansers, toners, and moisturizers, amongst others (Euromonitor International 2011d). Overall, demand for skin care products is concentrated in four categories: premium, herbal-based, natural/organic and whitening products. With their growing disposable incomes, Chinese consumers are starting to pay more for premium skin care products.

According to Euromonitor International, traditional distribution channels like hypermarkets, department stores and health and beauty retailers are still most popular for beauty and personal care products in 2014 (Euromonitor International 2011a). However, the online sales channel cannot be overlooked because of its explosive growth. Tmall.com, Jumei.com and Lefeng.com, which are the leading B2C online portals in China, have drawn the attention of skin care companies (Euromonitor International 2011d). Social media, with platforms such as WeChat and Sina Weibo, has become an indispensable tool for cosmetics brands to promote their products and interact with their customers (Li & Fung Research Center 2012).

Furthermore, a couple of newly issued regulations might favor CDIP product's launch in China, for both consumer products and raw oil. Since June 2015, a tariff on imported cosmetics and skin care products has been reduced to 2% from 5% (Burkitt 2015). This would be beneficial for CDIP's introduction of consumer products into China. Also, in June 2014, companies manufacturing cosmetics with pre-established ingredients inside China will no longer be required to provide samples of new products to the government for animal testing (Humane Society International 2013). According to this agreement between China and ASEAN, animal fat and oil exported to China would incur no tariff (China FTA Network 2009). This makes it more attractive for Chinese companies to buy raw crocodile oil from CDIP. However, according to the China Food and Drug Administration (CFDA), crocodile oil is not currently being used as a cosmetics ingredient. Consequently, a hygiene license granted by CFDA might be required for selling raw crocodile oil in China (CFDA 2002).

Skin Care Products in Indonesia

The skin care market in Indonesia is valued at $1.46B, with an annual growth rate of 14.2%, as of 2014. However, three multinationals – Unilever, Procter & Gamble and L'Oréal – accounted for about 69% of the market in skin care. Through 2014, local players such as Martha Tilaar Group, Vitapharm PT and Mustika Ratu Tbk PT witnessed declining market shares. Furthermore, mass market products account for 94% of the market (Euromonitor International 2011e). Despite the tough competition, there is great potential demand for CDIP's product. Crocodile oil has been used as a traditional medicine in Indonesia to treat burns, wounds, blisters, and skin irritation (Rodin 2013).

Products with lightening and whitening function were the most popular skin care products in 2014. Additionally, the anti-aging product segment was the fastest growing in the skin care market. With rising health awareness in Indonesia, increased use of skin care products containing natural ingredients, such as green tea, coffee or chocolate extract, has been observed (Euromonitor International 2011e).

Perhaps the largest uncertainty associated with entrance into Indonesia is how its significant Muslim population will perceive a product that contains crocodile oil. Many Muslims may be unwilling to use skin care products without halal certification. According to Law No. 33 on Halal Product Assurance ("Halal Product Assurance Law"), issued on October 17, 2014 by the Indonesian Parliament, halal certification will be mandatory for most consumable products, including skin care products manufactured, imported, distributed and/or traded in the Indonesian customs area by September 29, 2019 (Hadiputranto, Hadinoto & Partners 2015; ABNR 2015). Under Islamic law, crocodiles are considered haram, so they are not fit for consumption. That being said, there are currently products being sold on the Indonesian market that contain by-products from "haram" animals (Hussain 2014), so there is a possibility that CDIP could introduce their products successfully.

Skin Care Products in Japan

At $15.5B, the Japanese skin care market is the second largest in the Asia-Pacific region, just after the Chinese market. That said, growth prospects on the skin care market in Japan are not favorable as it is forecasted to remain stagnant for the next 5 years (Euromonitor International 2007).

Japan does not produce any crocodile oil domestically, hence any manufacturers using the oil as an input must acquire the raw material from an international supplier. Additionally, Japanese consumers tend to be loyal to domestic brands, creating an environment where large Japanese brands thrive, while foreign brands have difficulty breaking into the market. As a result, Shiseido, a Japanese company, claims 13% of the market, whereas foreign multinationals rarely achieve more than a 1% share (Euromonitor International 2007).

Mass products are performing better than premium products in the liquid, cream, gel and bar cleanser categories. However, moisturizer sales showed a different trend: premium products grew at a rate of 4% compared to 3% for mass products. Premium moisturizers are also sold in high-end department stores where sales agents have the opportunity to upsell their benefits. Additionally, all-in-one moisturizers have also gained popularity. Japanese consumers care about the ingredients in their skin care products, and they prefer organic materials. However, due to the lack of certification for organic materials in Japan, foreign certifications such as USDA Organic certificate have gained a foothold in the Japanese market. Japanese firms have been trying to use this trend to market organic products formulated for Japanese and not Western skin types (Euromonitor International 2007). Nonetheless, it is unclear how CDIP can tap into this trend.

Contrary to many other countries, Japan has a highly regulated skin care industry due to recent incidents involving skin-whitening products (Euromonitor International 2007). In 2013, Japan's second largest cosmetics company, Kanebo, recalled more than 4 million of its items after its patented whitening ingredient, Rhododenol, caused "clearly visible blotches" on thousands of users (Negishi 2013). As a result, it might be more difficult to comply with local rules and laws in Japan than anywhere else in the ASEAN+3 region.

Skin Care Products in the Philippines

Although the Philippines is one of the smaller economies in the region, with a total GDP of $299B in 2014 and GDP per capita of $2,950 (Euromonitor International 2011b), its GDP growth is high, at 6%, and is expected to remain strong in the next few years (Euromonitor International 2011h). The overall skin care market is also on the smaller end, at $0.75B. Additionally, growth in the segment is low, at 2.56% CAGR from 2014 to 2019. The industry has recently been trending towards online sales, although traditional brick and mortar sales are still dominant. Furthermore, the skin care market for men has been growing at a very high rate, while growth of the market for women has remained low.

Competition is strong for consumer products. Three companies, all international, control 51% of the market. There are some smaller domestic manufacturers that have significant market shares. Competition amongst the larger corporations is fierce, and it can be difficult for smaller firms to enter the market (Euromonitor International 2011b). Consumers are split between the price-sensitive mass market and brand-loyal high-end market. Both domestic and multinational firms compete across all segments, but multinationals dominate the mass market (Euromonitor International 2011b).

Consumers demand natural and organic products, both plant- and animal-based. Individuals are also very open to using new compounds, and potentially crocodile oil (Euromonitor 2011). Therefore, it could possibly be profitable for CDIP to enter the Philippine market, since crocodile oil products have begun to gain popularity in the country. For example, Philicillin crocodile oil sells their products online and in stores. There is also some supply from larger crocodile farms, but it is more limited than in other countries. Most large manufacturers are not using crocodile oil, but smaller niche firms may be interested in CDIP's raw material.

The low regulation of the skin care and cosmetics industry in the Philippines provides CDIP with an easy entry into this market. The FDA of the Philippines is responsible for ensuring safety, quality, and purity of all skin care products sold in the country (Food and Drug Administration of the Philippines 2013). However, since 2008, the country's FDA has adopted the ASEAN Cosmetic Directive (ACD), which standardizes the skin care and cosmetics regulatory scheme and eliminates the restrictions of trade for these types of products throughout the ASEAN+3 region (Health Sciences Authority 2008).

Persistent Challenges

Although CDIP has the potential to be a first mover in Asian markets with its crocodile oil products, several challenges remain. First, CDIP does not have enough knowledge about its potential end-consumers, meaning that they would need to start international market research from scratch. Second, the demand in the Asian skin care industry is dominated by products that provide whitening, anti-aging, and acne treatment functions. Since crocodile oil's functions are antimicrobial, antifungal, and collagen stimulating, CDIP needs to adapt its products to fit the market demand at large by combining crocodile oil with other inputs and utilizing their extensive R&D experience. Third, crocodile oil-based products are subject to future regulations from CITES, which could threaten CDIP's crocodile oil supply (CITES 2013). Lastly, CDIP needs to ensure that its perception as a high quality OEM does not diminish due to its divergence into B2C channels.

Though he is aware of the aforementioned obstacles, Pissanu knows that CDIP can remain in a strong position thanks to its high-quality R&D, relationship with academic institutions at TSP, and agreement with SCF.

Future Steps

CDIP has the capacity to produce two categories of products: raw crocodile oil for its B2B channel and consumer goods for its B2C channel. Pissanu knows that the lack of knowledge surrounding crocodile oil based products makes it difficult to sell these products to other manufacturers, but he is also aware of his limited experience in B2C markets. In order to stimulate demand from manufacturers, Pissanu may need to begin by introducing a crocodile oil based consumer product first, and start selling raw oil to manufacturers as the demand develops. Finding the right balance is essential, because operating in both markets at the same time will turn potential partners into competitors and CDIP must tread carefully.

CDIP could cannibalize its own products by providing competitors with high-quality oil.

Moreover, Pissanu is struggling to decide which country to enter first with his crocodile oil products. The crocodile oil product has the potential to be extremely successful as the benefits are more diverse and robust than competing products such as coconut oil, but the right market must be found within ASEAN+3. The pros and cons of each country make the decision exceedingly difficult. CDIP has extensive experience and a deep understanding of the Thai market, which will help decrease the risks associated with this venture yet entering Thailand first could cause CDIP to miss large and lucrative foreign markets. China is the country with most revenue potential, but herbal products, rather than animal based products, remain prominent in the skin care market. The rapid growth of Indonesia's skin care market is attractive, but the product could be rejected by the large Muslim population. In addition, despite their potential profits, the Japanese and South Korean skin care markets are constrained by high regulations, competition, and sense of nationalism. Lastly, the Philippines, although not lucrative when compared to other ASEAN+3 countries, is attractive due to low regulation and high growth in the skin care industry. Taking into consideration the pros and cons of each market, Pissanu needs to make a decision on how to proceed. CDIP is heading towards its IPO. Successfully expanding revenue streams, proving the firm's ability to take full ownership of a product, will contribute towards this goal. What should he do?

References

ABNR. 2015. New Halal Law Makes Halal Certification Mandatory. [Online]. [Accessed 20 March 2016]. Available from: http://.abnrlaw.com/news_detail.php?send_news_id=260&year=2015.

Amore Pacific. [no date]. Our Ingredients. [Online]. [Accessed 20 March 2016]. Available from: https://us.amorepacific.com/about-amorepacific/our-ingredients.

Burkitt, L. 2015. China to Cut Taxes on Some Imported Consumer Goods to Spur Spending. The Wall Street Journal. [Online]. 25 May. [Accessed 20 Mar 2016]. Available from: http://.wsj.com/articles/china-to-cut-tariffs-on-some-imported-consumer-goods-to-spur-spending-1432538808.

CDIP Thailand. 2015. Wān tāl deīyw StaLeaf. [Online]. [Accessed 23 Mar 2016]. Available from: http://cdipthailand.com/th/innovation-thai/innovation-product/64-staleaf.html.

Central Mosque. [no date]. The Fiqh of Halal and Haram Animals. [Online]. [Accessed 20 March 2016]. Available from: http://.central-mosque.com/index.php/General-Fiqh/the-fiqh-of-halal-and-haram-animals.html.

China Food and Drug Administration (CFDA). [Online]. [Accessed 20 March 2016]. Available from: http://eng.sfda.gov.cn/WS03/CL0755/.

China FTA Network. 2009. Overview. [Online]. [Accessed 20 Mar 2016]. Available from: http://fta.mofcom.gov.cn/topic/chinaasean.shtml.

Chu, K. 2015. Cosmetics Industry Applies Asian Trends to West. The Wall Street Journal. [Online]. 5 May. [Accessed 20 March 2016]. Available from: http://.wsj.com/articles/cosmetics-industry-applies-asian-trends-to-west-1430838068.

CITES (Convention on International Trade in Endangered Species of Wild Flora and Fauna). 2013. CITES at work. [Online]. [Accessed 20 March 2016]. Available from: https://.cites.org/.

Euromonitor International. 2007. Japan. [Online]. [Accessed 20 March 2016]. Available from: http://.euromonitor.com/japan.

Euromonitor International. [Accessed 20 March 2016]. Avialable from: http://.euromonitor.com/.

Euromonitor International. 2011a. Beauty and Personal Care in China. [Online]. London: Euromonitor International. [Accessed 20 March 2016]. Available from: http://.euromonitor.com/beauty-and-personal-care-in-china/report.

Euromonitor International. 2011b. Beauty and Personal Care in the Philippines. [Online]. London: Euromonitor International. [Accessed 20 March 2016]. Available from: http://.euromonitor.com/beauty-and-personal-care-in-the-philippines/report.

Euromonitor International. 2011c. Men's Grooming in South Korea. [Online]. London: Euromonitor International. [Accessed 20 March 2016]. Available from: http://.euromonitor.com/mens-grooming-in-south-korea/report.

Euromonitor International. 2011d. Skin care in China [Online]. London: Euromonitor International. [Accessed 20 March 2016]. Available from: http://.euromonitor.com/skin-care-in-china/report.

Euromonitor International. 2011e. Skin care in Indonesia. [Online]. London: Euromonitor International. [Accessed 20 March 2016]. Available from: http://.euromonitor.com/skin-care-in-indonesia/report.

Euromonitor International. 2011f. Skin care in South Korea [Online]. London: Euromonitor International. [Accessed 20 March 2016]. Available from: http://.euromonitor.com/skin-care-in-south-korea/report.

Euromonitor International. 2011g. Skin care in Thailand. [Online]. London: Euromonitor International. [Accessed 20 March 2016]. Available from: http://.euromonitor.com/skin-care-in-thailand/report.

Euromonitor International. 2011h. Skin care in the Philippines. [Online]. London: Euromonitor International. [Accessed 20 March 2016]. Available from: http://.euromonitor.com/skin-care-in-the-philippines/report.

Euromonitor International. Skin Care. [Online]. [Accessed 20 March 2016]. Available from: http://.euromonitor.com/skin-care.

Euromonitor International. South Korea. [Online]. [Accessed 20 March 2016]. Available from: http://.euromonitor.com/south-korea.

Export.gov. [no date]. Leading Sectors for U.S. Export and Investment. [Online]. [Accessed 20 March 2016]. Available from: http://.export.gov/southkorea/doingbusinessinskorea/leadingsectorsforusexportsinvestment/index.asp.

Fernquest, J. 2011. Thailand's crocodile industry. Bangkok Post. [Online]. 3 November. [Accessed 19 March 2016]. Available from: https://www.bangkokpost.com/learning/learning-news/264588/thailand-crocodile-industry%5D.

Food and Drug Administration of the Philippines. 2013. ASEAN Cosmetic Directive. [Online]. Muntinlupa City: Food and Drug Administration of the Philippines. [Accessed 20 March 2016]. Available from: http://.fda.gov.ph/industry-corner/downloadables/197-asean-cosmetic-harmonization/15782-asean-cosmetic-directive.

Fung Business Intelligent Center. 2015. China's cosmetics market. [Online]. [Accessed 20 March 2016]. Accessed from: http://.iberchina.org/files/cosmeticos_china_fung.pdf.

Genno Lab. [no date]a. About Us. [Online]. [Accessed 20 March 2016]. Available from: http://www.gennolab.com/wp/eng/company-2/about-us/.

Genno Lab. [no date]b. History. [Online]. [Accessed 20 March 2016]. Available from: http://.gennolab.com/wp/eng/company-2/history/.

Hadiputranto, Hadinoto & Partners. 2015. Halal Product Assurance Law. [Online]. [Accessed 20 March 2016]. Available from: http://www.bakermckenzie.com/-/media/files/insight/publications/2015/01/halal-product-assurance-law/files/read-publication/fileattachment/al_jakarta_halalproductassurance_jan15.pdf.

Health Sciences Authority. 2008. Agreement on the ASEAN Harmonized Cosmetic Regulatory Scheme. [Online]. [Accessed 20 March 2016]. Available from: http://www.hsa.gov.sg/content/dam/HSA/HPRG/Cosmetic_Products/AGREEMENT%20ON%20ASEAN%20HARMONIZED%20COSMETIC%20REGULATORY%20SCHEME.pdf.

Humane Society International. 2013. China's Cosmetics Animal Testing FAQ. [Online]. [Accessed 20 March 2016]. Available from: http://.hsi.org/assets/pdfs/bcf_china_cosmetics.pdf.

Hussain, S. 2014. All Natural Muslim Beauty Option? Yes! Eluxe Magazine. [Online]. [Accessed 20 March 2016]. Available from: http://eluxemagazine.com/beauty/muslim-beauty-options-halal-yes/.

Issuu. 2014. Global Cosmetic Industry, GCI October 2014. Global Cosmetic Industry Magazine. [Online]. 182(8). [Accessed 20 March 2016]. Available from: https://issuu.com/yvesrocherdemx/docs/gcimagazinegci201410-dloctubre.

LG Household & Health Care. 2014. Beautiful R&D. [Online]. [Accessed 20 March 2016]. Available from: http://.lgcare.com/global/company/rnd/rnd1.jsp.

Li, H. L., Chen, L.P., Chen, Q. X., Hu, Y.H., Liang, G., Qin, Y., and Xiong, Y. X. 2012. Crocodile oil enhances cutaneous burn wound healing and reduces scar formation in rats. Acad Emerg Med. [Online]. 19(3), pp.265-73. [Accessed 20 March 2016]. Available from: http://.ncbi.nlm.nih.gov/pubmed/22435858.

Li & Fung Research Center. 2012. China's cosmetics market, 2011. [Online]. Hong Kong: Li & Fung Research Center. [Accessed 20 March 2016]. Available from: http://.funggroup. com/eng/knowledge/research.php?report=industry&version=archive.

Malaysia Ministry of International Trade and Industry. 2015. Questions On ASEAN - Korea (AKFTA). [Online]. [Accessed 20 March 2016]. Available from: http://fta.miti.gov. my/index.php/pages/view/24.

Manager 360° Magazine (website in Thai) 2002. 20 Mar. 2016. Available from http://. gotomanager.com/.

Mizon. [no date]a. All in One Snail Repair Cream. [Online]. [Accessed 20 March 2016]. Available from: http://eng.mizon.co.kr/product/product_detail.asp?prod_num=1790.

Mizon. [no date]b. Water volume aqua gel cream. [Online]. [Accessed 20 March 2016]. Available from: http://eng.mizon.co.kr/product/product_detail.asp.

Negishi, M. 2013. Recall in Japan Blemishes Skin-Whitening Industry. The Wall Street Journal. [Online]. 28 July. [Accessed 19 March 2016]. Available from: https://www.wsj. com/articles/SB10001424127887323971204578629382236288570.

Reportlinker. 2015. China Cosmetics Market Report, 2014-2017. Cision PR Newswire. [Online]. 2 March. [Accessed 20 Mar 2016]. Available from: http://.prnewswire.com/ news-releases/china-cosmetics-market-report-2014-2017-300043914.html.

Rodin, M. 2013. Genuine Crocodile Oil for Treatment of Burn Wounds and Blisters. Indo Magic. [Online]. [Accessed 20 March 2016]. Available from: http://.indomagic.com/blog/ genuine-crocodile-oil/.

Sriracha Farm. 2015. Company Profile. "Company Profile - Sriracha farm." [Online]. [Accessed 20 March 2016]. Available from: http://.srirachafarm.com/home/index.php/ company-profile.

Thailand Law Forum. 2011. Thailand Cosmetic Law. [Online]. [Accessed 20 March 2016]. Available from: http://.thailawforum.com/database1/cosmetic-law-3.html.

The World Bank. 2010. GDP growth (annual %). [Online]. [Accessed 20 March 2016]. Available from: http://data.worldbank.org/indicator/NY.GDP.MKTP.KD.ZG.

WHO (World Health Organization). 2013. Traditional Medicine in Kingdom of Thailand. [Online]. [Accessed 20 March 2016]. Available from: http://www.searo.who.int/entity/ medicines/topics/traditional_medicines_in_the_kingdom_of_thailand.pdf.

Yano Research Institute. 2015. Cosmetic Market in Japan: Key Research Findings 2014. [Online]. Tokyo: Yano Research Institute. [Accessed 20 March 2016]. Available from: https://.yanoresearch.com/press/pdf/1316.pdf.

Chapter 8

RiverPRO's Environmentally-Friendly Paper: Growing Through Sustainability

Pimbucha Rusmevichientong,[1] Rosamy Albornoz,[2] Susan Chen,[2] Jinwen Lin,[2] Kulapa Kudilok,[3] and Ravissa Suchato[3]

Introduction

One afternoon in January 2015, RiverPRO Managing Director Mr. Sumrit Yipyintum was visiting the Thanatarn paper factory examining a run of his company's new product, unbleached, recycled tissue paper. As the name suggests, recycled, unbleached tissue is made from recycled materials and does not pass through the bleaching process that white tissue products go through, which reduces pollution and energy use associated with paper production. Having launched the product two years ago, RiverPRO is the only paper company in Thailand to produce recycled, unbleached tissue products. Sales of the product has doubled since 2014; RiverPRO is planning to produce more of it.

RiverPRO was established in 1966 as Thailand's first tissue producer. The company's first plant, the Thanatarn factory, is located in an area that was once a peripheral industrial zone but is now part of urban Bangkok. As the plant is near residential areas, RiverPRO's management is concerned that nearby communities could perceive the facility as a source of pollution and possibly call for a government shutdown of the factory. To avoid this, Sumrit has worked tirelessly to make manufacturing processes more sustainable. He hopes that the recycled, unbleached tissue paper can show the government and the community that RiverPRO is committed to sustainable operations and to sustainable communities.

However, Sumrit's ambition for his company does not end at sustainability. He also hopes that this new product will enable RiverPRO to compete more effectively against larger international corporations that have

[1]College of Health and Human Development, California State University, Fullerton.
[2]SMART Program, Cornell University.
[3]Department of Agriculture and Resource Economics, Kasetsart University.

established strong brands in Thailand. RiverPRO is considering going public to harness more financial support, business talent, and brand recognition. To accomplish this goal, RiverPRO first needs to prove its viability to the Securities and Exchange Commission of Thailand by increasing the company's market share and revenues. Sumrit expects that the recycled, unbleached tissue paper can be one of the keys to helping the company take second place in the tissue market.

Those thoughts raced through Sumrit's mind as he wondered if this new product would be attractive enough to Thai consumers. He had convinced RiverPRO's board of directors that launching the recycled product paper would strengthen the eco-friendly image of the company while increasing its market share. However, it is unclear whether customers will support the new eco-friendly paper product with its unfamiliar brown color. Sumrit knows that to launch a successful marketing strategy, his company needs to understand clearly what consumers want.

Welcome to Thailand

A constitutional monarchy established in 1932, Thailand is the only Southeast Asian country that was never a European colony. With a population of over 67 million, Thailand is the third most populous country in Southeast Asia. As of 2016, 54% of the population resided in urban areas, up from 38% in 2005 (The World Bank 2017). Its capital, Bangkok, is home to 8.3 million people (UN data no date).

Currently the second largest economy in Southeast Asia, the country enjoyed the world's highest economic growth rate from 1985 to 1996. During this period, Thailand became primarily an export-based economy, with manufacturing, agriculture, and tourism as its leading sectors. It is a member of the Association of Southeast Asian Nations (ASEAN). Thailand's GDP in 2015 was $395 billion U.S. dollars with a growth rate of 2.8% (World Bank 2017). Thailand ranks relatively high on the United Nations Human Development Index (HDI) among ASEAN countries; in 2015 it was ranked 87th (UNDP 2017). The percentage of the population living under the poverty line has decreased from 42.6% in 2000 to 12.6% in 2012 (United Nations Development Programme 2012). Despite the impressive progress in development, the country has experienced economic instability in recent years due to political and civil unrest.

Thailand's retail tissue paper industry

Although the country has suffered from political chaos and signs of an economic slowdown since 2008, the retail tissue paper industry has experienced strong growth, recording historic retail sales of around $230 million in 2014. The fastest growing product category is toilet paper, with an average annual growth rate of more than 5% between 2011 and 2013 (Statista). Most people in rural areas still use traditional 'squat' toilets and water for cleaning. With growing urbanization, "Western-style" toilets are becoming more common, and, along with them, the use of toilet paper. In addition, consumers like using toilet paper for general cleaning purposes as well. Because of the reliance on toilet paper, paper towels are not very popular. Facial tissue (mainly boxed) has experienced a 4.89% average annual growth rate from 2011 to 2013, and is projected to continue on this path for a while. Napkins have also seen strong growth driven primarily by demand from restaurants (Statista).

The Thai tissue industry caters to two markets: the domestic-use market and the industrial-use market, the latter comprised of public facilities such as hospitals, schools, and restaurants. Both markets have experienced growth in recent years, with the industrial-use market growing at a faster rate. Many companies retail their own brands and make products for other retailers as well under different brand names.

In terms of consumer groups, the Thai tissue market has four segments: Premium, Medium, Economy, and Super Economy. The more expensive premium tissue products are especially soft and are made of 100% virgin fiber pulp. In contrast, super economy products target low-income, price-conscious consumers, most of whom live in rural areas. With rapid urbanization, the demand for toilet paper will continue to grow, presenting opportunities in the market.

Retail tissue products are distributed through multiple channels: the modern trade channels of hypermarkets, supermarkets, and convenience stores, and the more traditional channel of small grocery retailers. Urban consumers tend to purchase tissue products in the modern outlets, while rural consumers shop mostly at traditional retailers.

Competitive Landscape

The tissue industry of Thailand is dominated by Berli Jucker Cellox (BJC) and Kimberly-Clark Thailand, both of which own a diversified product portfolio and enjoy high levels of brand awareness and abundant financial resources. RiverPRO Pulp & Paper Co. is the third largest producer in the market; the company faces challenges from not only Berli Jucker Cellox and Kimberly-Clark Thailand but also from other local companies.

Kimberly-Clark Thailand Co. (KC)

Kimberly-Clark Thailand Co., the number one tissue manufacturer at present, is the Thai branch of the transnational personal care product corporation Kimberly-Clark. The company has 1200 employees and two modern production facilities located in Thailand. Their brands include Scott, Kleenex, and Kimberly-Clark Professional. The company has the greatest variety of products in the Thai tissue market and is aiming to promote one of its mainstream products, Kimberly-Clark Professional, as a business-to-business product across mainland Southeast Asia. The company expects that this market will comprise up to 30% of its total sales in the next five to seven years.

Berli Jucker Cellox (BJC)

Founded in 1882, Berli Jucker Cellox holds second place in the market. It is a subsidiary of Berli Jucker PCL, one of the biggest and oldest companies in Thailand. Berli Jucker Cellox's has a regional distribution network in ASEAN countries. It owns two factories in Thailand, which have an annual production capacity of 45,000 tons, and a production facility in Vietnam, which produces 14,440 tons per year. In August 2013, BJC established a joint venture to support business expansion, sales and distribution in other Southeast Asian countries.

BJC recorded a 31.7% sales share within retail tissue in 2014 with sales of 2.2 billion TBH in the tissue and hygiene industry in 2013. The company has outperformed every other Thai tissue company and continues to be the leading domestic company in Thailand.

BJC's main brands include Cellox, Zilk, Dion, Belle, Maxmo, Melona and Yori. Even though its marketing expenditure is low compared to Kimberly-Clark Thailand Co., BJC has particularly strong brand awareness in Thailand partly because Berli Jucker was awarded the privilege of using the Royal Emblem of Thailand on their products. The company has started to expand to rural areas also.

Private label brands

Although a small sector, private labels owned by supermarket chains are another, growing, competitor in the Thailand tissue industry. Private label products are available from Big C, Tesco Lotus, Tops Supermarket of Central Retail, Home Fresh Mart of the Mall Group, Watsons, and Boots. Those products target low-to-middle income consumers and consist of tissues, cotton buds, and diapers. Because those products do not incur slotting fees and advertising costs, supermarkets set their prices lower than other brands.

Environmental considerations in the tissue industry

According to the Thailand Fiber and Paper Association, the consumer demand for fiber and paper products is on the rise. While tissue products only account for 2.5% of Thailand's total fiber and paper production in 2010, it is growing in terms of sales value (Thailand Pulp and Paper). Increasing public awareness of environmental issues has led to a growing demand for eco-friendly products.

A number of recycled tissue products are already present in Thailand. Some companies have actively sought a "Green Label"certificate from the Thailand Environment Institute, which guarantees that the product is manufactured through an environmentally-friendly process. Most tissue products also have enhanced environmentally-friendly images, such as Kimsoft, Wypall, and Scott, which are produced by Kimberly-Clark Thailand.

Products from RiverPRO also show strong consideration for the environment. The products all carry the Green Label, and are fluorescent-free. The packaging cartons are made of materials that can be recycled or used as fertilizer. In contrast, similar products by Kimberly-Clark Thailand

and Berli Jucker Cellox use plastic and unbleached paper for wrapping and containers.

Recycled tissue products include recycled, unbleached tissue (brown), recycled pink (dyed) tissue, and recycled white (bleached) tissue in napkin and roll formats. In terms of quality, compared to products made from virgin pulp, recycled products have a less smooth texture and are less efficient at absorbing moisture. RiverPRO's recycled, unbleached paper is a commitment to environment protection; it is the most eco-friendly of all the recycled paper products.

Aside from having an environmentally-friendly production process and producing recycled tissue, manufacturers such as Kimberly Clark Thailand try to promote this eco-friendly concept to their customers as well. The company holds an event to give certificates to organizations that choose to purchase products from the company for six consecutive years. This certificate certifies that the organization supports the idea of environmentally-friendly tissue and hygiene products. This helps with creating brand awareness and also in convincing more customers to buy products from Kimberly-Clark Thailand.

RiverPRO Pulp & Paper Company

Company history

River Group, commonly known as RiverPRO, was founded in 1966 as the Mai Nam Paper Industry Limited by a Japanese-Taiwanese entrepreneur, Kamol Yipyintum, the grandfather of Sumrit, the current Managing Director. Mai Nam Paper Industry Limited was the first paper mill in Thailand. Its first facility was located in the Samutprakarn Province, just outside Bangkok. The plant still operates today as the Thanatarn Pulp & Paper Company. (See Box 1 for detail on company's philosophy.)

Mai Nam Paper Industry Ltd. started production with two second-hand machines brought from Japan with a combined capacity of five tons per day, the equivalent of 55 thousand of rolls per day. Being the first domestic tissue paper producer in Thailand, RiverPRO had a competitive advantage in terms of cost and this has contributed to the company's rapid initial growth.

Box 1. RiverPRO's Corporate Vision, Mission, and Philosophy

Vision

"Be the second in Thailand market and get recognition in Indo-china market with balanced happy stability and sustainability by 2020".

Mission

- Manufacture and sell environmentally-friendly hygienic disposable products.
- Be a home and big family for employees who would like to improve their life.
- Encourage good citizenship.
- Be a role model in adopting the PSE.
- Gain reasonable return on investment to be a sustainable organization.

Philosophy

"Be a learning organization based on ethics and excellent management system according to the principle of the Philosophy of Sufficiency Economy in order to have happy employees providing better quality of life, sharing to societies and contributing to the environment."

In 1979, RiverPRO expanded its capacity to 20 tons per day by installing a new Japanese machine with state-of-the-art technology and equipment for the De-Inking Process (DIP). At the time, the DIP was an innovation that allowed companies to turn office paper, cardboard, and even cotton fabric into raw material for recycled pulp, which in turn could be used to make napkins, toilet, and tissue papers. In 1992, the company invested in another new machine from Italy, which improved the quality of the company's products.

RiverPRO's growing market share necessitated the expansion of production facilities, but lack of space at the Thanatarn Plant made this impossible. As an alternative, in 2003, RiverPRO opened a new plant in Saraburi Province. The new plant has two machines from Germany and Sweden, which provide a production capacity of 115 tons per day.

Corporate organization and culture

RiverPRO has 800 employees, 350 at the Thanatarn Plant and 450 at the Saraburi Plant. The company is majority-owned by the Yipyintum family; the employees collectively own 10% of the company. The company is overseen by a board of directors comprised of four members of the Yipyintum family and three other individuals. Figure 1 outlines the company's organizational structure, and shows the various departments and Board Committees.

RiverPRO has a clearly articulated vision, mission, and philosophy, which centers on running a sustainable enterprise that strives to balance making profit with being a good environmental steward and corporate citizen. Many of these ideas have grown out of the "Philosophy of Sufficiency Economy" (PSE), a school of thought articulated and promoted by Thailand's monarch King Bhumibol Adulyadej during the 1970s and further gaining prominence in the 1990s.

"Gaining momentum in Thailand after the 1997 financial crisis, the Sufficiency Economy thinking has increased in importance over the years, right up to this year of political transition. The thinking advocates growth with economic stability over rapid but unbridled growth. It emphasizes sustainable development, sound macroeconomic policies, and the equitable sharing of the benefits of economic prosperity. At the

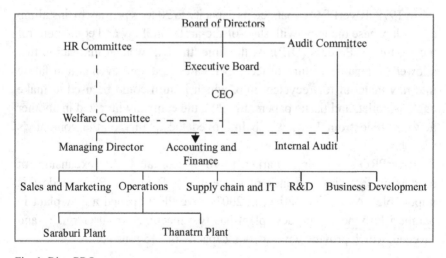

Fig. 1: RiverPRO organogram.

Box 2. About Sufficiency Economy

Philosophy of Sufficiency Economy

"Sufficiency Economy is a philosophy that stresses the middle path as an overriding principle for appropriate conduct by the populace at all levels... To achieve sufficiency, an application of knowledge with due consideration and prudence is essential. In particular, great care is needed in the utilization of theories and methodologies for planning and implementation in every step. At the same time, it is essential to strengthen the moral fiber of the nation, so that everyone, particularly public officials, academics, and business people at all levels, adhere first and foremost to the principles of honesty and integrity."

Office of the National Economic and
Social Development Board (Thailand)
(*Source*: Piboolsravut and Sathirathai, 2004)

same time, it shuns excessive risk-taking, untenable inequalities, and the wasteful use of natural resources" (UNDP 2007).

The philosophy has its roots in Thailand's prominent Buddhist religion, and it also speaks to the need to strive for sustainability, a principle that has gained prominence in the face of global challenges such as balancing development with mitigating the adverse affects of climate change. RiverPRO's management subscribes to this philosophy, which underlies their commitments to community development and environmental stewardship. (See Box 2.)

Business

RiverPRO has had sustained growth over the last 10 years (Figure 2). An important factor in the rapid growth of RiverPRO is the opening of the Saraburi Plant in 2004 that increased capacity by almost 350%. This has enabled the company to compete directly with Berli Jucker Cellox and Kimberly-Clark.

In line with RiverPRO's vision to become the second largest tissue producer in the Thai market, the company is planning to use the expanded production capacity to begin supplying industrial clients, such as manufacturers of diapers and sanitary napkins. While this could represent a significant opportunity for RiverPRO, the company does not have a clear sense of the market size and demand at this point.

The company has a mixed commercialization strategy with 50% of their sales from retail products, 25% from OEM products, and 25% from the away-from-home (AFH) market. However, even with half of its revenue coming from retail products, RiverPRO has not been able to build a significant presence in the retail tissue market. The company has witnessed encouraging growth in the AFH market and has successfully sold its recycled, unbleached tissue products to restaurants, hospitals, hotels and airlines. The company captured the interest of its customers in the AFH market by delivering an "eco-friendly" image to consumers. Moreover, the company sees these public facilities as chances to educate Thai consumers that recycled, unbleached tissue is just as hygienic as white tissue. RiverPRO produces different types of paper products sold to Thailand's market, and also exports some brands to Laos, Cambodia, and Myanmar.

RiverPRO is in a difficult position: while competing against Berli Jucker Cellox and Kimberly-Clark, the company is also threatened by rising private labels. As a mid-size manufacturing company, it is difficult for RiverPRO to receive loans from banks and collect accounts receivable from distributors and clients in a reasonable time period. The lack of backup cash has contributed to the company's plan to list itself on the stock market exchange in the next 10 years.

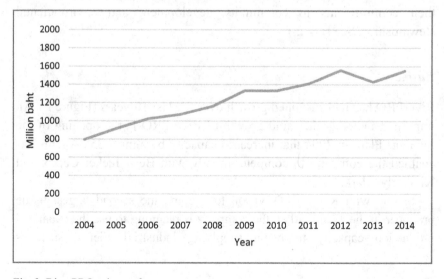

Fig. 2: RiverPRO sales performance.

Brand portfolio

All RiverPRO's products are made from raw material sourced from environmentally sustainable recycled fibers from office paper and cardboard, plantation forests, and sugar cane trees. Pinn and Tendre are the biggest brands of the company. Pinn is made from 100% recycled fibers while Tendre is made from sugar cane trees. Premium brands are made from fibers sourced from plantation forests.

As mid- and low-end products contribute to the majority of the company's revenue, RiverPRO has no plan to expand its investment on Primrose and Mild Ultra, their two premium brands, since the profit margin is low. Conversely, the company has shown an increasing interest in the Middle segment—a segment that it thinks will grow fastest in the future due to the high urbanization rate. (See Table 1 for a list of RiverPRO's brands.)

Table 1. The RiverPRO brands matrix.

Brand	Price category
Primrose	Premium (high quality-high price)
Mild Ultra	Premium (high quality-high price)
Tendre	Upper Medium (high quality-moderate price)
Pinn Plus	Medium (value for money)
Pinn	Economy (fair value-low price)
Mild	Economy (fair value-low price)
Smile	Economy (fair value-low price)
Paula	Economy (fair value-low price)

(*Source:* RiverPRO)

Branding, marketing and distribution

Branded products are sold through a distributor to modern trade channels including major supermarket chains and traditional trade channels (private grocery stores, street stores and floating market stores). Although branded products are sold via distributors, RiverPRO negotiates retail prices, space and position on the shelf, and promotions directly with stores. Brand prices are set according to the quality of the product. RiverPRO also sells its products to other mainland Southeast Asian countries through distributors, but the sales generated only account for a small portion of its revenue.

OEM sales are negotiated and shipped directly to clients. The most important OEM clients for RiverPRO are the modern trade stores, Tesco, Lotus, and Big C. Negotiations in the AFH market are made for mid- and long-term contracts and are allocated through bidding processes. Some clients of RiverPRO in the AFH market are Siriraj Hospital, Ramathipbordi Hospital, Siam Paragon Mall, Thai Airways, Air Asia, and others.

The company sells its branded products through distributors and only promotes their brands via price promotion or events at the point of sale. Despite Kimberly-Clark and Berli Jucker Cellox having commercials in television, RiverPRO is not advertising in this channel. Based on his decades of professional expertise in the tissue industry, Sumrit is certain that consumers prefer promotions at the point of sale given paper products are fast moving consumer goods. But he also recognizes RiverPRO's relatively weak brand recognition and loyalty compared to Berli Jucker Cellox and Kimberly-Clark. In order to save money on promotion, a clear and unique brand image must be delivered to the consumers via packaging.

RiverPRO's recycled, unbleached tissue

To maintain their current relationship with urban communities around their factories, RiverPRO is reinforcing their environmentally friendly image by producing recycled, unbleached tissue products as an extension of the Pinn line.

Recycled, unbleached tissue paper products are produced from recycled office paper and cardboard. Those products have a characteristic brown color because they do not go through the process of bleaching, while white paper products must be bleached to achieve their color. There are white tissue paper products in the market made from recycled materials, the difference is that they are bleached (such as RiverPRO's brand: Pinn) to change their color. An important difference between recycled, unbleached tissue paper and recycled bleached tissue paper is that recycled bleached tissue paper is softer. Recycled, bleached tissue paper is softer because the bleaching process breaks down pulp fibers making the paper softer. However, it still has the same strength as recycled, unbleached tissue paper, which is usually sold in the medium price category, leading the company to position it in the middle-end segment.

The production process of recycled, unbleached paper is more environmentally friendly in two aspects. Firstly, it uses recycled materials, helping to reduce the use of trees as raw material. Secondly, it eliminates the need to bleach the pulp saving water, chemicals and energy used in the process. Table 2 below shows that resources are saved when producing one metric ton of recycled tissue paper and one metric ton of unbleached recycled tissue paper if compared to the production of one metric ton of white tissue paper.

Table 2. Savings related to the production of one metric ton of recycled paper versus one metric ton of white paper made from virgin pulp.

Recycled Paper	Unbleached Recycled Paper
17 Trees	25 Trees
26,500 Liters of water	29,000 Liters of water
378 Liters of oil	490 Liters of oil
27.5 Kg. of polluted air	27.5 Kg. of polluted air
4,000,000 Watts	4,000,000 Watts
2.75 m³ of landfill	2.75 m³ of landfill

(*Source:* RiverPRO)

In theory the production cost of recycled, unbleached paper is lower than the production cost of white tissue paper because it does not use raw virgin pulp. However, economies of scale have an important role in production costs. In RiverPRO's case, recycled, unbleached paper volume represents about 13% of the total volume of a converting machine, which raises operational costs. As a result, the cost to produce recycled, unbleached paper products is approximately the same as producing white paper products. Currently, RiverPRO is selling unbleached, recycled paper at the same price as their white paper products. This means that RiverPRO has the same gross margin over both types of products. However, if the volume of recycled, unbleached paper increase, so will its margin.

First-mover advantage

An important aspect of recycled, unbleached tissue is that it is new to the Thai market. Previously there was only "brown" tissue paper import-ed from China, which is white tissue dyed to look brown. RiverPRO's unbleached recycled paper should be more competitive than these imported products due to lack of importing logistical costs and a less complex production process. RiverPRO is the first mover of the eco-friendly tissue market. Sumrit believes the company will have a long lifespan in this specific market since the strongest competitors, Kimberly-Clark and Berli Jucker Cellox, are not going to launch recycled, unbleached tissue paper in the short term. His main arguments are that the market is too small for much larger firms to capitalize on, and that larger firms do not have the production flexibility required to be profitable at such a low volume. This is based on the fact that RiverPRO is producing the product in a small machine while KC and BJC operate larger machines with much longer changeover times. However, Sumrit knows that it is impossible to predict whether or not the competitors will jump into this market in the future.

RiverPRO not only wants its product to be the first recycled, unbleached tissue in Thailand, but also wants it to be the first in the Indochina market. Since Indochina countries all belong to ASEAN, which allows member countries to export and import goods from each other without tariff, RiverPRO will be able to develop the product outside of Thailand. Witnessing Berli Jucker Cellox's and Kimberly-Clark's increasing investment in the Indochina market, such as the new production facility Berli Jucker Cellox built in Vietnam, RiverPRO is attracted to the large profits that entering these market might be bring. However, Cambodia, Laos and Myanmar are less developed than Thailand. The penetration rate of tissue paper is still low but increasing due to rapid economic development and urbanization.

Being a first mover in the new market is also risky, and the biggest challenge is the lack of knowledge on consumer perceptions. Even though the company launched the recycled, unbleached tissue two years ago, whether people will use it at home is still an unknown. According to the company's market survey, most of the current recycled, unbleached sold in the last two years were bought by local coffee shops who follow Starbuck's strategy of providing "recycled, unbleached tissue" to give a "high-end" image. However, as the product is moving to the retail market targeting in-household usage, what household consumers think about the recycled, unbleached tissue remains a question.

Consumer Preferences

Sumrit thinks that a more sustainable production process along with the corporate social responsibility initiatives currently taken by the company can improve consumer impressions of the company and its brands. RiverPRO's recycled, unbleached paper is already on the market, but the company is unsure of how to promote it. Realizing that a better understanding of consumer attitudes towards recycled, unbleached tissue products was needed, Sumrit commissioned research about consumer preferences to most efficiently bridge the gap between what RiverPRO produces and what consumers seek.

To gain insight into Thai consumer behavior, Mr. Sumrit Yipyintum hired a consulting team to investigate consumer preferences. The team conducted a survey targeted at urban consumers in Bangkok. As a result, findings are more applicable to urban consumers.

Based on a questionnaire to random people in central Bangkok, preliminary results indicated most consumers that participated in the research obtained at least a Bachelor's degree and had monthly incomes of roughly 15,000 TBH to 50,000 TBH. Survey respondents most frequently purchased tissue paper products in supermarkets, with hypermarkets being the second most popular channel to buy tissue products.

The survey also specifically asked about consumer perception of unbleached tissue products. In general, consumers perceive unbleached recycled tissue as unhygienic, unattractive, and rough (as shown in Figure 3). They also believe it to be less suitable for personal use than white tissue and should not cost more than white tissue. Consumers who exhibit a willingness to try or switch to unbleached tissue indicated that eco-friendliness and quality were important attributes of the products.

To determine what motivated consumers to use unbleached tissue paper, consumers were asked to rank unbleached paper attributes on a Likert scale of importance with one indicating the least importance and five indicating the greatest importance. As seen in Figure 4, results suggest that the two most important attributes for consumers were quality and eco-friendliness. However, most of the attributes had average ratings of roughly 4.0 to 4.5, suggesting all of these factors are important to consumers.

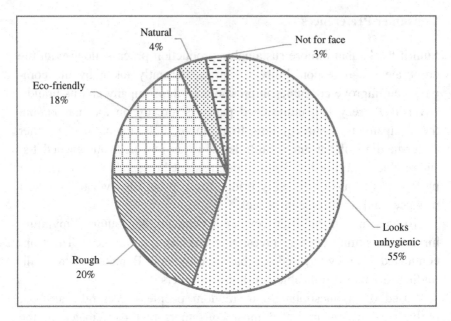

Fig. 3: Consumer perceptions of recycled tissue.

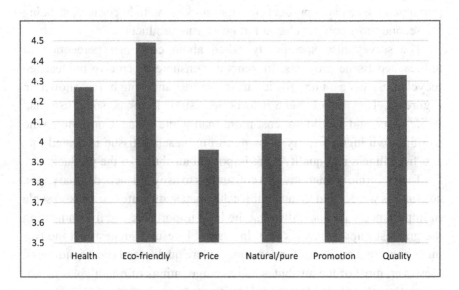

Fig. 4: Consumers' perceptions of tissue paper attributes.

Challenges

Looking at the busy workers in the plant, Sumrit feels a big burden on his shoulders. He knows that the company is at a crossroads. The competition within the tissue industry is fierce and RiverPRO is not in a good position. Can RiverPRO build up its "eco-friendly" image successfully and thus deliver a positive image to the community and the government? Would recycled, unbleached tissue be profitable and help the company move to the number two market share in the industry? Mr. Sumrit Yipyintum knows he has to make a choice now.

References

Mongsawad, P. 2010. The Philosophy of the Sufficiency Economy: A Contribution to the Theory of Development. *Asia-Pacific Development Journal.* 17(1). pp. 123-43. [Accessed 27 November 2017]. Available from: http://www.unescap.org/sites/default/files/apdj-17-1-5-Mongsawad.pdf.

Piboolsravut, P. 2004. Sufficiency Economy. ASEAN Economic Bulletin. [Online]. 21(1). pp. 127-34. [Accessed 27 November 2017]. Available from: http://www.jstor.org/stable/25773806.

Piboolsravut, P. and Sathirathai, S. 2004. Sufficiency Economy and a Healthy Community. For 3rd IUCN World Conservation Congress Bangkok. Retrieved from: https://issuu.com/sayasat/docs/sufficiency_economy_and_a_healthy_community.

Statista. [no date]. Tissue and Hygiene Paper: Thailand. Retrieved from: https://www.statista.com/outlook/80000000/126/tissue-and-hygiene-paper/thailand#.

Thailand Pulp and Paper Industry in 2010. Report for An Binh Paper Corporation. Retrieved from: http://www.anbinhpaper.com/userfiles/file/SO%20LIEU%20THONG%20KE/Thailand.pdf.

UN data. [no date]. City population by sex, city and city type. [Online]. [Accessed 27 November 2017]. Available from: http://data.un.org/Data.aspx?d=POP&f=tableCode%3A240.

United Nations Development Programme. [no date]. About Thailand. [Online]. [Accessed 27 November 2017]. Available from: http://www.th.undp.org/content/thailand/en/home/countryinfo.html.

World Bank. [no date]. Thailand Data. [Online]. [Accessed 27 November 2017]. Available from: http://data.worldbank.org/country/thailand.

World Bank. [no date]. Urban population (% of total). [Online]. [Accessed 27 November 2017]. Available from: http://data.worldbank.org/indicator/SP.URB.TOTL.IN.ZS.

World Bank. [no date]. Countries and Economies. [Online]. [Accessed 27 November 2017]. Available from: https://data.worldbank.org/country.

Chapter 9

Zenxin: Organic Produce Trailblazer in Malaysia

Lin Fu,[1] Sarah Byrne,[1] Wangyue Guo,[1] Quinn Kolar,[1] Sonia Sadaf,[1]
Chris Wien,[1] Jinwen Zheng,[1] and Kit Chan[2]

Introduction

Tai Seng Yee recalls his first trip with his father to the Cameron High-lands to visit the area's organic farmers in the early 2000s. He distinctly remembers, "On that trip, we tasted the local organic cabbages and were impressed by the freshness and flavor." Tai's father had just started an organic compost factory. At the time, the concept of organic was still new to most of Malaysia, so the company initially had difficulty finding cus-tomers for its organic fertilizer. Thinking to look for potential customers among the farmers in the Cameron Highlands, father and son made that trip together. After tasting the local organic produce, Tai and his father were inspired to grow and sell organic vegetables in addition to producing organic fertilizers. The family business now includes organic produce and has become a leader in the Malaysian organic market.

Today, Tai is the managing director of Zenxin Agri-Organic Food (Zenxin). The company has been selling organic produce ever since that fateful trip to the Cameron Highlands in the early 2000s. Although Zenxin is doing well overall, its company-owned farms are not as profitable as expected. Tai just had a meeting with his father, Zenxin's founder, where the two discussed this very issue again. Moreover, their latest sales figures showed that they were now 50:50 in terms of domestic market vs. international market exposure. Domestic demand in Malaysia for organic produce and products has increased over the years, but consumer awareness about organic goods remains relatively low in comparison with other countries. Given the still low levels of domestic consumer demand, Tai wondered if it would be better to focus more on exports for now.

[1]SMART Program, Cornell University.
[2]K-Farm, Malaysia.

As Tai waited for the latest shipment of organic tomatoes from one of their contract farmers in the Cameron Highlands, he pondered which direction he should take Zenxin.

Country Context: Malaysia

Malaysia is a country in Southeast Asia with a population of around 30 million people. With a GNI (Gross National Income) per capita of just under US$11,000, it is considered an upper middle income country. Wealth disparity is still an issue, but the situation has improved slightly over the past decade. In 2004, Malaysia's Gini coefficient was 0.46; in 2014, its Gini coefficient dropped to 0.40. Also of concern are the country's persistent inter-ethnic tensions and gender equality issues (UNDP 2013; Lee and Khalid 2016).

Malaysia is a member of the Association of Southeast Asian Nations (ASEAN). In 2015, Malaysia's total trade with ASEAN was RM401.33 billion, which represented more than one quarter of the country's global trade. Exports to ASEAN totaled RM219.29 billion, or about 28% of Malaysia's total exports, making ASEAN Malaysia's single largest regional export destination. In recent years, the country has benefited from increased inter-company linkages, cross-border investments, and outsourcing within the region. Within ASEAN, Singapore is Malaysia's largest trading partner, followed by Thailand, Indonesia, and Vietnam. Exports to Singapore, Thailand, and Indonesia collectively account for around 83% of Malaysia's total exports to ASEAN (MATRADE, 2015).

Malaysia currently has an estimated 7.75 million hectares (ha) available for agricultural production. This land is largely devoted to economically lucrative plantation crops like palm oil and rubber, which are the country's primary exports. Malaysia's top food imports include maize, wheat, soy, and onions. The country's recent increased focus on agricultural policy, however, has emphasized food security as a goal. Due to the growing national population, government agencies are stressing the need for farmers to produce more food crops instead of cash crops so as to improve Malaysia's food security situation (FAOSTAT no date; Razak *et al.* 2013).

Under its Third National Agricultural Policy (1998–2010), Malaysia focused on improving productivity while sustainably using natural resources. Additionally, the Third National Agriculture Policy recognized the importance of organic agriculture as an export opportunity and also as a way to benefit small scale producers. For this reason, the Ninth Malaysia Plan (2006-2010) made the organic industry a focus area and called for 20,000 ha of land to be converted to organic production (Murad *et al.* 2008). It was during this period of time, as the organic industry in Malaysia was just beginning to take shape, that Zenxin became influential in the industry.

Malaysia's Organic Food Industry

Organic agriculture in Malaysia

Organic agriculture was first introduced to Malaysia by the Center for Environment, Technology, and Development (CETDEM) in 1985. CETDEM is a non-profit focused on promoting sustainable development with particular attention to organic agriculture and alternative energy sources. Since then, the number of organic farms in the country has grown. In 2010, the number of farmers involved in organic farming was 900; by 2015, that number was more than 1500. In 2001, only 131 hectares of farmland in Malaysia were organic farms; in 2014, that number was 1700 hectares. Nonetheless, Commercial organic agriculture is still considered a relatively new and small industry in Malaysia (Somasundram *et al.* 2016; Suhaimee *et al.* 2016).

Since 1985, Malaysia has seen a tremendous increase in the demand for organic produce in its food market, largely due to rising incomes and increased consciousness about consuming healthy food (Ahmad and Juhdi 2010). According to a 2010 study conducted by the Malaysia Agricultural Research and Development Institute (MARDI), more than 90% of Malaysian consumers knew about organic products and associated it with positive qualities like being chemical-free, healthy, and all-natural (Suhaimee *et al.* 2016). Although the domestic demand for organic food is increasing, the sector is still not well established in Malaysia. A few major players, including Zenxin, make up the entirety of the industry.

Organic certification in Malaysia

In 2003, Malaysia's Department of Agriculture introduced a national organic certification scheme known as Skim Organik Malaysia (SOM), which governs the production, processing, labeling, and marketing of organically produced plant-based foods. SOM certification is relatively inexpensive compared to foreign organic production certifications like Australia's NASAA (see Box 1). The SOM manual, available to farmers at the Department of Agriculture's local offices across the country, outlines the necessary steps and standards to become certified as organic under the SOM scheme. Farms usually go through a two-year conversion period before their produce can be labeled as organic under this scheme. At the end of 2014, a total of 142 farms had obtained organic certification through SOM (Suhaimee et al. 2016; DOA no date).

SOM has not gained traction with either farmers or with other stakeholders along the value chain. Some farmers find the certification extremely stringent and difficult to follow. The strict bookkeeping requirement has proven to be a particular challenge for many farmers. At an even more basic level, many farmers are unable to read and understand the SOM manual because it is only available in English and Malay. Although Malay is the official language of Malaysia, many ethnic Chinese farmers in rural communities do not have a strong grasp of the language. In the Cameron Highlands, an important area for vegetable and flower production and now for organic farming, a majority of the farmers are of Chinese origin. A combination of onerous financial record requirements and inaccessibility of certification materials has made it difficult to persuade farmers to switch from conventional to organic farming. Moreover, Malaysian wholesalers prefer foreign organic certifications over SOM. They consider the Australian certification (see Box 1) standards and process more reliable and prefer to keep imported organic produce in their shops over the local organic produce.

Box 1: Australian Organic Standards

Global organic certifications have become very prominent in Malaysia's organic agriculture, partly due to SOM's lack of customer appeal. Australian certifications, in particular, are often referenced. Australia has an extensive organic certification process that is regularly re-evaluated so as to be current with global trends in organic production and consumer demands. Since the Australian Department of Agriculture, Fisheries, and Forestry (DAFF) has accredited seven different organizations to certify products as organic, there are actually seven different types of labels that might appear on organic food. This can be confusing for consumers both inside and outside Australia (Chang *et al.* 2005).

The National Association for Sustainable Agriculture, Australia (NASAA) is one of the seven DAFF-accredited organizations. To be certified as organic by NASAA, individual operations (as opposed to grower collectives) must adhere to the NASAA Organic Standard. The most important aspect of the inspection and review process is the producer's ability to provide documentation of an organic management plan. Only after a "conversion to organic" period, can products be sold as organic with the NASAA seal. The conversion period can be significantly shortened if farmers can prove that they have been following an organic plan for at least three years. NASAA already conducts certifications in Malaysia. Since the NASAA certification process is conducted only in English, many Malaysian farmers are at a disadvantage due to language barrier issues.

Zenxin requires that their contract farmers use NASAA certification and help farmers through the certification process. With NASAA certification, the produce can then be marketed abroad, most often in Singapore and the Middle East. Since NASAA certification is widely recognized, it also makes wider product distribution possible, if and when Zenxin decides to pursue additional markets.

Lack of organic agricultural extension support

Although the Tenth Malaysia Plan signaled the intent to support the domestic organic industry, the research and extension services to help encourage domestic organic agriculture are just not there. For MARDI, which is responsible for researching agriculture, food, and agro-based industries in general, organic agriculture is not a priority research area, and, consequently, it does not receive much research funding. As a result, few experts there conduct research that could be helpful for organic farmers. Of the few MARDI specialists dedicated to organic farming, fewer still are approached for help by organic farmers. Organic farmers are reluctant to seek assistance from MARDI's regional offices because the process to request research support is extremely time consuming. All requests go to the headquarters—submitters rarely receive a satisfactory response or any response at all through this channel.

At MARDI and at public universities in Malaysia that engage in agriculture-relevant research, there are very few people who work specifically on organic agriculture. As a subject matter, organic agriculture must compete with other topics, like food security and issues facing conventional farming, both of which are better funded by government agencies. The lack of interest in organic agriculture from a research perspective is partly due to lack of funding and partly due to lack of associated researchers, though the latter is largely a consequence of the former. This is why most organic farmers prefer to seek research support from either the companies with which they contract, like Zenxin, who disseminates information about good practices to its contract farmers, or from research institutions in neighboring countries.

Organic retail and nascent domestic organic demand

The availability of organic produce in supermarkets and other grocery stores in Malaysia varies tremendously. Some supermarkets have large organic produce sections with offerings that match almost all the same varieties of fruits and vegetables found in their conventional produce section. Some stores only carry one or two organic products and some have the organic produce mixed in with the conventional produce. At many retail locations, even those that stock large amounts of organic produce, the organic produce may be mixed in or placed right next to products labeled "hydroponic" or "natural." Many customers are confused as to what the "organic" label actually means and how it differs from products labeled as natural or hydroponic. Due to this confusion, many consumers seem unwilling to pay a premium for organic products (prices for organic products in Malaysia are much higher than conventionally farmed options, sometimes up to three or four times more expensive).

Consumers are generally unaware of organic certifications, what the certification process entails, and what the certification labels mean. Consumers have less confidence in SOM certification as compared with international certifications because they do not think the SOM labeling standards are clear. Additionally, many organic labels only use an acronym, e.g., NASAA and SOM, which does not work well in situations where customers are not already familiar with these certification systems. As a result, it has been difficult to demand higher prices for organic products and the domestic organic food industry in Malaysia is still small. More than 60% of the organic food products in the country are imported.

Malaysia's organic food industry faces several challenges. As the disposable income of Malaysian citizens have risen, they are increasingly interested in making educated purchasing decisions. Consumers who prefer organic cite health reasons or motivations based on environmental impact (Ahmad and Juhdi 2010). The demand for organic food in Malaysia is growing, but the supply of local organic products is inconsistent. The variety of local organic food options is also limited. To address some of these challenges, MARDI has recently initiated various program and activities in support of the organic farming sector (Somasundram *et al.* 2016).

Zenxin Agri-Organic Food

Vision and mission

Zenxin has been the leading producer, distributor and retailer of organic fruits and vegetables in Malaysia since 2001. According to its mission statement, the company is "committed to produce organically-grown products of the highest quality by disallowing the use of chemical fertilizers and pesticides." Seeing organic as the future of farming, Zenxin pledges to strive to "make our earth and human beings greener and healthier."

Zenxin has been an active promoter of organic food and agriculture in Malaysia since its inception in 2001. Company employees strongly believe in the concept of organic and actively try to influence their friends and acquaintances to learn more about organic certification processes in order to build trust in organic labels. In addition to its efforts to convert more traditional farmers to organic production, Zenxin also engages in public outreach through the company's recreational organic park in Malaysia, the first and largest of its kind in the country. At the Zenxin Organic Park, visitors can learn about organic farming, tour an actual organic farm, and engage in various recreational activities within the park grounds like biking and fishing.

Zenxin controls a complete organic production chain, from compost factory to organic farms and organic wholesalers. The company is certified organic under both NASAA and SOM and is also a member of the International Federation of Organic Agriculture Movements (IFOAM). With a long history, strong market presence, and solid brand recognition, Zenxin views itself as without domestic peers for now in Malaysia. "We compete with ourselves. We see ourselves as a platform, an industry, instead of just an organic food company," says Tai.

Current products

Headquartered in Kluang, Malaysia, Zenxin's business includes its own organic farms, many more contract farms, an organic compost and fertilizer factory, the recreational organic park, and also ten retail outlets across Malaysia and in Singapore. These retail outlets sell Zenxin's own organic produce and products as well as imported options. Within Malaysia and Singapore, their organic produce can also be found in the Jaya Jusco, Giant, Cold Storage, and Shop n Save outlets.

Zenxin offers more than 60 varieties of organic produce, which it claims is "the widest and most complete" selection in Malaysia. The top items by sales volume vary due to produce seasonality, but on that list are choy sum, siew pak choy, cabbage, bananas, and lettuce. About half of Zenxin's organic vegetables and fruits are consumed locally, while the other half is exported to Zenxin's Singapore branch, relabeled, and exported again to other parts of the world, such as the Middle East. The company's main export markets are Singapore and Hong Kong.

In 2009, the company launched an organic food products line with the brand name "Simply Natural." This product line offers organic foodstuffs made without artificial additives and preservatives. Simply Natural organic products include oats products, sprouted rice products, noodles, honey, healthy snacks, energy bars, spices, and wine. All products are processed and/or packaged in Zenxin's own NASAA-certified organic facilities that include a dedicated cold room for food repacking.

Current operations

As "the premier name in organic produce," Zenxin prides itself on its complete organic value chain. Currently, their business includes an organic compost factory, five company-owned farms, 25 contract farms (with more than 200 workers), ten organic food stores, three distribution centers, and an organic park and restaurant. The compost factory turns waste from the parent company's other industries into organic fertilizer and compost to be used by farmers. This organic fertilizer is used at Zenxin's own farms as well as its contract farms to grow the organic fruits and vegetables that are later packaged in the company's own packing centers, which are dedicated solely to organic products. Packaged products are distributed within 24 hours by the distribution centers to supermarkets and to the Zenxin retail stores, where they reach the end consumers. About 50% of Zenxin's organic produce comes from its own farms and the other 50% from its 25 contract farms. The entire production process of Zenxin has been certified by NASAA and SOM since 2007, making it the only company in the region with completely organic-certified operations.

At the farm level, Zenxin recognizes room for improvement. At Zenxin's five organic farms, farmers are divided into different groups, each with three or four workers and each focusing on different crops. Farm supervisors decide what to grow, but feel hampered by the lack of industry research available. Zenxin also works with 25 contract farmers in the Cameron Highlands area of Malaysia. Together, these 25 farmers manage more than 60 hectares of land. Of these 25 contract farmers, ten were already organic farmers before entering into a contract farming agreement with Zenxin, 13 converted to organic after being approached by Zenxin, and the remaining two are still in the conversion period. To incentivize farmers to use organic production methods, Zenxin not only helps them in their NASAA certification process, but also covers the associated costs.

Although Zenxin offers additional training to all its farmers, its contract farmers seldom travel to Kluang for these trainings and the company does not send the specialists to the Cameron Highland on a regular basis.

Ongoing challenges

Production shortfall

At present, Zenxin's profits from its own organic farms do not look promising. The location of the company-owned farms is less than ideal: the farm is in a lower altitude area, where temperate vegetable crops struggle to grow. Also, various pest and disease problems within the greenhouses are arising. Zenxin finds that the contract farmers, even those in lower altitudes areas, are generally more productive when it comes to vegetable production. Consequently, Zenxin is considering whether to transition to act solely as the middleman, i.e. buying produce from the contract farmers and then bringing that produce to market, instead of being actively involved in farming as well. Zenxin has also had some difficulty adding to its number of contract farmers. Although organic farmers would be able to sell their organic crops at a higher price, the sequencing of events is a tough sell for many: farmers must convert to organic methods first before being able to sell a single item to Zenxin. In what is perhaps classic loss aversion behavior, the loss of income up-front is felt more and has a greater influence on farmers' decision-making than the more than equivalent gains in the future.

Low public awareness

Despite the efforts of Zenxin and other stakeholders in the organic food space in Malaysia, general public awareness of the health and environmental benefits of organic products is still relatively low. Many consumers cannot distinguish between authentic organic foods from non-organic ones. As the only company in the region with an organic certified value chain, Zenxin is threatened by products with vague labels like "chemical free" and "green" that try to pass themselves off as organic.

Box 2: Mr. Li, A Zenxin Contract Farmer

Mr. Li is an organic farmer in the Cameron Highlands and since 2009, a contract farmer for Zenxin. Although he was educated as a mechanical engineer, he decided to start farming in 1998 and transitioned to organic farming in 2004. At the time, the market for organic produce was limited. After two years, he decided that organic farming on his own was too difficult and expensive and so, he returned to traditional farming.

Most traditional farmers in the Cameron Highlands have 50 to over 100 hectares of land to grow vegetables; Mr. Li only has one hectare. On his one hectare, Mr. Li grows mustard, spinach, cauliflower and tomatoes. He uses seeds saved from his own farm or imported from Taiwan, Japan, and Korea. Mr. Li considers his partnership with Zenxin a valuable one because he has been able to get NASAA and SOM certification. He has also been able to improve his profitability and productivity.

Zenxin pays its contract farmers a fixed price per produce item. The company has its own standards for the organic products that it buys from its contract farmers. If the fruits and vegetables produced by contract farmers do not meet Zenxin's standards, then the company will not buy them. For Mr. Li, the inability to sell to Zenxin would be a major financial loss because Zenxin is his only customer. Though there is a market nearby that is accessible by well-maintained roads, the local people are usually not willing to pay a premium price for organic.

Mr. Li is passionate about testing different ways to improve the productivity and performance of his organic farm. When he encounters problems, he usually turns to agents or professors from Taiwan and Japan for help. He has only limited dealings with Malaysian research institutions, universities, and agricultural departments. He would like to be able to access new trainings and techniques from different organizations, but does not find such a support system in place in Malaysia. Like other farmers in the Cameron Highlands, Mr. Li worries about soil erosion, especially during the rainy season. When there is sustained heavy rainfall, farm productivity can be negatively affected. A well-constructed drainage system is needed to support the greenhouses and coverings that individual farmers already use.

Policy Barriers

Zenxin is indirectly affected by two major policy barriers faced by contract farmers, namely immigration policy and land ownership policy. Farmers in the Cameron High-lands recruit laborers from foreign countries, such as Bangladesh, because of domestic labor shortages as well as the lower cost of foreign labor. The immigration procedure for temporary foreign laborers is a complicated one. It involves several different government offices and the probability of a failed application is high. Since farmers rely on this low-cost foreign labor pool to keep their own costs down, many farmers take the risk of recruiting and hiring illegal laborers from foreign countries.

Many farmers, especially those in the Cameron Highlands, do not hold ownership rights to the land that they farm. Instead, they hold a temporary occupancy license, which is essentially a renewable lease from the government. The owner of the lease can occupy and use the land, but cannot transfer it or benefit from improvements made to it because the land still belongs to the government. The government is under no obligation to renew the lease (Kadouf 2011). The instability inherent in temporary occupancy licenses can make it difficult for farmers to obtain and maintain organic certification. Non-permanent land use may affect the consecutiveness of an organic plot, which is one of the elements in the evaluation process for organic certification. Additionally, to convert a conventionally-farmed parcel into an organic one requires high inputs in terms of time and money; if farmers do not have ownership rights over their land and cannot benefit from any improvements made, then they have little incentive to invest the required time and money to convert to organic.

Looking Forward

As the awaited shipment of organic tomatoes arrive from the farm of Mr. Li in the Cameron Highlands, Tai is no closer to making a decision on the direction that Zenxin should take. The success of Zenxin is intimately linked with its ability to be profitable at several points along the value chain. Improving productivity and profitability is critical, but so too is continuing the company's mission to be a platform for healthier living and lifestyles through organic food. Tai hopes that more and more Malaysian consumers will learn to appreciate the benefits of organic food from both a health and environmental impact perspective.

References

Ahmad, S. N. B. and Juhdi, N. 2010. Organic Food: A study on Demographic Characteristics and Factors Influencing Purchase Intentions among Consumers in Klang Valley, Malaysia. *International Journal of Business and Management.* **5**(2). pp.105-118.

Chang, H. S., Zepeda, L. and Griffith, G. 2005. The Australian Organic Food Products Market: Overview, Issues and Research Needs. *Australasian Agribusiness Review.* **13**(2005). p.15.

Department of Agriculture, Malaysia (DOA). [no date]. *Malaysian Organic Scheme Certification (SOM).* [Online]. [Accessed 21 November 2017]. Available from: http://www.doa.gov.my/index.php/pages/view/377?mid=70.

FAOSTAT. [no date]. *Crops.* [Online]. [Accessed 21 November 2017]. Available from: http://www.fao.org/faostat/en/#data/QC.

Kadouf, H. A. 2011. Land administration and the right of access to land: An analysis of the concept of temporary occupation license under Malaysian land law. *Malayan Law Journal.* [Online]. **3**. pp.80-101. [Accessed 21 November 2017]. Retrieved from: http://irep.iium.edu.my/17804/1/mlj_2011_3_lxxx.pdf.

Lee, H. A. and Khalid, M. A. K. 2016. *Is inequality in Malaysia really going down? A puzzle explored.* [Online]. Kuala Lumpur: University of Malaya. [Accessed 21 November 2017]. Available from: http://pubdocs.worldbank.org/en/285151475547874083/Is-Inequality-in-Malaysia-Really-Going-Down.pdf.

Malaysia External Trade Development Corporation (MATRADE). 2015. *Malaysia's Trade with ASEAN.* [Online]. [Accessed 27 November 2017]. Available from: http://www.matrade.gov.my/en/malaysian-exporters/services-for-exporters/trade-market-information/trade-statistics/152-malaysian-exporters/going-global/asean/3507-malaysia-s-trade-with-asean.

Murad, M. W., Mustapha, N. H. N. and Siwar, C. 2008. Review of Malaysian Agricultural Policies with Regards to Sustainability. *American Journal of Environmental Science.* **4**(6). pp.608-614.

NASSA. 2016. *NASAA Organic and Biodynamic Standard.* [Online]. [Accessed 21 November 2017]. Available from: https://www.nasaa.com.au/documents/standards/6-nasaa-organic-standard/file.html.

Razak, M.I., Hamzah, A.S., Abas, N., Idris, R. and Ibrahim, Z. 2013. Sustaining Food Production for Food Security in Malaysia. *Journal of Economics and Development Studies.* **1**(2). pp.19-25.

Somasundram, C., Razali, Z. and Santhirasegaram, V. 2016. A Review on Organic Food Production in Malaysia. *Horticulturae.* **2**(3). p.12.

Suhaimee, S., Ibrahim I. Z. and Wahab, M. A. M. A. 2016. *Organic Agriculture in Malaysia.* [Online]. [Accessed 21 November 2017]. Available from: http://ap.fftc.agnet.org/ap_db.php?id=579.

United Nations Development Program (UNDP). [no date]. *About Malaysia.* [Online]. [Accessed 21 November 2017]. Available from: http://www.my.undp.org/content/malaysia/en/home/countryinfo/.

Chapter 10

A Primer on Enterprise Upgrading

Aimée Hampel-Milagrosa[1]

In developing countries, micro, small, and medium enterprises (MSMEs) make up a large part of the industrial fabric, which is why policy makers and scholars alike look at small scale entrepreneurs as important development agents in society. MSMEs provide livelihoods to millions of people worldwide by offering possibilities to gain income, training and work experience (Altenburg and Eckhardt 2006). Small scale entrepreneurship has been heralded as a driver of private sector development with research suggesting that increases in MSME productivity and enterprise growth are the most effective instruments behind private sector development and economic growth (Gomez 2008). However, a larger body of literature shows that MSME growth is the exception rather than the rule.

Empirical evidence suggests that most small enterprises never grow beyond a certain scale and only a handful will upgrade their businesses to the next level of productivity, income and employment (Berner *et al.* 2008). What we commonly observe is that those enterprises that are large-sized typically started large (for example, through Foreign Direct Investment) or graduated from a specific group of entrepreneurs (for example, from professionals or elite groups) (Eifert *et al.* 2005). Literature refers to the few well-performing MSMEs who manage to grow organically as "gazelles".

Although there is a substantial amount of research on enterprise growth, literature on the dynamics of upgrading of "gazelles" is rather thin. The most common understanding refers to "upgrading" as a transfer from informal to formal modes of operation through business registration and compliance with all legal requirements. Most of the studies discuss the advantages and disadvantages of formalization and how the business environment enables upgrading (see for example, De Soto 1989; La Porta *et al.* 2011). Within this area is a smaller strand of literature that views

---

[1]Asian Development Bank (formerly German Development Institute).

enterprise upgrading as a movement from stagnant levels of productivity, income and employment towards higher levels of productivity and increased income or employee numbers, regardless of level of formality.

This section presents a short overview of the literature behind enterprise upgrading and identifies the strands of literature that contribute to the topic. We begin with a definition. While growth refers to "an increase in amount" (for example, of productivity, income or employment), here, upgrading refers to an "increase in amount due to the introduction of something new," or in short, "growth through innovation." Economic innovation is described as the gradual and cumulative process of introducing ways of doing business differently from one's competitors. These could be through new products, processes, functions, sectors or markets and marketing strategies. Thus, enterprise upgrading implies a creative and cumulative process of introducing new things rather than just a "scaling up" of operations.

Against this background, we shall use the following formal definition of enterprise upgrading, to wit:

Enterprise upgrading entails qualitative improvements in products, processes and ways of organizing production enabling the entrepreneur to capture innovation rents as a result of being faster than the competition. Capturing rents allows the entrepreneur to increase firm income, productivity or number of employees." (See Schmitz and Knorringa 2000; Altenburg and Eckhardt 2006).

Based on the formal definition, there are two qualifiers that make an upgrader. First, the upgrader has introduced an innovation to the enterprise or its market (qualitative qualifier) and second, the upgrader, through this innovation, experienced a measurable growth that was faster than the growth of its competitors (quantitative qualifier). Therefore, "upgraders" are the handful of exceptional entrepreneurs whose enterprises have managed to progress from micro to small, or small to medium-sized during a specific period of time as a result of various innovation strategies. These kinds of innovation strategies could be in the form of:

- Product innovation—the creation of new products;

- Process innovation—improvements in the way products are created;

- Function innovation—taking over other functions in the enterprise's value chain;

- Sector innovation—branching out to other sectors;

- Marketing and market innovation—implementation of a new marketing strategy or selling in new markets.

Such innovative measures lead to a capture of "innovation rents" which are profits that are superior to what the competition earns in the same period. Such profit increase jump-starts enterprise growth and leads to higher productivity, greater income and more employees (see Figure 1).

Note that it is possible that the introduction of innovation in itself does not lead to enterprise growth. Fierce competition or weak property rights can lead to lower-than-expected rents and fail to provide the higher returns needed to cover innovation investments. This study is limited

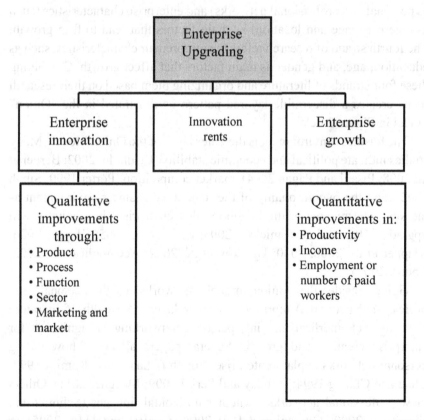

Fig. 1: Conceptual framework for enterprise upgrading (*Source:* Hampel-Milagrosa, 2014).

to the types of innovation that resulted in growth, where captured rents led to measurable increases in profits, productivity, sales or number of employees. Innovation-led increases in profits, sales, or number of employees are the type of growth that distinguishes sporadic growth from sustainable growth. It is the latter that characterizes a productive enterprise that effectively contributes to national economic growth.

What Drives Innovation in a Firm?

There are four strands of research that attempt to explain how innovation led enterprise growth occurs. The first strand refers to the business environment, for example, business registration, as the main explanatory factor for firm growth. The second and third strands point to networks (such as personal and professional networks) and enterprise characteristics (such as enterprise age and location) as main factors that lead to firm growth. The fourth strand of research refers to entrepreneur characteristics, such as education, age, and gender as main factors that affect growth. Combining these four strands of literature and organizing them based on their research focus creates a discernible layered pattern as illustrated in the "Onion" model in Figure 2 below.

The business environment is the outer layer of the Onion Model. Many studies indicate political and economic stability (Liedholm 2002; Berner *et al.* 2008; Pisani and Pagan 2004), market competition (Porter 1990; Singh 2002), and the overall quality of the regulatory business environment as the key determinants of the likelihood that enterprises in a country will upgrade (Klein and Hadjimichael 2003; Beck *et al.* 2005; Klapper 2006; Klapper *et al.* 2006, 2010; Djankov *et al.* 2002; Acemoglu *et al.* 2002; Rodrik 2005).

Going inside the Onion model, networks (both personal and professional networks) represent an inner layer. A wealth of literature suggests that interfirm and interpersonal networking is significant for enterprise creation and growth. Several papers allude to how strong personal networks explain enterprise growth (Chan 2001; Romijn 1997; Chan and Chiang 1994; Hobday and Perini 2009; Meagher 2011). Others view professional networks—whether horizontal linkages (Schmitz and Knorringa 2000; Giuliani and Bell 2005; Conley and Udry 2005) or vertical linkages (Humphrey and Schmitz 2000; Aw 2002; Gereffi 1999; Pietrobelli and Rabellotti 2004)—as more useful agents that bring about an increase in enterprise size.

Further inside the Onion model, enterprise characteristics are used as explanatory factors that influence upgrading. These include enterprise age (Banerjee and Duflo 2000; Jovanovic 1982; Evans 1987), location (Piore and Sabel 1984; Pyke *et al.* 1990), sector (Mead and Liedholm 1998; de Mel *et al.* 2008), formality (La Porta *et al.* 2011; Sleuwagen and Goedhuys 2002), access to finance (Akoten *et al.* 2006; Fafchamps *et al.* 2011), and internal research and absorptive capacity (Cohen and Levinthal 1990; Nadvi 1999; Zahra and George 2002).

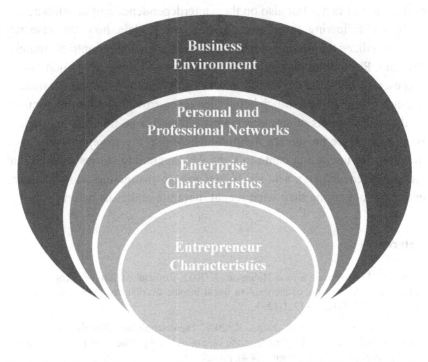

Fig. 2: Determinants of micro, small and medium enterprise (MSME) upgrading – the Onion Model (*Source:* Reeg 2013).

At the core of the Onion model are entrepreneur characteristics that many researchers' view as the explaining factor in an enterprise's capacity to upgrade. Authors identify the entrepreneur's age (Cortes *et al.* 1987;

de Mel *et al.* 2008; McPherson 1996), gender (Mead and Liedholm 1998; Ramachandran 1993; McPherson and Liedholm 1996), education (Tan and Batra 1995; Burki and Terell 1998) and work experience (McPherson 1992, 1996; Parker 1995; Ramachandran and Ramnarayan 1993; Eifert *et al.* 2005), motivation (Berner *et al.* 2008; Cotter 1996; Olomi *et al.* 2001; de Mel *et al.* 2008), and risk-taking ability (de Mel *et al.* 2008) as important factors for enterprise upgrading.

In the Onion model, these four layers of factors are taken all together in the analysis. Thus, unlike other research that singles out certain strands of factors as determinants for enterprise growth, the Onion model approach analyses these factors altogether in order to explain enterprise upgrading. The analysis of the Onion model not only focuses on the contribution of each strand of factor but also on their interdependence and interlinkages.

In the following three case studies, we explain how the research operationalized the Onion model in field research in three countries, namely, Vietnam, Philippines and India. As the stories will show, the Onion model successfully captured the totality of strategies that the entrepreneur used to upgrade his or her firm, much better than other growth models that focused on the contributions of singular factors alone. Across the three upgrading stories that were presented, the pivotal role that the entrepreneur played in enterprise upgrading came to light. The upgrading stories showed that the entrepreneur plays a much bigger role in instigating and sustaining enterprise upgrading than what recent literature makes us believe.

References

Acemoglu, D., Johnson, S. and Robinson, J. 2002. Reversal of fortune: geography and institutions in the making of the modern world income distribution. *Quarterly Journal of Economics.* **117**(2002). pp.1231-1294.

Akoten, J. E., Sawada, Y. and Otsuka, K. 2006. The determinants of credit access and its impacts on micro and small enterprises: the case of garment producers in Kenya. *Economic Development and Cultural Change.* **54**(4). pp.927–944.

Altenburg, T. and Eckhardt, U. 2006. *Productivity enhancement and equitable development: challenges for SME development.* Vienna: UNIDO Combating marginalization and poverty through industrial development (COMPID) Research Program.

Aw, B. Y. 2002. Productivity dynamics of small and medium enterprises in Taiwan. *Small Business Economics.* **18**(1). pp.69–84.

Banerjee, A. V. and Duflo, E. 2000. Reputation effects and the limits of contracting: a study of the Indian software industry. *Quarterly Journal of Economics.* **115**(3). pp.989–1017.

Beck, T., Demirguc-Kunt, A. and Maksimovic, V. 2005. Financial and legal constraints to growth: does firm size matter? *The Journal of Finance.* **60**(1). pp.137–177

Berner, E, Gomez, G. M. and Knorringa, P. 2008. *Helping a large number of people become a little less poor: the logic of survival entrepreneurs.* Helsinki: UNU WIDER.

Burki, A. A. and Terell, D. 1998. Measuring production efficiency of small firms in Pakistan. *World Development.* **26**(1). pp.155–169.

Chan, K. 2001. *Chinese business networks: state, economy and culture.* Singapore: Prentice Hall.

Chan, K. and Chiang, C. 1994. *Stepping out: the making of Chinese entrepreneurs.* New York: Centre for Advanced Studies of the National University Singapore: Prentice Hall.

Cohen, W. and Levinthal, D. 1990. Absorptive capacity: a new perspective on learning and innovation. *Administrative Science Quarterly.* **35**(1). pp.128–152.

Conley, T. and Udry, C. 2005. *Learning about a new technology: pineapple in Ghana.* [Online]. New Haven: Yale University. [Accessed 7 July 2013]. Available from: http://www. econ.yale.edu/~cru2/pdf/july2005a.pdf.

Cortes, M., Berry, A. and Irhaq, A. 1987. *Success in small and medium-scale enterprises: the evidence from Colombia.* New York: Oxford University Press for the World Bank.

Cotter, J. 1996. Distinguishing between poverty alleviation and business growth. *Small Enterprise Development.* **7**(2). pp.490–452.

De Mel, S., McKenzie, D. and Woodruff, C. 2008. *Who are the microenterprise owners? Evidence from Sri Lanka on Tokman v. de Soto.* Washington, D.C.: The World Bank.

De Soto, H. 1989. *The other path: The invisible revolution in the third world.* New York: Harper and Row Publishers Inc.

Djankov *et al.* 2002. *Going informal: benefits and costs.* Draft. Washington, D.C.: The World Bank Group.

Eifert, B., Gelb, A. and Ramachandran, V. 2005. *Business environment and comparative advantage in Africa: evidence from the investment climate data.* Working Paper. Washington, D.C.: Center for Global Development.

Evans, D. S. 1987. The relationship between firm growth, size, and age: estimates for 100 manufacturing industries. *Journal of Industrial Economics.* **35**(4). pp.567–582.

Fafchamps, M., McKenzie, D., Quinn, S. and Woodruff, C. 2011. *When is capital enough to get female enterprises growing? Evidence from a randomized experiment in Ghana.* Working Paper. Washington, D.C.: The World Bank.

Gereffi, G. 1999. International trade and industrial upgrading in the apparel commodity chain. *Journal of International Economics.* **48**(1). pp.37–70.

Gomez, G. M. 2008. *Do micro enterprises promote equity or growth?* Gorinchem: Institute of Social Studies.

Giulani, E. and Bell, M. 2005. The micro-determinants of meso-level learning and innovation: evidence from a Chilean wine cluster. *Research Policy.* **34**(1). pp.47–68.

Hampel-Milagrosa, A. 2014. *Micro and small enterprise upgrading in the Philippines, the role of entrepreneur, enterprise, networks and business environment.* Bonn: German Development Institute.

Hobday, M. and Perini, F. 2009. *Latecomer entrepreneurship: a policy perspective.* Oxford: Oxford University Press.

Humphrey, J. and Schmitz, H. 2000. *Governance and upgrading: linking industrial cluster and global value chain research.* Working Paper. Brighton: University of Sussex: Institute of Development Studies.

Jovanovic, B. 1982. Selection and the evolution of industry.*Econometrica.* **50**(3). pp.649–670.

Klapper, L. 2006. *Entrepreneurship: how much does the business environment matter?* Washington, D.C.: The World Bank Group.

Klapper, L., Laeven, L. and Rajan, R. 2006. Entry regulation as a barrier to entrepreneurship. *Journal of Financial Economics.* **82**. pp.591–629.

Klapper, L., Lewin, A. and Delgado, J. M. Q. 2010. *The impact of the business environment on the business creation process.* [Online]. Washington, D.C.: The World Bank. [Accessed 6 July 2013]. Available from: http://www-wds.worldbank.org/servlet/WDSContentServer/WDSP/ IB/2009/ 05/19/000158349_20090519094645/Rendered/PDF/WPS4937.pdf.

Kelin, M. and Hadjimichael, B. 2003. *The private sector in development: entrepreneurship, regulation, and competitive disciplines.* Washington, D.C.: The World Bank.

Liedholm, C. 2002. Small firm dynamics: evidence from Africa and Latin America. *Small Business Economics.* **18**(3). pp.227–242.

La Porta, R., Lopez-De-Silanes, F. and Shleifer, A. 2011. *The unofficial economy in Africa.* Working Paper. Cambridge: National Bureau of Economic Research.

McPherson, M. A. 1992. *Growth and survival of southern African firms.* East Lansing: Michigan State University.

McPherson, M. A. 1996. Growth of micro and small enterprises in southern Africa. *Journal of Development Economics.* **48**(1996). pp.253–277.

McPherson, M. A. and Liedholm, C. 1996. Determinants of small and micro enterprise, registration: results from surveys in Niger and Swaziland. *World Development.* **24**(3). pp.481–487.

Mead, D. C., and Liedholm, C. 1998. The dynamics of micro and small enterprises in developing countries. *World Development.* **26**(1). pp.61–74.

Meagher, K. 2011. *Identity economics: social networks and the informal economy in Nigeria.* Woodbridge: James Currey.

Nadvi, K. 1999. Collective efficiency and collective failure: the response of the Sialkot surgical instrument cluster to global quality pressures. *World Development.* **27**(9). pp.1605–1626.

Olomi, D., Nilsson, P. and Jensson, J. 2001. *Evolution of entrepreneurial motivation: the transition from economic necessity to entrepreneurship.* Wellesley: Babson College Kauffman Foundation.

Parker, J. 1995. *Patterns of business growth: micro and small enterprises in Kenya.* East Lansing: Michigan State University.

Pietrobelli, C. and Rabellotti, R. 2004. *Upgrading in clusters and value chains in Latin America: the role of policies.* Washington, D.C.: Inter-American Development Bank.

Piore, M. J. and Sabel, C. F. 1984. *The second industrial divide: possibilities for prosperity.* New York: Basic Books.

Pisani, M. J. and Pagan, J. A. 2004. Self-employment in the era of the new economic model in Latin America: a case study from Nicaragua. *Entrepreneurship & Regional Development.* **16**(4). pp.335–350.

Porter, M. E. 1990. *The competitive advantage of nations.* New York: Free Press.

Pyke, F., Becattini, G. and Sengenberger, W. 1990. *Industrial districts and inter-firm cooperation in Italy.* Geneva: International Institute for Labour Studies.

Ramachandran, K. 1993. Poor women entrepreneurs: lessons from Asian countries. *Small Enterprise Developmen.* **4**(1). pp.46–49.

Ramachandran, K. and Ramnarayan, S. 1993. Entrepreneurial orientation and networking: some Indian evidence. *Journal of Business Venturing.* **8**(6). pp.513–524.

Reeg, C. 2013. *Micro, small and medium enterprise upgrading in low and middle income countries: a literature review.* Bonn: DIE.

Rodrik, D. 2005. Institutions as the fundamental cause of longrun growth. In: Aghion, P. and Durlauf, S. N. (eds.). *Handbook of economic growth, 1A.* Amsterdam: North Pole, pp.386–414.

Romijn, H. 1997. Acquisition of technological capability in development: a quantitative case study of Pakistan's capital goods sector. *World Development.* **25**(3). pp.359–377.

Schmitz, H. and Knorringa, P. 2000. Learning from global buyers. *Journal of Development Studies.* **37**(2). pp.177–205.

Singh, A. 2002. *Competition and competition policy in emerging markets: international and developmental dimensions.* [Online]. Geneva: United Nations. [Accessed 14 December 2013]. Available from: https://www.g24.org/wp-content/uploads/2016/01/18.pdf.

Sleuwagen, L. and Goedhuys, M. 2002. Growth of firms in developing countries, evidence from Côte d'Ivoire. *Journal of Development Economics.* **68**(1). pp.117–135.

Tan, H. W. and Batra, G. 1995. *Technical efficiency of SMEs: comparative evidence from developing economies.* Washington, D.C.: The World Bank.

Zahra, S. A. and George, G. 2002. Absorptive capacity: a review, reconceptualization, and extension. *Academy of Management Review.* **27**(2). pp.185-203.

Chapter 11

Malagos Farmhouse Cheese: Crafting Cheese at 38°C

Aimée Hampel-Milagrosa[1] and Karen Dall[2]

Introduction

This incredible upgrading story of Malagos Farmhouse Cheeses comes from the Philippines, an archipelago in Southeast Asia and home to almost 100 million people. What makes this story unique is that, being a tropical country, cheese production would have been unthinkable if not impossible, but Olive Puentespina, owner of Malagos, saw the potential of artisanal goat and cow cheese-making in the country. Her upgrading story traces her lowly beginnings crafting cheeses in the family garage up until the time she began to supply to the business class of Philippine Airlines, the country's premier flag carrier. Her story will not only inspire but also shed light on the following research question: *what are the constraints to enterprise upgrading and what explains her firm's ability to overcome these barriers?*

We will use the "Onion" model to analyze Olive's narrative. The Onion model was developed by Reeg (2013) and has been subsequently used to analyse enterprise upgrading in India, Egypt, and the Philippines (Hampel-Milagrosa *et al.* 2013). The Onion model puts together four different strands of research on factors impacting enterprise growth into one multi-layered model. These layers represent the business environment, personal and professional networks, enterprise characteristics, and entrepreneur characteristics. Compared to previous approaches to enterprise growth, the Onion model looks at how the entrepreneur combines all of these layers to create a growth strategy for his or her firm. The upgrading analysis follows an evaluation of the interlinkages of these four layers with one another.

In the interview with the entrepreneur, we were on the lookout for various types of innovation that the entrepreneur introduced in the firm and on how these innovations impacted the company's productivity,

---

[1]Asian Development Bank (formerly German Development Institute).
[2]United Nations University Institute for Environment and Human Security.

profits or employee size. Throughout the interview, we constantly referred to the Onion model to trace the origin of the innovation and to confirm whether the strategy came from one or from many layers of the model. We wanted to make sure of three things: that an innovation was introduced to the company, that the introduced innovation has positively impacted enterprise growth through an increase in employee numbers, and that this resulting growth was sustainable above and beyond those of the company's competitors.

Analysis of the Malagos' Farm House Cheese upgrading story showed that Olive had to overcome not only constraints in tropical cheese production but also constraints to enterprise upgrading itself. Tropical conditions in the Philippines that hampered cheese production added to her main upgrading constraint of being an anonymous local producer that challenged established European and American cheese imports. To address these challenges, Olive used a combination of success factors from across four layers of the Onion model to create sector-specific upgrading strategies. Underneath all her strategies, however, we see that human capital endowment, motivation and risk-taking attitude were the main driving forces in overcoming barriers to the enterprise's success. Olive began as an informal entrepreneur before deciding to register her business, and her success story has important implications for policy makers who want to increase the productivity of the private sector through business environment reforms.

This case study is organized as follows. First, we begin with an introduction about the Philippines and the Filipino economic context. We show that although the Philippines has made significant economic improvements since it ended the Marcos era in the mid 1980s, the country still faces a long way towards a developed country status. Then we show that the Philippines is slowly transitioning to a more service-oriented economy, manifested through an increasing number of people leaving agriculture. A discussion of the government's efforts to improve the business environment to make the country an investment destination follows. Here we shed light on the situation of Filipino women entrepreneurs who, despite representing half of proprietors in the country, are still faced with lack of access to productivity-increasing resources. After a short description of how Olive Puentespina was identified in the Methodology, we tell her story using her own words, in her own perspective. We then use the Onion model to analyse her upgrading strategy and end with lessons learned and conclusions.

The Filipino Economic Context

The Republic of the Philippines with over 7000 islands and its diverse population that speaks more than 80 languages is among the most dynamic economies in Southeast Asia. From 1986 until 2015, after democracy was restored, the Gross Domestic Product per capita has doubled to US$2600 and the country reached average growth rates of above 5% in the past decade (Worldbank 2016a; Ringuet and Estrada 2003). Market liberalization, joining the World Trade Organisation (WTO) and the Asia Pacific Economic Cooperation (APEC) and its Poverty Alleviation Plans further paved the way to economic growth (WTO 1999). Rapid population growth led to a shift in the Philippines' position from a food exporter to a food importer, and the share of agriculture of the GDP and agricultural exports have been declining on the way to a middle income country (Briones 2013).

Today the Philippines is transitioning from an agriculture-based to a more service-oriented economy with the service's share of the GDP increasing to about 58%, while agriculture accounting for only about 10% share (Worldbank 2016). Another pillar of the Filipino economy is remittances: they constitute approximately 10% of the GDP, which equaled US$25 billion in 2015 (Chipongian 2016). One commonly mentioned advantage of Filipinos is their proficiency in English (even in remote areas) and the high educational level: 94% of Filipino adults are literate (Worldbank 2016).

While the Philippine industrial sector is shaped mostly by the manufacturing of electronics and other high-tech components, the remaining agricultural sector ranges from small subsistence farming to large commercial holdings which focus on exports (PSA 2016; Worldbank 2016). Some 30% of the Filipino workforce is still employed in agriculture and approximately 55% of the total population lives in rural areas. Since the 1960s when the rural population was about 70% of the total population, the share has decreased significantly, indicating the global trend of urbanization. However, poverty is still most severe and widespread in rural areas: out of the 38% of the population living on less than US$3.10 a day (Worldbank 2016), 80% live in rural areas. Against this background, the development of the agricultural sector is a major priority of the government as a means to alleviate poverty (IFAD 2016).

The Philippines ranks 115 in the Human Development Index and belongs to the category of "medium development" like its neighbors Indonesia and Vietnam (UNDP 2015a). Since 1980, the country's rank has improved mainly due to higher life expectancy (68.2 years) and due to the Gross National Income per capita, which has increased by about 79.5%. Nevertheless the Philippines still ranks below the average (with 0.710 HDI) among countries in East Asia and Pacific (UNDP 2015b).

Agriculture and Agribusinesses in The Philippines

Agriculture still plays a significant role in the Filipino economy both in exports as well as in livelihood provision. Crops (60%) are the largest commodity group of Filipino agriculture followed by 23% livestock and poultry, and 17% fishing. Major crops are coconut, sugarcane, banana and pineapple, and the major staple crop is rice (PSA 2013; Briones 2013). Borras and Franco (2005) call this type of agriculture "low value, high volume."

Poverty in the country remains high, especially among households dependent on agriculture even if the same sector has been regarded the most efficient in job creation and poverty reduction (Worldbank 2016a). For this reason, the Filipino government developed a strategy to support rural microenterprises and agribusinesses through the provision of credit, technology, and market support. Some 3 million microenterprises in rural communities that lack access to credit have been targeted by this strategy (IFAD 2016).

In addition to a lack of finances, smallholders have to deal with poor infrastructure. Severe weather events have made road conditions in many rural parts of the country impassable. As the Philippines consist of over 7000 islands, commodities often need to be transported via air or water. This increases marketing costs and marketing margins and commonly leads to a lower share of the farmer in the final selling price.

The country's geography tends to cut off many smallholders from access to modern technology and knowledge. Despite this, smallholders are largely predicted to survive. Firstly smallholders have been found to be very efficient in terms of labor per productivity output; secondly they have extensive local knowledge, which is highly valuable especially in times of adverse climatic conditions; and thirdly smallholders can tap into relatives' remittances in times of need, as about 40% of overseas migrants come from rural areas (Estacaan 2013).

With regard to women in agriculture, although the Philippines holds rank 7 in the Global Gender Gap Index of the World Economic Forum (2015), women's agribusiness opportunities are particularly constrained by their limited access to land. In general women own less land than men and they are further limited through inheritance norms, land titling systems and their restricted ability to purchase land. Thus, just 11% of Philippine landholders are female and since only landholders can benefit from the governmental Comprehensive Agrarian Reform Program (CARP), many women are automatically excluded. Furthermore, since women are traditionally responsible for subsistence crops, they tend to receive less training and agricultural extension services, less credit and fewer access to high quality inputs (ADB 2013). An overarching agriculture strategy to include women in commercial agriculture would be beneficial as they make up more than 50% of the agricultural workforce.

The Filipino Business Environment – A Woman´s Perspective

The Philippines is a lower middle income country that ranks 103 out of 189 in the World Bank's Ease of Doing Business Index, a global ranking of the ease of starting and running businesses. This rank indicates a negative change of six ranks in comparison to 2015 rankings, lower than the regional average of East Asia and the Pacific, but higher than the rankings of Indonesia and Laos PDR. The World Bank's Doing Business calculates an indicator for specific elements of a business life and ranks countries accordingly. For example, opening a formal enterprise in the Philippines is time and resource-consuming as it takes 16 procedures, on average 29 days and 16% of the income per capita (the country ranks 165 in the Starting a Business indicator). More obstacles can be found in

Registering Property (rank 112), Getting Credit (rank 109), Enforcing
Contracts (rank 140) and Paying Taxes (rank 126); the latter accounts for
almost 200 hours per year per person. In contrast, the Doing Business
report ranked the Philippines as comparably excellent in terms of Getting Electricity (rank 19) (Worldbank 2016b). PricewaterhouseCoopers
commended the Philippines' investment potential due to its strategic geo-
graphical location, its large and educated workforce and its liberal, mar-
ket-oriented economy (Pwc 2015).

The Philippines has already undergone structural reforms in the past
decade, but more reforms are still needed to enhance property rights through
more systematic and administrative adjudication of land and through
the simplification of business regulation to encourage overall business
growth (Worldbank 2016a). The government views entrepreneurship as an
important tool to empowering the poor and reducing poverty. As stated in
the Philippine Development Plan, the government aims to support micro,
small and medium-sized enterprises in particular (MSME), which account
for 99.6% out of all 830,000 business enterprises in the Philippines and for
38% of total job growth (Evangelista 2013).

A total of 4 out of 10 adult Filipinos are engaged in business, of whom
45% are female. According to the Philippine Institute for Development
Studies (PIDS) the Philippines has the second highest percentage
worldwide of entrepreneurially active women (PIDS 2015). PIDS (2015)
states that women are mostly engaged in microenterprises in the informal
sector, reflecting the traditional structure of men as principal income
earners in established enterprises while women are informal supporters
of family income. The tension between a women's business and her
household responsibilities leads to a superior number of men owning
businesses although more women start businesses. Furthermore, access
to official business development services is more difficult for women than
for men; for example access to credits and financing, or access to (market-)
information. Thus, women tend to enter markets with low entry barriers
like retail trade, food stalls and personal services, which also tend to have
low productivity (PIDS 2015).

Methodology

The Philippine approach involved two rounds of interviews, the first one for upgraders and the second one for non-upgraders. The upgrading story of Olive Puentespina was discovered in the first round of interviews. During this first round, the objective was to interview founders and owners of small or medium-sized enterprises that grew from micro or small-size, respectively, and trace back their success stories. To determine how the Philippine government categorized enterprise size, the study first sought the assistance of the Bureau of Micro, Small and Medium-sized Enterprises Development (BMSMED) under the Department of Trade and Industry of the Philippines (DTI). After consulting with DTI experts, we found that their formal definition of MSME was based on capitalization and does not fully capture the proportion of micro enterprises in the Philippine economy. We decided to establish a definition of Philippine MSMEs based on size, and reached the following categorization, to which the DTI, for the purposes of our research, agreed to:

- Micro sized enterprises are those with 1-5 regular employees
- Small sized enterprises are those with 6-10 employees
- Medium sized enterprise are those with 11-99 employees and
- Large sized enterprises as those with greater than 100 employees.

Since upgrading is an exceptional feat, sampling has to be conducted purposively. To find upgraders, three methods were used. First, several agency officers from the BMSMED, DTI, Center for International Trade Expositions and Missions (CITEM), Department of Tourism (DOT), National Economic Research and Business Action Center (NERBAC), Manufacturer's Associations and Chambers of Commerce and Industries at the national and regional level were approached with the purpose of obtaining a list of enterprises from the Food Processing sector. Second, we held interviews and focus group discussions (FGDs) with heads of the Davao Food Processors Association and requested to be referred to other members of their organization who were willing to be interviewed. Third, industry and academia experts' interviews were also used as opportunities to acquire the names and contact details of more entrepreneurs.

Once we had a list of potential respondents, we still had to filter out upgraders from those enterprises that started large. Based on our ongoing definition of upgrading and qualitative/quantitative qualifiers, we considered an upgrader as a micro enterprise that have increased their workforce size to small (or from small to medium size enterprise) in the last 12 years from date of interview. Moreover, enterprises should have exhibited an above-average quantitative change in total asset or sales / returns or production area size within the same time period, acquired through significant and verifiable innovation in products, processes or ways of organizing production.

The Story of Malagos Farm House Cheese

This upgrading story is about Malagos Farmhouse Cheese, proudly owned and operated by Olive Puentespina, a young vibrant mother of three. Her enterprise is located in Davao city in southern Philippines and she is a pioneer producer of artisanal goat and cow cheese in the Philippines. In this story, we will first use Olive's perspective of how she grew her firm before proceeding to analyse her upgrading strategy.

> My name is Olive Puentespina. I originally came from Batangas, from Luzon island, but have been living in Davao for many years. I came from a middle class family, meaning I did not grow up poor, but I did not grow up rich either. My father worked as a banker at the Philippine National Bank. I can remember that we did not have electricity at home until I was 10 years old and had to constantly rely on a generator for electrical power.

> My husband and I met when we were both students at the University of the Philippines in Los Baños (UPLB). He came from Davao, in southern Philippines, where we also decided to settle down after marriage. His family is into agribusiness such as orchid and plant propagation and eco-tourism and it was just natural for us to help in maintaining the business. In 2003, my husband and I decided to acquire 30 goats because we thought it would be nice to have some animals roaming around in the farm. In 2006, the thirty goats were already numbering 100 and were

requiring high overhead costs for their maintenance. I was thinking, these goats are always getting something from us so it would just be fair to also get something from them in return. Plus, they were producing so much milk that there had to be something done about it. I did not want to let the milk to waste.

In the beginning, I tried to make soap out of goat milk but found out that you actually use very little goat milk in the milk soap. I was still throwing out a lot. It was then when I decided to make cheese. I was a graduate of Bachelor of Animal Science in UPLB and actually worked for some time at the Dairy Training and Research Institute (DTRI) of UPLB so I knew the basics of cheese making. However, having spent so many years in Davao, I have forgotten how to do it.

I went back to Los Baños and spent two days training with a former colleague on how to make cheese. I bribed her into teaching me cheese making by bringing wine for us to drink during our sessions. I wrote everything down because soon enough I was on my own, experimenting by myself. I did a lot of experiments and spent hours in my small laboratory to be able to produce different types of cheeses. "Laboratory" is actually an exaggeration. I asked my father-in-law for a space in the family's large garage where I could conduct my cheese experiments. He offered to put up a temporary wall that would separate the vehicles from the garage with my laboratory and installed a water source for me. The water is very important for the cheese making.

The hours I spent experimenting on how to make cheese were extensive. Sometimes, I went back to the lab after the family dinner to try to make some more cheese. I took notes of everything I did and documented everything I have done in my years of cheese making into what I call my protocol diary. I am very proud of my first two products from goat milk. They were feta cheese and kesong puti. Kesong puti (white cheese) is a type of fresh cheese that is usually produced from cow's milk. It is widely known in the Philippines and has a huge consumer base in the country, particularly in Luzon. It took me three months to make my first feta from my kitchen using normal kitchen utensils.

I wanted to learn more about cheese making, so with the help of family based abroad, I went in 2008 on a one month tour of artisanal cheese makers in the US, travelling from Wisconsin to northern California. I would have wanted to go to Europe to learn about cheese making there, knowing that the cheese there are excellent, but finances were tight and the lack of family members in Europe meant that this was not an option. Back in the Philippines, I kept on making cheeses, tweaking them to the Filipino palate as to not assault the Filipinos who are not used to aggressive cheese aromas. I always use locally available materials for ingredients except for the "cheese starter" which I import since it is not available locally.

My husband Dr. Bo is a veterinarian and I asked him for help to increase our goat milk production in order to supply milk for my experiments. He decided to help me by crossbreeding imported Boer goats and Anglo-Nubian goats to produce the "Bo-Ang" goats that were excellent milk producers. Every time I produce some type of cheese, my family, especially my three kids are my "guinea pigs". I ask them to taste and rate my newly produced cheeses. I like that they are always honest! Aside from experimenting, I also attended countless seminars, trainings and trade fairs in the Philippines and abroad. In trade fairs that I previously attended, I gave away so many samples that my cheese stock is always depleted but I did not generate significant business deals.

However, during one of the local trade fairs I got to know two people who were to change my life: the Head Chef of Philippine Airlines (PAL) and a half-Swiss half-Filipino food distributor named Karin Roelli Carmona. The Head Chef of Philippine Airlines liked my cheeses and my story so much that he asked me to create cheese especially for PAL's business and first class international flights. At that time I told the Chef that I am is still experimenting and actually I was working alone. It might take some time before I can get it right and develop samples, let alone supply the volume that the flagship carrier was willing to buy. Fortunately the head Chef of PAL said he was willing to wait. After several months I produced exclusively for PAL my now-famous mango chevre.

Karin Roelli Carmona, in the meantime, asked to be the exclusive distributor of my cheeses, even before I started going commercial. She currently distributes my cheeses to high end supermarkets in the country. Back then she asked if she can bring my cheese to Switzerland when she goes there for a vacation to which I agreed. While on vacation, Karin showed my cheeses to two "cheese masters" who were impressed with the quality of my product and the situation with which I produced them. They arranged to visit me in Davao, without any idea of what to expect. They told me that the moment they landed on Philippine soil, the first thing they said were "You cannot make cheese in this country! It is too warm and humid!" So I showed them how I did it. For two weeks, the two cheese masters exchanged ideas with me and observed my work. After two weeks, they asked me to teach them my technique in exchange for teaching me theirs.

The two cheese masters went back to Switzerland and wrote a report about me for a local newspaper. The excerpt goes: "Cheese at 38 degree temperature, extremely high humidity and a non-existing cheese cellar is anything but easy. In spite of the difficult production circumstances, the Philippine cheese master creates the highest quality in her production. All employees wear gloves, the necessary kitchenware are always sterilized with hot water, and the cheese are hidden in a plastic bag to ripen. The talent to improvise is also demanded. Instead of the cellar, the cheese is stored in sterile plastic boxes".[3]

Thus I continued to approach cheese making, guided with basic theory and with lots of improvisation. I have since produced 22 different types of cheese, including the Blue Pepato with green peppercorns and the Blush, a 2-month aged cheese dipped in Bignay wine. Bignay is a red wine made from local berries. To appease the Filipino palate, my Chevre

---

[3]The original report in German reads: "Kaesen bei 38 Grad Lufttemperatur, extreme hoher Luftfeuchtigkeit und einem fehlenden Kaesekeller sei alles andere als einfach. Den schwierigen Produktionsumstaenden zum Trotz achte die philippinische Kaesemeisterin auf hoechste Qualitaet bei der Produktion. Alle Angestellten tragen Handschuhe, das benoetigte Geschirr wird immer mit heissem Wasser sterilisiert und zum reifen werden die Kaese in einen Plastiksack gesteckt. Auch Improvisationstalent ist gefragt. Anstatt im Keller lagern die Kaese in sterilen Plastikboxen."

is not as heavily salted, the Feta Tricolor with chili and rosemary has a unique herb blend suited to local tastes and the Queso Rustico is similar to the Spanish Manchego. I have also produced cheese with dried mangos and dried pineapple bits that are produced locally. Of course I also have the usual cheeses aged in blue or white mold, or both.

I am very rigorous with my products. I conduct cheese analysis every six months instead of the usual once-a-year evaluation and have fully adapted cheese production to Philippine conditions. From an initial production of 3 to 6 kilograms of cheese per week, I now produce between 20 to 100 kilograms per week of different cheeses, half of which is supplied to Philippine Airlines. I have updated my equipments and have expanded my cheese lab from circa 4 sqm to 75 sqm.

What explains my success? I have lots of ideas and I know where I would like to go with my business. I believe in mentoring, and I thank the Swiss cheese masters for sharing their expertise with me. If I don't know anything, I go out and learn it. I even bought a book called Accounting for Dummies just to learn how to do bookkeeping for my cheese sales. I love what I do! I have carpal tunnel syndrome, tennis elbows and herniated disks but I still wake up every morning excited to work on my cheeses. It is hard manual labour, carrying the milk vats and so on. However, it is also important to know when to back off.

I remember being "thick faced" during the beginning of my enterprise. I used to call people up to ask them to invite me to trade fairs or to supply me with stuff I need for my cheese. I remember I called up people to provide me with plastic boxes to store my ripening cheese and for my deliveries. Nobody wanted to supply me with just a few pieces - I only needed less than 1000 boxes - because the suppliers usually sell to companies in terms of at least 10,000 pieces of plastic boxes per order. Finally I found this one Chinese businessman who agreed to supply me with my needed boxes. Now that I am successful, I still buy my boxes from him even though other suppliers are now offering their boxes at sometimes a cheaper price.

I have innovated in the packaging too. If you buy at least 1 kilogram of Malagos Farm House Cheeses, you would get a cheese cooler package that allows you to transport the cheese without spoilage and with style. The little square bag has the Malagos Farmhouse Cheese ensignia printed on the front. I also have started to incorporate some European style cheese making techniques that I learned from the two Swiss cheese masters.

As compared to when I started, the situation for micro entrepreneurs now is way better. The government now listens to us—to the small entrepreneurs—although you still have to make the trip to various government offices. Belonging to an association helps because the members help each other in the process of documentation and accreditation.

To give back to the community, I also take in employees who are handicapped who otherwise would not have a chance in the Philippine labour market. I have an employee who is blind in one eye, and one employee who is deaf. Although it is not my responsibility anymore, I even pay for their health check-up and other medical examinations. I treat them with respect so that they acquire self worth. Looking back, I would not hesitate to go through the growth path again because it is a good learning process.

Analysis of Upgrading Strategy

In this section we break down Olive Puentespina's story using the framework of the Onion model to explain how she managed to overcome the odds and upgrade her company. We will begin from the outermost part of the Onion going inwards: starting from the business environment, working towards personal and professional networks, on to enterprise characteristics and finally, entrepreneur characteristics. As the analysis will show, while the entrepreneur used a combination of strategies across all layers of the Onion model, Olive drew upon the innermost layers the most. Moreover, the analysis of her story also highlights the fact that enterprise upgrading could occur without being formalized first.

A. Business environment

When Olive stated that the situation for micro entrepreneurs is now much better than when she started her cheese making sometime in 2006, she is actually right. MSMEs in the Philippines now enjoy a more favorable policy environment to increase their productivity and upgrade. The most crucial legislation in support of MSMEs is RA 9501, otherwise known as the 'Magna Carta for Micro Small and Medium Enterprises (MSMEs)'. It was presented to parliament in 1991 and was approved in 2008. RA 9501 acknowledges SMEs' role in creating employment and economic growth and providing a self-sufficient industrial framework for the country. The Magna Carta for MSMEs announced the State's support for developing MSMEs with all available means. This includes a directive to all lending institutions – as defined by the Central Bank of the Philippines (BSP) – to reserve at least 8 per cent of their total loan portfolio available for MSEs and MSME credit. The Department of Trade and Industry was tasked to be the main coordinator for the development of Philippine MSMEs. DTI offices, line offices and regional centres all over the country were mobilized to support MSMEs' various business needs (Hampel-Milagrosa 2014).

Although Olive mentioned that the business environment has dramatically improved, some things have not changed. She still had to make several trips to various government offices whenever she needed to have administrative and legal matters sorted out. Also, information about and prospects of participation in trade fairs—facts that she needed as a startup—was rather difficult to obtain such that she had to contact friends to obtain information.

The topic of red tape came up during our discussion and Olive mentioned that it is an unavoidable part of being an entrepreneur. However she explained the dynamics of red tape in a different way. She said entrepreneurs are always in a rush and in a country where documentation is pretty bureaucratic; entrepreneurs tend to appreciate when a fast lane is opened for them. This fast lane comes at a price, which fortunately is a manageable sum for her. What derails the business is the uncertainty of the length of administrative procedures, with or without bribes.

B. Personal and professional networks

Networks, mostly in her personal circle, but also in her professional group, played a strong role in Olive Puentespina's upgrading strategy. Most of the support that has allowed Olive's innovative element to come out originated from Olive's personal network who fully supported her from the time she was struggling until now. For example, her former colleague and friend obliged to refresh her memory in preparing cheese in exchange for a bottle of wine. Her father-in-law relinquished a section of the family's garage to allow her to conduct her experiments. Her husband bred hybrid goats for her in order to augment her goat milk supply as soon as her experiments started taking off. Her extended family in the USA adopted her while she took a month-long sojourn across several states to learn more about cheese making.

> I wanted to learn more about cheese making, so with the help of family based abroad, I went in 2008 on a one month tour of artisanal cheese makers in the US, travelling from Wisconsin to northern California. (-Olive Puentespina)

Her immediate family in the Philippines allowed her to return to her laboratory at night to continue with cheese making and continue to serve as her straightforward critics when it comes to the taste and quality of her cheese products. Clearly, her success would not be possible without the encouragement and backing of her personal network.

Her professional network provided the necessary support to Olive when her micro enterprise started to thrive. Olive is a member of the Food Processors' Association of Davao (FPAD), a dynamic organization of micro and small entrepreneurs in her city that are engaged in the food processing industry. FPAD is recognized by the Department of Trade and Industry, the Department of Tourism, the Department of Science and Technology and the Davao City Chamber of Commerce and Industry. Within this association, its members are well organized and make sure to inform each other of various events, developments and opportunities in their field. Although several members have overlapping businesses (for example, there are several processors involved in dried mango production) the spirit in the association is of helping each other and not of rivalry.

C. Enterprise characteristics

Implicit in Olive Puentespina's story is the fact that she did not begin as a formal entrepreneur. She began implementing her ideas before officially starting and registering her business. She preferred to conduct her experiments until she reached a level of mastery and production that would allow her to confidently market her cheese. Business formalization occurred before joining trade fairs, and only because she had to be a registered business in order to participate. It was after her fortunate meeting with Mrs. Karin Roelli Carmona and the PAL Chef that her business really took off.

Two other factors that contributed to her upgrading were her enterprise's location and her product portfolio. Olive benefited from the fact that the family was into agribusiness and therefore had an initial number of goats whose milk she could start experimenting with. Though the climate was not ideal for cheese production, her family's farm in Davao provided her with enough physical space to establish her cheese laboratory and to support the reproduction of goats to augment her milk supply.

In a short span of time, Olive was able to increase her product portfolio from two (her Feta and Kesong puti) to 22 different kinds of cheeses. A wide product portfolio helped her to capture the interest of many other buyers who are intrigued by locally made cheeses. One strong strategy that Olive employed was to tweak her cheeses in such a way that the flavours appeal to local tastes. She created cheeses that were not too salty or too ripe, as well as cheeses that were infused with various local wines, berries and fruits.

Although the Philippines is well advanced in terms of labour laws and equality in employment, there is still a lot of workplace discrimination occurring in reality. During the interview, Olive divulged that she does not hesitate to hire physically challenged people in her company because otherwise these people would not have any opportunity for formal work at all. She also goes beyond her duties as employer by financially covering check-ups and medical examinations for her employees. This is an excellent employment strategy because her employees will in return, stay loyal to her, and remain highly motivated in their jobs.

I have an employee who is blind in one eye, and employee one who is deaf. Although it is not my responsibility anymore, I even pay for their health check-up and other medical examinations. (-Olive Puentespina)

D. Entrepreneur characteristics

While Olive grew up in a middle class setting, her family had no access to electricity until she was ten years old. This, together with other childhood experiences of a typical middle class Filipino lifestyle, has instilled in her a sense of economy and resourcefulness.

I was always conscious of recycling the family's agribusiness' trash. I did not want anything to go to waste. In fact they called me the trash woman ("basurera") of the family. (-Olive Puentespina)

Olive possesses the necessary education and work experience to equip her with the basic knowledge and skills to create her cheeses. With her Bachelor of Science in Agriculture and her brief employment at the Dairy Training and Research Institute at the University of the Philippines at Los Baños she was able to not only learn the process but most importantly understand scientific concepts behind cheese making. Cheese can be produced from almost any type of milk through the activity of special bacteria and the aid of rennet, a preparation that contains rennin, a complex of enzymes that curdles the casein in milk. Thus critical steps in the cheese making process requires a basic understanding of the science behind sterilization, acidification, coagulation and salination which Olive, through her education and work experience, acquired.

Also, from listening to her story, Olive is a very determined and motivated woman. She acknowledged that she had forgotten most of her skills in cheese making due to the years she has spent living and working in the family's farm in Davao so she decided to go to Los Baños and learn from her former colleague. She diligently takes notes of her experiments in her protocol diary, from successful ones, to the mistakes, in order for her not to do them again. Her notes have been her fountain of ideas, information and inspiration, a major contributing factor to her success.

I told my husband that if I ever die, the first thing he should do is to go to my cheese lab and get my protocol diary! (-Olive Puentespina)

Her passion for her craft is so strong that despite having three young kids, Olive decided to go away for a month to learn more about cheese making. Furthermore her determination could be observed in the sheer amount of experimentation that she did and the number of trade fairs and seminars that she attended in order to garner attention to her products. Even if she kept on going back home without any business deal, she kept on persevering. Similar to other motivated entrepreneurs, her health condition is not a hindrance to her drive to succeed, although she tries to keep a healthy work-life balance.

I have carpal tunnel syndrome, tennis elbows and herniated disks but I still wake up every morning excited to work on my cheeses. It is hard manual labour, carrying the milk vats and so on. However, it is also important to know when to back off. (-Olive Puentespina)

Lessons learned and conclusions

The story of Olive Puentespina of Malagos Farm House Cheeses is unique not only in terms of the manner in which she upgraded her enterprise but also because her product of choice defies conventional production methods when produced in the Philippines. This means that Olive's main issues are to overcome constraints to production aside from overcoming constraints to enterprise growth. The tropical climatic conditions in the Philippines were obviously not the ideal conditions for cheese production. As a novice, Olive did not have the proper facilities and equipment to produce cheese so she had to do a lot of improvisation. She had to use non-conventional methods to produce her cheese and make do with whatever was available to proceed with her experiments (e.g., to use plastic sacks to store her cheese for ripening). The location of her laboratory near the family garage and the incredible ambient heat in Davao all worked against the processing of anything dairy-related. She used her scientific background to sterilize equipment to alleviate the environment's impact on her production. In addition, while Filipinos are not new to cheese consumption per se, the concept of Filipino-produced cheese was limited to the Kesong puti of the north. Olive had to overcome the absolute anonymity of her product and face direct competition against imported cheese from Europe and America. This was actually her greatest constraint in terms of enterprise growth. How do you introduce a locally produced new product to a market that is accustomed to imported high quality alternatives?

Olive drew upon a combination of success factors that allowed her to develop strategies that were built to overcome a range of difficulties. Clearly, Olive had the human capital endowment, the motivation and the risk-taking attitude to steer her company towards growth. She was also fortunate to possess the resources to support her earlier experimentation. The combination of these success factors was specific to challenges she faced in her sector and country, yet were all based on her strong resolve as an entrepreneur. Notice that across all upgrading strategies that she used to overcome her main constraint, a particularly consistent factor emerges: her determination to succeed. Her willpower to be successful bound all her upgrading strategies together and served as the foundation of all business decisions that she made. In this particular case, the entrepreneur was central to the upgrading dynamic and mattered most in the enterprise's success.

The regulatory environment of course matters, but seems to be a secondary factor in her upgrading story as most of the success factors point towards elements found at the inner layers of the Onion. Olive's upgrading case challenges the implied automatization of increased enterprise productivity following business formalization. Olive worked informally at first and her decision to formalize came when the advantages of formalization have outweighed the disadvantages of being informal (see Altenburg/Hampel-Milagrosa/Loewe 2017). For policy makers, this means that efforts to increase the productivity of the private sector that would lead to economic growth need not only concentrate on improving the business environment but also on creating a level field in terms of human endowments and access to resources. A quality educational system and easy access to resources are equally important as an efficient business registration system.

References

ADB (Asian Development Bank). 2013. *Gender equality in the labor market in the Philippines*. [Online] Mandaluyong City: Asian Development Bank. [Accessed 7 November 2016]. Available from: https://www.adb.org/sites/default/files/publication/31194/gender-equality-labor-market-philippines.pdf.

Altenburg, T., Hampel-Milagrosa, A., Loewe, M. 2017. A decade on: how relevant is the regulatory environment for micro and small enterprise upgrading after all? *The European Journal of Development Research*. 29(2), pp.457-475.

Borras, S.M. and Franco, J.C. 2005. Struggles for land and livelihood. *Critical Asian Studies*. 37(3), pp.331-361.

Briones, R. 2013. *Philippine Agriculture to 2020: Threats and Opportunities from Global Trade*. [Online]. Makati City: Philippine Institute for Development Studies. [Accessed 7 October 2016]. Available from: https://dirp3.pids.gov.ph/ris/dps/pidsdps1314.pdf.

Chipongian, L.C. 2016. *OFW remittances rech $25.8B in 2015*. [Online]. Manila: Manila Bulletin. [Accessed 7 August 2016]. Available from: http://www.mb.com.ph/ofw-remittances-reach-25-8b-in-2015/.

Evangelista, R. CIPE (Center for International Private Enterprise). 2013. *Entrepreneurship in the Philippines: Opportunities and challenges for inclusive growth*. [Online] Washington: Center for International Private Enterprise. [Accessed 7 October 2016]. Available from: http://www.cipe.org/publications/detail/entrepreneurship-philippines-opportunities-and-challenges-inclusive-growth.

Hampel-Milagrosa, A. 2014. *Micro and small enterprise upgrading in the Philippines: the role of the entrepreneur, enterprise, networks and business environment*. Bonn: German Development Institute.

Hampel-Milagrosa, A., Loewe, M., Reeg, C. 2015. The entrepreneur makes a difference: Evidence on MSE upgrading factors from Egypt, India, and the Philippines. *World Development*. 66(2), pp.118-130.

Hampel-Milagrosa, A., Loewe, M., Reeg, C. 2013. Which factors determine the upgrading of micro, small and medium-sized enterprises? Evidence from Egypt, India and the Philippines. Bonn: German Development Institute.

IFAD (International Fund for Agricultural Development). 2016. *Rural poverty in the Philippines*. [Online]. [Accessed 7 September 2016]. Available from: http://www.ruralpovertyportal.org/country/home/tags/philippines.

Estacaan, G. Oxfam. 2013. *Back in the game: Winning strategies for private sector investments on small producers in the Philippines*. [Online] Quezon City: Oxfam. [Accessed 7 November 2016]. Available from: https://philippines.oxfam.org/policy_paper/back-game-winning-strategies-private-sector-investments-small-producers-philippines.

Philippine Institute for Development Studies. 2015. *Challenges in the economic participation of women as entrepreneurs*. [Online] Makati City: Philippine Institute for Development Studies

[Accessed 7 October 2016]. Available from: https://www.pids.gov.ph/publications/5489 or https://dirp3.pids.gov.ph/webportal/CDN/PUBLICATIONS/pidspn1503_rev.pdf.

PSA (Philippine Statistics Authority). 2013. *Agriculture and Fisheries. Philippine Yearbook 2013*. [Online]. [Accessed 7 October 2016]. Available from: https://psa.gov.ph/sites/default/files/2013%20PY_Agriculture%20and%20Fisheries.pdf.

PSA (Philippine Statistics Authority). 2016. *Poverty Incidence among Filipinos registered at 26.3%, as of the first semester of 2015*. [Online] [Accessed 7 September 2016]. Available from: https://psa.gov.ph/content/poverty-incidence-among-filipinos-registered-263-first-semester-2015-psa.

PWC (Pricewaterhouse Coopers). 2015. *Finding your way: Doing business and investing in the Philippines*. [Online]. [Accessed 7 October 2016]. Available from: http://www.pwc.com/ph/en/business-guides/assets/documents/pwc-doing-business-in-the-philippines-2015.pdf.

Reeg, C. 2013. *Micro, small and medium enterprise upgrading in low- and middle-income countries: a literature review*. Bonn: German Development Institute.

Ringuet, D.J. and Estrada, E. 2003. Understanding the Philippines' Economy and Politics since the Return of Democracy in 1986. *Contemporary Southeast Asia: A journal of International and Strategic Affairs*. [Online] **25**(2), pp.233-250. [Accessed 7 September 2016]. Available from: https://muse.jhu.edu/article/387730/pdf.

The World Heritage Foundation. 2016. *Economic Freedom Snapshot*. [Online]. [Accessed 7 August 2016]. Available from: http://www.heritage.org/index/country/philippines.

UNDP (United Nations Development Program). 2015. *International Human Development Indicators*. [Online]. [Accessed 7 September 2016]. Available from: http://hdr.undp.org/en/countries.

UNDP (United Nations Development Program). 2015. *Human Development Report 2015: Philippines*. [Online]. [Accessed 7 September 2016]. Available from: http://hdr.undp.org/sites/all/themes/hdr_theme/country-notes/PHL.pdf.

Worldbank. 2016. *World Development Indicators*. [Online]. [Accessed 7 September 2016]. Available from: http://databank.worldbank.org/.

Worldbank. 2016. *Philippines overview*. [Online]. [Accessed 7 August 2016]. Available from: http://www.worldbank.org/en/country/philippines/overview.

Worldbank. 2016. *Doing Business 2016: Economy Profile 2016 Philippines*. [Online]. Washington: Worldbank. [Accessed 7 October 2016]. Available from: https://openknowledge.worldbank.org/handle/10986/23370.

World Economic Forum. 2015. *The Global Gender Gap report 2015*. [Online]. Switzerland: World Economic Forum. [Accessed 7 November 2016]. Available from: http://www3.weforum.org/docs/GGGR2015/cover.pdf.

WTO (World Trade Organization). 1999. *The Philippines: September 1999*. [Online] [Accessed 7 October 2016]. Available from: https://www.wto.org/english/tratop_e/tpr_e/tp114_e.htm.

Chapter 12

Lingzhi Mushroom Company:
Not Your Typical Mushroom Management

Aimée Hampel-Milagrosa,[1] Pham Van Hong,[2] Karen Dall,[4]
and Michael Bruentrup[3]

Introduction

This chapter portrays the noteworthy upgrading story of the Lingzhi Mush-room Company (LMC), established in 2001 and headed by Mrs. Nguyen Thi Chinh of Hanoi, Vietnam. The LMC is a first-mover in the introduction of non-endemic mushroom species in the country, and is also a pioneer in research into the pharmaceutical potential and manufacture of medici-nal mushroom-based products in Vietnam. The company's upgrading story from a struggling microenterprise into a large-sized firm that leads raw mushroom and mushroom-based product manufacture in the country is told in her own words, using her own perspective. Her story provides insight into the following research questions: *what are the constraints to enterprise growth and what explains her firm's ability to overcome these barriers?*

Following her narrative, we analyse her case using an enterprise upgrading model. The enterprise upgrading model examines enterprise growth from a systemic development perspective. It provides evidence that sustainable firm growth is brought about by the conglomeration of four levels of factors: the business environment, professional and personal business networks, enterprise and entrepreneur characteristics. These four levels of factors were juxtaposed to form a concentric circle similar to the layers of an onion; hence the upgrading model is referred to as the "Onion model". Enterprise upgrading is characterised by the introduction of an innovation (or a series of innovations) that may not necessarily be new to the world, but is definitely new to the firm and the immediate market where

[1]Asian Development Bank (formerly German Development Institute).
[2]Vietnam National University.
[3]German Development Institute.
[4]United Nations University Institute for Environment and Human Security.

the firm operates. The introduced innovation allows the enterprise to reap innovation rents ahead of its competitors, and therefore grow, much faster than the rest. This analytical approach—growth through innovation—explains firm growth as a phenomenon that is proactively induced by the firm. It distinguishes internally-induced enterprise upgrading (due to innovation) from types of growth that could be stimulated externally (due to monopoly or due to an increase in overall demand). Upgrading is seen as a more sustainable form of firm growth, because the innovating firm continues to reinvent itself and not only responds to, but also influences market demand.

The enterprise upgrading analysis in this case shows two important findings: First, the entrepreneur used a combination of strategies that are found in various layers of the Onion model in order to address barriers to growth. She complements one strategy with another, to fill in gaps or to create synergies and to strengthen the impact of this combined strategy against the growth barrier. Second, enterprise upgrading heavily banks on a "super entrepreneur"[3] that could spell the difference between stagnation and success of different entrepreneurs within the same setting.

This chapter is organized as follows. We set the stage by presenting a short overview of Vietnam and its agribusinesses, its business environment and the resulting economic participation of women, and in light of LMC's engagement in the pharmaceutical sector, the health situation of the Vietnamese. We follow this with an explanation on how we operationalized this model in the methodology. Next, the story of LMC as told by its owner is presented, followed by an analysis of her account using the "Onion". This chapter ends with conclusions and policy recommendations that could provide guidance to entrepreneurs and policy makers facing similar situations.

---

[3]Hampel *et al.* (2015) defines the concept of super entrepreneur in enterprise upgrading as: "…where the entrepreneur is better endowed with human capital; has higher motivation and risk-taking ability; is willing to invest in human resource development, R&D and market research; and possesses personal wealth or easy access to family finance."

Vietnam, Agribusiness, and Women Entrepreneurs

The Socialist Republic of Vietnam thirty years ago was one of the poorest countries in the world with an annual per capita income around US$100 (Worldbank 2016a). Today this Southeast Asian country is often presented as a perfect but rather quiet development success story (Davis 2016; Breu 2012)—a country jumping from a centrally planned economy towards more market orientation due to political and economic reforms known as Đổi Mới in 1986 (Fritzen 2002). The average annual income today is almost US$2000 (UNdata 2015), while the economy grew consistently at a rate of 5.5% or greater since 1990 (Worldbank 2016b). The end of the US economic embargo 1993 paved the way for the entry of international investments. In addition, in subsequent years Vietnam joined the Association of Southeast Asian Nations (ASEAN) in 1995, the Asia-Pacific Economic Cooperation (APEC) in 1998 and World Trade Organisation (WTO) in 2007 (Chaponniere *et al.* 2008; APEC 2016).

Although the Vietnamese economy is still shaped primarily by the Vietnamese Communist Party that develops Five Year Plans through the plenary sessions of the Central Committee and national congresses, it is one of Asia's most open economies and has become a major exporter of agricultural products (VIETRADE 2014; FAOSTAT 2016). Looking at the Human Development Index (HDI), Vietnam ranks lower than the regional average; it shares its rank (116) with South Africa and El Salvador, and is comparable to the Philippines (115) and Thailand (93) (UNDP 2015). The share of people living in extreme poverty (US$1.90/day) has dropped drastically from ~50% in 1990 to 3% today, although 14% still live below the national poverty line (Worldbank 2016a, 2016b), and 14% of the population is undernourished (FAO 2015). Future economic challenges include the ongoing transformation, as well as income disparities between urban and rural areas. Despite the growth of urban populations, 67% of the population live in rural areas, where agriculture is still the major employer (~47% in 2013). Despite being a major source of income, the share of agriculture in the GDP is only for 18% (Worldbank 2016a, 2016b).

Agriculture and agribusinesses in Vietnam

The Vietnamese agriculture sector (including related agribusinesses) consists mainly of farming (72.2%) and livestock (26.5%), while Agriservices—agrochemicals and agriproduct retailing—account for only 1.3%. The overall market size of the Vietnamese agriculture sector is almost 40 billion US$ (2011). One major challenge for local businesses is the competition from larger foreign firms; an example of this would be the industrial feed market, where foreign forms currently have a 60% market share and thus can influence prices heavily (Stoxplus 2014).

Similar problems occur in the sugar sector: Although Vietnam is the fourth largest sugar producer in South East Asia, the sugar market is highly underdeveloped. It has no formal distribution system, which leads to an non-competitive sugar sector (Business Monitor International 2014). Kim Son (in Vietnamnet 2015) argues that one of the major problems of Vietnam's agriculture is the quality and not the quantity of agricultural products. If the quality and diversity were higher, more investments would be made and income would increase.

Other obstacles in agribusiness for small-scale farmers in general are high production costs, low technology or old-fashioned cultivation technologies, inconsistent quality standards and a lack of *"contract farming, multi-actor collaboration, improved transparency, accountability and enhanced support from the local government"* (Ha 2015a). What is needed are more linkages between all players along the value chain and less bureaucracy. A potential sector for improving these linkages is organic food production, as organic agriculture is done only on 0.2% of the country's total agricultural land and increasing due to local and international demand (Viet Nam News 2016). On the other hand, farmers have to face new challenges regarding international standards regarding hygiene and safety and certifications. The example of organic agriculture illustrates quite well the problems in the agribusiness sector as better infrastructure, knowledge and support and policies from the government is needed. Finally, a general distinction between rural and urban population is to be made: While urban areas have seen significant growth, small-scale farmers in rural areas still struggle with constraints like insufficient market access, poor infrastructure, and a lack of information, production inefficiencies, and a lack of capital (Ha *et al.* 2015a; Steer and Sen 2010). The significance of these constraints became more apparent especially after Vietnam joined the WTO in 2007 (Ha *et al.* 2015b).

State of Vietnam's public health

The Linghzhi Mushroom Company operates in the Vietnamese pharmaceutical sector. To provide context to its relevance and contribution, a short overview of the state of the country's health sector is presented here.

The overall state of public health in Vietnam is good, when looking at the life expectancy at birth (76 years) in comparison with other countries in Western Pacific (also 76 years) or the World Bank income group (66 years). The under-5 and maternal mortality rate dropped enormously since 1990 to 24 per 1000 live births and 140 per 100,000 live births, respectively. This positive trend also applies for the population using improved drinking-water sources (>90%) and improved sanitation facilities (~75%), although in rural areas these figures are a bit lower (~70%). The top five causes of death are stroke, ischemic heart disease, chronic obstructive disease, lower respiratory infections, and road injuries, of which stroke was the leading cause of death killing 112.6 thousand people in 2012. Adult risk factors are high blood pressure, which applies to about 25% of the population and tobacco use by men (46%) (WHO 2015).

Tuberculosis still ranks among the top ten causes of death, but the overall number of deaths caused by tuberculosis, malaria, or HIV decreased from the year 2000 to 2012. Expenditure on health per capita is $300, which counts in total for 6% of the GDP in 2013. This figure is relatively low when compared to Thailand, which spends more than $650 per capita on health, but high when compared to Laos, which spends $95. There are 1.2 physicians per 1,000 people, which is close to the regional average (Worldbank 2016b).

The business environment and women entrepreneurs

In the World Bank's Ease of Doing Business Index from 2016, Vietnam ranks 90th out of 189 countries; which is higher than the regional average for East Asia and the Pacific (EAP), but lagging behind Malaysia (18) and Thailand (49) (Worldbank 2016c). In comparison to Doing Business 2015[4] where it ranked 93rd, Vietnam improved especially in the field of "getting electricity" (108) and "getting credit" (28) though the actual costs of getting electricity still lie far above the average income. Paying taxes (rank 168) is one of the major constraints of doing business as it takes in average 770 hours per year to prepare, file and pay the taxes (EAP: 200 hours). To register a firm in Vietnam also requires more than the double number of procedures (10) in comparison with OECD countries (4.7). Time and costs for import and exports exceed values of the OECD countries many times over, but compare favorably with the regional averages (Worldbank 2016d). These complex and often changing conditions and regulations therefore hinder potential entrepreneurs from starting a business. Nevertheless, Vietnam is one of the most attractive regions for foreign investment because of its stable macroeconomic (exchange rate and level of inflation) and political environments (PwC 2015). Moreover, it has a young, energetic, and well-educated population and oil and coal reserves in addition to other minerals (Ernst & Young 2013).

According to Thanh Nien News (2015) more than 300 businesses were launched in Vietnam every day in July and August 2015. According to Akram-Lodhi and van Staveren (2003) 1200 new SMEs are registered every month. Steer and Sen (2010) also state that enterprises increased fifty-fold since 1992. In 2012, there were a total of 332,672 active enterprises, 67.6% were micro, 28% were small, 2% were medium and 2.4% were large (ITCILO 2015).

The introduction of the Law on Enterprises in 2005 (No. 60/2005/QH11) recognized the strong role of the private sector in pushing Vietnamese economic growth and commits itself to the private sector's long-term development. The law also provides rights, obligations and procedures with regard to the establishment, operations and interactions of businesses in Vietnam. In addition, based on a 2006 national survey on challenges to Vietnamese women entrepreneurs conducted by the International Finance Corporation Gender and Entrepreneurship Markets division and

---

[4]The World Bank's Doing Business reports provide objective measures of the ease of doing business for firms in 189 economies all over the world. The annual report covers reforms conducted in the previous year, across 10 indicators (see www.doingbusiness.org).

the Mekong Private Sector Development Facility, Vietnam introduced the Law on Gender Equality (LGE) in 2009 (No. 73/2006/QH11 of November 29, 2006) (IFC and GEM 2006). The LGE provides for legal equality between men and women in all fields of social and family life. In 2007, the ILO together with the Vietnamese Women Entrepreneurs Council (VWEC) studied patterns and constraints to women-owned businesses in Vietnam and their demand for business development services (ILO 2007). This paved the way for the introduction of two additional decrees in 2009: Decree 48 (No. 48/2009/ND-CP of May 19, 2009) and Decree 70 (No. 70/2008/ND-CP of June 4, 2008) which both laid out responsibilities and coordination among agencies implementing the Gender Equality Law (see Hampel-Milagrosa *et al.* 2010).

Though it seems that the institutional environment favorable female entrepreneurship, a more recent study by Zhu *et al.* (2015) shows that Vietnamese women entrepreneurs still identify several elements of the institutional environment as their main obstacles to growth. These are high competition, high employee turnover rates *vis-a-vis* inability to attract and retain high quality employees, weak economy, lack of market training and limited access to financial capital.

In addition, despite the progressive new legal frameworks, household responsibilities are still left mostly to women. In addition, as women's businesses usually support their family's livelihood and are security-oriented instead of being growth-oriented, possibilities for women are still limited (ILO 2007). Only around 30% of business owners in Vietnam are women (Zhu *et al.* 2015). Women are mostly active in trading food, beverages, textiles and garments and their enterprises are generally smaller. Although women entrepreneurs tend to provide employment for other women, they also tend to have lower profits on average (Akram-Lodhi and van Staveren 2003). Along with the World Bank's Ease of Doing Business Index report, another study was conducted by the United Nations Industrial Development Organization (UNIDO) in cooperation with the ILO and the VWEC (see Hampel-Milagrosa *et al.* 2010). The study evaluated whether regulatory business environment reforms in Vietnam conducted a lá Doing Business created an impact on women's economic participation. In terms of starting a business, men and women are equal by law when it comes to registered land ownership and savings, although women's education is lower in average and they would consult their families more for business decisions (Hampel-Milagrosa *et al.* 2010). Although the government officially intends to promote gender equality in employment, incentives like tax benefits are missing (IFC MPDF and GEM 2007) and the gender wage gap is still at 86% (Akram-Lodhi and van Staveren 2003).

Methodology

The selection of Lingzhi Mushroom Company, owned and operated by Mrs. Nguyen Thi Chinh, follows our definition of "growth through inno-vation." In accordance with this definition, her enterprise had to surpass two quantitative thresholds and meet two qualitative criteria (for innova-tion) to be classified as an upgrader. Specifically, it must have:

- Been a micro, small enterprise (MSE) at least five years ago but have become a medium-sized enterprise in the meantime (i.e., passed the threshold between micro and small or small and medium-sized[5]);
- Increased its employment by at least 10% annually during these five years;
- Made documented efforts to innovate;
- Grown substantially faster than its respective competitors (again, in terms of the number of employees) in order to validate that its growth was not merely due to external effects, such as increase in demand, but mainly to innovation.

Her qualification for these criteria were checked prior to the interview.[6]

Upgraders are one of a kind. Therefore, we had to follow purposive sampling techniques in order to identify the original pool of potential upgraders. In the selection of Lingzhi Mushroom Company, we were generously assisted by the Vietnamese Chamber of Commerce and Industry (VCCI) and the Vietnamese Women Entrepreneurs' Council

---

[5]In Vietnam, enterprise size classification is as follows: micro (<9 employees), small (10-49 employees), medium (50-199 employees), large (200-299 employees).
[6]For a more thorough description of a similar methodology that was employed to evaluate upgrading of micro and small enterprises on Egypt, India and the Philippines kindly see Hampel-Milagrosa *et al.* (2015).

(VWEC). We initially conducted a semi-structured interview with Mrs. Nguyen Thi Chinh that was followed up with a site visit. As much as possible, we allowed the entrepreneur to tell her story freely, with minimum interruption. During the interview, we clarified or reconfirmed issues that were unclear using a checklist of upgrading factors based on the Onion model. In addition, we consulted documents provided by the entrepreneur and used news reports found in the internet to substantiate the interview.

The Story of Lingzhi

The following is the story of the Lingzhi Mushroom Company (LMC) in the words of its owner, Mrs. Nguyen Thi Chinh. She begins with the origins of the firm and elaborates the difficulties encountered by the company after its establishment: being relatively unknown, having a small market for its product, having low sales and low raw material supply and finally, low production capacity. She also elaborates how she introduced drastic changes in the company to address these constraints.

> When I established the company on May 18, 2001, I was still a full-time professor at the Vietnam National University in Hanoi. On top of my teaching responsibilities, I was also conducting several small projects for different companies at that time. My projects involved testing different kinds of raw plant materials for their molecular properties. This included, among others, testing various kinds of mushrooms for their anti cancer properties, extracting these healing elements safely and harnessing them in tea, powder, or capsule form. One day, my husband suggested that instead of always testing in the laboratory, we should turn my test results into a real business. I was hesitant at first because I was occupied with my job at the university but I told my husband to go ahead and register our business. I assumed the position of director and scientific / technical adviser while my husband was the business manager and public relations officer.

> It sounds easy when I tell the story now, but I was confronted with many problems at the onset. I had to open our office at our home because we did not have a proper office at that time. I also had very limited raw material

supply because we did not have adequate space for planting mushrooms. Moreover, although I had a university laboratory at my disposal, my own company did not have adequate space for my experiments. I therefore decided to set up my own laboratory in one floor of our house in Hanoi, in order to be able to do independent research and development at home. This floor was exclusively for my own and my students' use. Being a university teacher, I could team up and train Masters and Ph.D. students in my laboratory. In return, I supervised them in the research and allowed them to use our lab results for their dissertation topics. Altogether, we were eight people working for my company when we began.

Eventually we launched three products; Nam Linh Chi (NLC), Nam Van Chi (NVC) and the Cordyceps militaris (CM), named from the specific kind of mushroom where they were harnessed from. Each product had two product lines; in tea form and either capsule or powder form. Immediately after launch, LMC received recognition for the Vietnam Innovation of Science and Technology Award (VIOTEC) in 2002. At that time, and actually until now, not many people were—or are—aware of mushroom-based products, and particularly about anti-cancer properties of mushrooms. So despite the innovation award and having almost no competition, the market for our products turned out to be very small! It was catastrophic loss for us because our mushroom capsules, teas, and powders had a short shelf life and we had to throw out a lot when they expired.

We didn't get any financial support from the government in setting up and running the business and are strongly against loaning money from the bank. My work at the University kept us financially afloat during those trying times. I continued to churn out new mushroom-based products, to train and supervise students, but I also decided that I needed additional knowledge and skills in order to make my business thrive. I decided to participate in several training courses (for example, in Brunei) and showcase my products in trade fairs (for example, in China) that were specific to mushroom products. At that time, such courses and fairs were only offered outside of Vietnam. It is only recently in our country that we have the Vietnam Association for Mushroom that offers domestic conferences, training and trade fairs.

My operations remained pretty small for several years and suffered a further blow in 2006. I remember a South African firm with its headquarters in Hamburg, Germany that wanted to partner with me. I would supply them with mushroom teas and capsules that they would then distribute through their networks, worldwide. Unfortunately, I was still operating on the 3rd floor of my 100 square meter house in Hanoi and could not keep up with demand. They eventually cancelled the orders and looked for another partner. My husband died soon after and the business was all left to me to handle. It was at this lowest point of my company and my life I that I decided to take the risk and reorganize and expand my business.

I made four drastic changes: First, I leased two farmlands totaling 15,000 square meters in Hanoi in order to increase and stabilize my raw material supply. Second, I imported several varieties of mushrooms into the country. I wanted to be able to cultivate my own supply of mushrooms and at the same time, introduce these different kinds of mushrooms to the Vietnamese people. Third, I hired my son, a university graduate, to be responsible for the farmlands, quality assurance, and supply chain management. I also appointed my daughter, also a university graduate, to be the director of our company. She is now in charge of the business and marketing element of LMC. I stepped down to vice director and remain the scientific / technical adviser, but I am happy to be able to focus my energies on my laboratory tests. Fourth, we opened shops / showrooms, in Hanoi and in HCMC to increase consumer and public awareness about our products.

After these management changes, we received a big order for our products from a pharmaceutical company from Thailand. Our relationship has become very successful and continues until today. In Thailand, it seems, mushroom teas against cancer are widely accepted and well known. I have numerous walk-in clients who come all the way from Thailand to buy my products in bulk. Business has been booming ever since. Our biggest production and demand is for Lingzhi products, but we have developed a total of 15 unique mushroom / non-mushroom products as supplementary treatment for various kinds of cancer, HIV, hepatitis, heart disorders, allergies, colitis, diabetes and blood pressure regulation. Now LMC has a total of 80 employees in the company (part time and full time, in Hanoi and HCMC) and have currently three shops / showrooms in Hanoi and two shops / showrooms in HCMC in full operation.

In 2012, I received the Gold Medal from the World Bank as one of the seven winners of the "Mekong Region Business Women Contest" for my Lingzhi Mycelia Powder. In 2013, I again received recognition from the government: I was given not only the Hanoi Creative Women Award but also the Vietnamese Creative Women Award. Through my hard work, I have also received various recognitions for product quality and innovation. But to be honest, the achievement that I am most proud of is that I am able to help sick patients, particularly the poor ones who could not afford expensive medical treatment. I provide my teas, capsules, and powders to Vietnamese hospitals at a lower cost, so that poor patients could supplement medical treatment with these cheaper, locally produced medicines.

In the next section, we will break down Mrs. Thi Chinh's success story using the Onion model. Additional information about the LMC that were obtained from the site visit and a separate questionnaire will be incorporated in the analysis.

Analysis of Upgrading Strategy

This section presents an analysis of Mrs. Thi Chinh's upgrading strategy. We divide the case and interview analysis in the order of the Onion model presented in the previous section, beginning with the business environment, followed by the networks and going deeper into the layers of enterprise and entrepreneur characteristics. Analysis of her upgrading story shows how Mrs Thi Chinh used a combination of strategies to strengthen her response to challenges facing her business. She typifies a "super entrepreneur" who willingly took on multiple roles in the enterprise to steer it towards upgrading.

A. Business environment

In general, the business environment of Vietnam is favorable for women entrepreneurs, as the country has been actively introducing laws and decrees as well as implementing reforms to this effect. A national study showed that the majority of women entrepreneurs found registering their business a relatively easy and uncomplicated procedure (Hampel-Milagrosa *et al.* 2010). This has also been Mrs. Thi Chinh's experience, who says: "When I started the company, our immediate decision was to register it because it was not difficult anyway. It is even easier now to register businesses, with the current reforms that the government has made."

In 2015, she changed the legal form of her enterprise from sole proprietorship to a limited liability company. In comparison to a sole proprietorship where there is no legal distinction between the company and its owner, a limited liability company delimits the company's repayment responsibilities for its debt to the extent of the amount of capital they invested. It essentially protects the private property of Mrs. Thi Chinh from being affected by bankruptcy. According to Mrs. Thi Chinh, this process was also easy.

Although she was positive about the business environment in Vietnam in general, she criticized the overall weak support from government in terms of business development services for micro and small enterprises. Her situation reflects findings of the VWEC (2007) national study that showed the need for business development services among entrepreneurs, in particular, on how to professionalize service delivery, how to link up with business associations, how to network with professionals. She responded to these constraints by personally seeking out possibilities for networking and self improvement. These come in the form of trainings, participation in trade fairs and conferences. We will discuss her strategy in more detail in the next sections on networks and entrepreneur characteristics.

B. Personal and professional networks

The upgrading of LMC would not have been possible if not for Mrs. Thi Chinh's husband who supported and encouraged her. She acknowledged that the idea to start a business using her research findings from the laboratory originated from her husband. They both registered the business, with Mrs. Thi Chinh as the legal proprietor. But, since she was busy with responsibilities at the university, the husband stepped up and managed the business. It was mutually agreed that her husband would act on her behalf. Her two children, though also supportive, were not engaged in the business during its starting years. The turning point came when Mrs. Thi Chinh lost a potentially large contract because of LMCs inability to respond to an order, and her husband died. It was at this point that she decided to restructure the business, starting with hiring her own two children to manage it. Her son manages the farm while the daughter has taken up directorship.

> I hired my own children because they know the business since it began and are acquainted with how it operates. We have constant communication among us. They are also both highly education [sic] so I have full trust in their judgment and intention to see the business succeed. (-Mrs Thi Chinh)

Her work and her family life have become so intertwined that her friends and colleagues fondly call her the "Mushroom Queen" of Vietnam. Thus it was no surprise to them when she became one of the founding members of Vietnam's first mushroom association in the mid-2000s. Due to the increasing popularity of mushroom production in Vietnam, several mushroom associations have formed in the country. Mrs. Thi Chinh recalls the difficulties she encountered in finding people with similar passion and interest in mushroom production and marketing (horizontal linkages). This was one of her main reasons for establishing the mushroom association: to create her own professional network. To date, LMC not only participates but also provides financial support to conferences, seminars, and activities of other mushroom associations in the country. Mrs. Thi Chinh does not consider them as competition but as comrades in the fight against Vietnamese poverty and health issues.

Mrs. Thi Chinh coupled this strategy by attending trade fairs and conferences at her own expense. In these conferences, was she not only able to showcase her research outputs and introduce her product to the market, but she was also able to widen her professional networks. We will touch on this strategy again in the section on entrepreneur characteristics.

In the interview Mrs. Thi Chinh disclosed that, although her capsules, teas, and powders had scientifically proven medicinal properties, there is no better institution to validate her products' healing properties than a hospital that treats cancer patients. Thus, began LMCs engagement in various hospitals in Vietnam that take the form of a combination of charity work, networking, and marketing activities (vertical linkages).

> LMC has donated medical mushroom products to many cancer patients treated in hospitals: 39 late-stage liver cancer patients at K hospital, 10 HIV / AIDS patients at Dong Da hospital in Hanoi, 10 diabetic patients at Polyclinic Ha Tay, 10 cancer patients from Thach Son, Phu Tho province and 135 children, poor patients and women exposed to late stage HIV / AIDS that are being treated in Ba Vi Hospital in Ha Tay. We have also treated a few foreign patients. (-Mrs. Thi Chinh)

Through the engagement of LMC in hospitals, not only has Mrs. Thi Chinh increased her company's professional network but she also ensured that the company was in the right network that offers her firm prospects for growth. As her company's products became more trusted, even more consumers became aware of her medicinal mushroom products. This strategy could also fall into the Onion layer of "enterprise characteristics" because of the philanthropic activities of the firm. However, since the main purpose of the initial charity work was to build up its network and build up product validation the strategy was discussed here.

C. Enterprise characteristics

At the LMC's foundation is the conduct of research and product development activities. The company's laboratories—officially called Centre for Research and Development of Mushroom and Biological Products—is equipped with state-of-the art equipment that serves as an extension of Mrs. Thi Chinh's official laboratory at the Vietnam National University. Together with MSc and Ph.D. students that she trains under her wing, they regularly provide fresh scientific inputs into the company. She pointed out during the interview that, without exception, the company carries out three levels of testing for every mushroom product:

We conduct three levels of tests for our products: first in the laboratory, then with mice, and finally with volunteers. (- Mrs Thi Chinh)

Due to the sensitivity of the sector that the company is in, Mrs. Thi Chinh also made sure that the management team itself is multifaceted and composed of professionals:

> The management team of the company consists of high professional (sic) persons with long-time experiences in production, business management and scientific research. Especially there is an associated professor (the proprietor), three doctors, some MSc students and people who have graduated from universities. (-Mrs Thi Chinh)

The company also prides itself on the fact that most of its top level management is composed of women. They find this an advantage rather than a disadvantage because from LMC's experience, "the women play well the role of leaders for the development of the company". Another factor Mrs. Thi Chinh finds extremely important is communication within the company, particularly at the management level. The fact that her own children occupy senior management positions in the company makes communication easier. She sees to it that she keeps an open communication line with her daughter (managing director) and with her son (farm and supplies manager). However, she also makes herself available for discussions with other employees from managers to office employees, from sales people to farm personnel. In an effort to create – and maintain – a high quality work environment, Mrs. Thi Chinh has kept salaries and social payments consistent for her staff, even during the early, more challenging, times.

> Imagine, despite low sales, I was paying my employees' salary and keeping all my social payments such as health and other insurance on time. So after the initial launch, my business was struggling to survive. (-Mrs Thi Chinh)

However, now that the business is successful and expanding, selecting more strategic locations for LMC shops is necessary. The company has opened three shops in Hanoi (one of the economic capitals) and two shops in Ho Chi Minh City (the political and economic capital of Vietnam), while obtaining supply from two farms in HCMC. The administrative process required for opening shops has been easy according to Mrs. Thi Chinh. Since the two major cities are excellently connected via air, rail and road, the company's two locations are optimal for current operations.

D. Entrepreneur characteristics

Mrs. Thi Chinh is highly educated, which is uncommon for women of her age in Vietnam[7]. In the beginning of the 1970s she already finished college, something unheard of for women at that time. Even more unusual, she went on to do graduate work, this time focusing on microbiology. It was at this time that her special interest in mushrooms developed. She obtained her MA degree in 1973 in the Czech Republic (Czechoslovakia at that time) and returned to Vietnam to locally cultivate high-yielding mushroom varieties that she got to know during her post-graduate studies. She taught at VNU and tried to apply techniques that she learned but found that her skills were still inadequate. So she decided to go back to her university in the Czech Republic to take a Ph.D. in microbiology, focusing on innovative, low-cost ways to produce mushrooms, motivated by concern for the economic situation of Vietnamese farmers.

According to her, it was during her stay in the former Czechoslovakia that she visited different mushroom farms and realized their double-barreled significance for poverty alleviation and for medicinal purposes. She said, *"[O]ne can recycle simple farm waste such as hay, sawdust or compost, invest a small amount into planting materials and obtain high yielding, high value mushrooms."* It was her motivation to harness the economic and medicinal potential of mushrooms that pushed her to follow this path.

Education aside, Mrs. Thi Chinh's connection with and work experience at the Vietnam National University not only honed her laboratory skills and technical knowledge but also created the outlet for projects that eventually led the way to starting her business. That she is a woman, she argued, could have played a role in obtaining scholarships for foreign education, but she maintains that her gender did not necessarily help or hinder her in

---

[7]In 1980, Vietnamese (men and women in total) had a mean of only 4.2 years of schooling (Human Development Index, Vietnam Country Briefing Note, HDR 2015).

any way in starting her business. The award that she won in 2012 from the World Bank (Mekong Region Business Women Contest) helped a great deal in advertising and gaining recognition for her company. Although the World Bank acknowledgement was the necessary boost she and the company needed at that time, the award was simply meant to recognize what the company had already achieved.

Mrs. Thi Chinh's motivation to search for networks, to make her products known, and to increase her knowledge has inspired her to seek out conferences, fairs, and seminars. As she pays the cost of her own travel and accommodation to participate in such events, she makes sure that she gets the most out of them:

> Vietnamese customers also starting asking for my products after a German doctor came to our country and made a well-publicized seminar about early cancer detection. I attended his seminar and contributed to the plenary discussion while citing examples from my laboratory tests and findings. I also used testimonies from cancer patients that took my teas, capsules or powder as supplements to normative cancer medicines and have been completely healed.

By nature, Mrs. Thi Chinh's doesn't consider herself a risk-taker. However, the dramatic loss of a large deal from a potential business partner made her realize that if she wanted the business to grow, she had to learn to take risks. She needed to start thinking strategically for the business and to treat the business as a real independent company, instead of an extension of her university work.

Lessons Learned and Conclusions

This chapter set out to study the enterprise upgrading story of Lingzhi Mushroom Company of Vietnam by tracing the company's growth and analyzing this growth using the four-layered Onion model. The Onion model evaluates enterprise upgrading (defined as growth through innovation) by conducting a systematic analysis of factors influencing growth: business environment, personal and professional networks, enterprise and entrepreneur characteristics.

Our analysis showed that the main constraint of the entrepreneur is the novelty of the product and its purpose. Although Vietnam is historically a tea drinking nation, mushroom teas were unheard of in Vietnam when Mrs Thi Chinh began her company in 2001. Moreover, the medicinal uses of mushroom, which is the main selling point for her products, were too novel for her intended market. Moreover, since LMC was initially operating on a small scale, it remained under the radar of the Vietnamese government and could not avail of business development services that it needed most. Additional minor constraints that needed to be overcome were the lack of knowledge, skills and technical equipment necessary to conduct laboratory testing of the different mushroom species.

The LMC, however, had several factors that worked to its advantage: its founder and first director had the education, skills, and work experience that provided the backbone for the activities it needed most: research. Financial resources for the enterprise did not pose the biggest constraint to growth. In fact, the university connections of Mrs. Thi Chinh (her MSc and PhD students) continue to provide the research and development necessary for innovation in the firm. While she initially had to assume multiple roles in the firm, family support, whether morally, provision of laboratory space in the household or family members taking roles in the management team, was critical in the firm's early years.

Evaluating the upgrading strategy, there are two lessons that could be learned from LMC that distinguished the company from other stagnating micro enterprises. First, Mrs Thi Chinh used a combination of strategies to overcome her initial constraints and second, her multiple roles as proprietor, manager, technician and motivation were pivotal to the company's success.

Combination of strategies. In order to overcome singular constraints, the entrepreneur used a combination of strategies that either complemented each other or strengthened each other's impact. For example, part of the reason why the company was struggling was because the entrepreneur played multiple roles in the firm: farmer, lab technician, technical and scientific adviser on top of her role as a university professor. The strategy she used was to step down on her directorial responsibilities, focus on R&D and delegate management to other people. In this way, the entrepreneur could focus her skills on what she does best, and that is conducting scientific research, documenting results and translating results into tangible medicinal products. Her lack of production space that impacted her raw material supply was addressed by strategically expanding sales and farm space. Her expansion was not random; she opened showrooms and farms in the northern (Hanoi) and southern (HCMC) economic / political capitals that she knew were easily accessible logistically. To make sure that mushroom and other material supplies remained stable, she delegated her son into the corresponding lead position. By supporting farmers and mushroom associations in the country, she makes sure that the varieties she uses are propagated elsewhere. To address the issue of her firm's anonymity and its related constraint of having a small market, the entrepreneur attended workshops and seminars, personally funding her travel both domestically and abroad. She also combined product advertisement with charity work in hospitals that validated the reliability of her mushroom products.

Multiple roles, the entrepreneur makes the difference. Analysis has confirmed that sustainable, innovation-driven enterprise growth relies on a highly motivated, risk-taking entrepreneur whose persona spells the difference between business stagnation and success. Mrs. Thi Chinh possessed the education, training and work experience that is crucial for the product and the sector that her company is in. She might have initially lacked the horizontal and vertical networks because of the product and its markets' novelty, but she actively sought these networks and established them. Her husband's death and the imminent failure of her business woke her up and made her take the necessary risks that prevented the company from failing. The business environment was not regarded as a major contributing factor to LMC's success although the preference of Mrs. Thi Chinh to formalize her business at the beginning indicates the ease of registration for firms in the country in general.

What does the case of LMC imply for enterprise upgrading in general? Though enterprise upgrading occurs among a select few, the government and the private sector have a strong role to play in fostering innovation among all micro and small enterprises. For instance, providing an enabling environment is crucial for all businesses but it is not only about improving ease of registration but also about providing support mechanisms. Citing the case of Lingzhi Mushroom Company, these mechanisms could be in the form of business development services that link entrepreneurs to relevant markets and networks in their field. To make enabling conditions for creating "super" entrepreneurs, the case of LMC shows the importance of education. This means that the promotion of quality education at all levels for public schools and the provision of training and vocational education opportunities are imperative. Work experience is critical for entrepreneurial success, therefore the provision of on-the-job training and exposure of graduates to lead firms is a fruitful source of entrepreneurship experience.

References

Akram-Lodhi, A. and van Staveren, I. 2003. *A gender analysis of the impact of indirect taxes on small and medium enterprises in Vietnam.* [Online]. Barbados: UN Women. [Accessed 13 June 2016]. Available from: http://gender-financing.unwomen.org/en/resources/a/g/e/a-gender-analysis-of-the-impact-of-indirect-taxes-on-small-and-medium-enterprises-in-vietnam.

APEC (Asia-Pacific Economic Cooperation). 2016. *Member economies.* [Online]. [Accessed 6 June 2016]. Available from: http://www.apec.org/about-us/about-apec/member-economies.asp.

Breu, M., Dobbs, R., and Remes, J. 2012. Taking Vietnam's economy to the next level. *McKinsey and Company.* [Online]. February. [Accessed 1 June 2016]. Available from: http://www.mckinsey.com/global-themes/asia-pacific/taking-vietnams-economy-to-the-next-level.

Breu, M., Dobbs, R., Remes, J., Skilling, D. and Kim, J. 2012. *Sustaining Vietnam's growth: the productivity challenge.* [Online]. New York: McKinsey Global Institute. [Accessed 1 June 2016]. Available from: http://www.mckinsey.com/~/media/McKinsey/Global%20Themes/Asia%20Pacific/Sustaining%20growth%20in%20Vietnam/MGI_Sustaining_growth_in_Vietnam_Full_Report.ashx.

Business Monitor International. 2014. Industry Trend Analysis – Vietnam's Uncompetitive Sugar Sector at Risk From AEC Integration. *Business Monitor International.* [Online]. September. [Accessed 8 June 2016]. Available from: http://www.agribusiness-insight.com/industry-trend-analysis-vietnams-uncompetitive-sugar-sector-risk-aec-integration-sept-2014.

Chapponiere, J. R., Cling, J. P. and Zhou, B. 2008. *Vietnam following in China's footsteps: The third wave of emerging Asian economies.* Helsinki: UNU World Institute for Development Economics Research (UNU-WIDER).

David, B. 2016. Vietnam: The Quiet Economic Success Story Of Asia. *Forbes Asia.* [Online]. 2 February. [Accessed 1 June 2016]. Available from: Available at: http://www.forbes.com/sites/davisbrett/2016/02/02/vietnam-the-quiet-economic-success-story-of-asia/#2e0d607c444a.

Ernst & Young. 2013. *Doing Business in Vietnam.* [Online]. Ho Chi Minh: Ernst & Young. [Accessed 6 June 2016]. Available from: http://www.ey.com/Publication/vwLUAssets/ Doing_Business_in_Vietnam/$FILE/Doing_Business_in_Vietnam_16000319.pdf.

FAO (Food and Agriculture Organization). 2015. *Regional Overview of Food Insecurity: Asia and the Pacific.* [Online]. Bangkok: Food and Agriculture Organization of the United Nations. [Accessed 8 June 2016]. Available from: http://www.fao.org/3/a-i4624e.pdf.

FAOSTAT. 2016. *Viet Nam.* [Online]. [Accessed 6 June 2016]. Available from: http://www. fao.org/faostat/en/#country/237.

Fritzen, S. 2002. Growth, inequality and the future of poverty reduction in Vietnam. *Journal of Asian Economics.* **2**. pp. 635-657.

Ha, T., Bosch, O. and Nguyen, N. 2015a. Necessary and Sufficient Conditions for Agribusiness Success of Small-scale Farming Systems in Northern Vietnam. *Business and Management Studies.* **1**(2). pp.36-44.

Ha, T., Bosch, O. and Nguyen, N. 2015b. Defining the real needs of women smallholder-farmers in Vietnam: The importance of grassroots participation and multi-stakeholder collaboration. *International Journal of Business Management Review.* **3**(2). pp.35-38.

Hampel-Milagrosa, A., Pham, V. H., Nguyen A. Q. and Nguyen, T. T. 2010. *Gender related obstacles to Vietnamese Women Entrepreneurs.* [Online]. Vienna: United Nations Industrial Development Organisation. [Accessed 6 June 2016]. Available from: https:// www.unido.org/fileadmin/user_media_upgrade/What_we_do/Topics/Women_and_Youth/ FMVIE09005_GOVERN_Report_final.pdf.

Hampel-Milagrosa, A. 2015. The entrepreneur makes a difference: evidence on MSE upgrading factors from Egypt, India and the Philippines. *World Development.* **66**(2). pp.118-130.

IFC (International Finance Cooperation) Mekong Private Sector Development Facility (MPDF) and Gender Entrepreneurship Markets (GEM). 2006. *Women business owners in Vietnam: a national survey.* Washington, D.C.: World Bank Group.

IFC (International Finance Cooperation) Mekong Private Sector Development Facility (MPDF) and Gender Entrepreneurship Markets (GEM). 2007. *Voices of Vietnamese Women Entrepreneurs.* [Online]. Hanoi: International Finance Corporation. [Accessed 8 June 2016]. Available from: http://www.ifc.org/wps/wcm/connect/1653bd8047adb354930 3f7752622ff02/VN-Voice-of-Women-Entrepreneurs-ENG.pdf?MOD=AJPERES.

ILO (International Labor Organization). 2007. *Women's Entrepreneurship Development in Vietnam.* [Online]. Hanoi: International Labour Organization. [Accessed 6 June 2016]. Available from: http://www.ilo.org/wcmsp5/groups/public/---asia/---ro-bangkok/ documents/publication/wcms_100456.pdf.

ITCILO (International Training Centre of the International Labour Organisation). 2015. *Women Empowerment Through Business Member Organizations.* [Online]. Turin: International Training Centre of the ILO. [Accessed 16 June 2016]. Available from: http:// www.itcilo.org/en/the-centre/programmes/employers-activities/hidden-folder/resources/ Women%20Empowerment_Country%20fact-sheet_Vietnam_2015.pdf.

PwC (Price Waterhouse Coopers). 2015. *Doing Business in Vietnam.* [Online]. 4th ed. Vietnam: Pricewaterhouse Coopers. [Accessed 6 June 2016]. Available from: https://www. pwc.com/vn/en/publications/2015/dbg_2015.pdf.

Steer, L. and Sen, K. 2010. Formal and Informal Institutions in a Transition Economy: The Case of Vietnam. *World Development.* **38**(11). pp.1603-1615.

Stoxplus. 2014. *Vietnam Agribusinesses: Sector Overview.* [Online]. Hanoi: Stoxplus. [Accessed 8 June 2016]. Available from: https://kinhteluongtdt.files.wordpress. com/2014/10/stoxplus-vietnam-agribusiness-sector-overview_20140715095708.pdf.

Viet Nam News. 2016. Organic Produce Becoming Popular, Lucrative. *Viet Nam News.* [Online]. 13 May. [Accessed 8 June 2016]. Available from: http:// vietnamnews.vn/economy/296702/organic-produce-becoming-popular-lucrative. html#i9vXEaRgd3X4CP5U.97.

The Law on Gender Equality (No. 73/2006/QH11). Vietnam: The National Assembly. [Accessed 6 June 2016]. Available from: http://www.ilo.org/dyn/travail/docs/934/Law%20 on%20Gender%20Equality%202006.pdf.

Than Nien News. 2015. Around 300 new businesses launched each day in Vietnam: report. *Than Nien News.* [Online]. 30 August. [Accessed 8 June 2016]. Available from: http:// www.thanhniennews.com/business/around-300-new-businesses-launched-each-day-in-vietnam-report-50734.html.

UNdata (United Nations Data). 2015. *Viet Nam.* [Online]. [Accessed 1 June 2016]. Available from: http://data.un.org/CountryProfile.aspx?crName=Viet%20Nam.

UNDP (United Nations Development Program). 2015. *Viet Nam.* [Online]. [Accessed 1 June 2016]. Available from: http://hdr.undp.org/sites/all/themes/hdr_theme/country-notes/ VNM.pdf (1.6.2016).

Vietnamnet. 2015. The challenges of Vietnam Agriculture. *Vietnamnet.* [Online]. 13 October. [Accessed 16 June 2016]. Available from: http://english.vietnamnet.vn/fms/ special-reports/143237/the-challenges-of-vietnam-agriculture.html.

VIETRADE. 2014. Challenges and new opportunities for Vietnam's agriculture in the international integration process. *Vietnam Trade Promotion Agency.* [Online]. 24 November. [Accessed 6 June 2016]. Available from: http://www.vietrade.gov.vn/en/index. php?option=com_content&view=article&id=2246:challenges-and-new-opportunities-for-vietnams-agriculture-in-the-international-integration-process&catid=270:vietnam--industry-news&Itemid=363.

WHO (World Health Organization). 2015. *Viet Nam: WHO Statistical Profile.* [Online]. [Accessed 15 June 2016]. Available from: http://www.who.int/gho/countries/vnm. pdf?ua=1.

WORLDBANK. 2016a. *Vietnam Overview.* [Online]. [Accessed 1 June 2016]. Available from: http://www.worldbank.org/en/country/vietnam/overview.

WORLDBANK. 2016b. *Worldbank data.* [Online]. [Accessed 1 June 2016]. Available from: http://databank.worldbank.org/data/reports.aspx?source=global-economic-prospects.

WORLDBANK. 2016c. *Doing Business 2016: Measuring Regulatory Quality and Efficiency, East Asia and the Pacific (EAP).* Washington, D.C.: World Bank Group.

WORLDBANK. 2016d. *Ease of Doing Business in Vietnam.* [Online]. [Accessed 6 June 2016]. Available from: http://www.doingbusiness.org/data/exploreeconomies/vietnam/#close.

Zhu, L., Kara, O., Chu, H.M. and Chu, A. 2015. Female Entrepreneurship: Evidence from Vietnam. *Journal of Business and Entrepreneurship.* **26**(3). pp.103-128.

Chapter 13

Mathesis Food Products Company: Bringing Back the Millet

Aimée Hampel-Milagrosa,[1] Karen Dall,[2] Mukesh Gulati,[3]
Sangeeta Agasty,[3] and Sangeeta Suresh[3]

Introduction

This upgrading story is about the Mathesis Food Products company, owned and operated by 35-year old Ms. Annapurna Kalluri of Hyderabad, India. Her company manufactures a host of cereal and millet-based snacks, breakfast foods, and instant foods under the brand name "Navya." While the case is about the growth of her millet processing enterprise, an interesting twist of Annapurna's upgrading story is her proactive involvement in the development of machinery that was needed to process millets. When she started looking for processing equipment during the early days of her company, the government could only offer limited support. She used her engineering background, the support of various agencies and the help of her father to develop the machinery that she would need for food manufacturing. In telling her upgrading story, she provides an answer to our research question: *What are her main constraints to enterprise growth and what allowed her firm to overcome these barriers?*

To evaluate her upgrading story, we use the Onion model. The Onion model analyses the various factors that contributed to the enterprise's growth. It consists of four layers. The outer layer expounds on the influence of the business environment to enterprise growth. This is followed by the network layer (personal and professional networks) and by enterprise characteristics layer. The last and final layer represents elements of the proprietor's personal characteristics that impacted the upgrading of the firm. The difference between the Onion model approach and previous studies conducted on enterprise growth is that the analysis takes the

---

[1]Asian Development Bank (formerly German Development Institute).
[2]United Nations University Institute for Environment and Human Security.
[3]Foundation for MSME Clusters.

impact of the four elements altogether. It also shows the interlinkage of these four factors. Moreover, in the Onion model, growth as a mere increase in productivity, profits or employees is not a sufficient measure of entrepreneurial success. Growth must originate from cumulative innovative activities of the entrepreneur that allowed them to reap innovation rents that are higher than those of their competitors.

Our analysis show that in the case of Annapurna, two factors significantly contributed to the upgrading of her enterprise, namely, her social background and the business environment. Annapurna possessed the necessary education and work experience in a lead firm that prepared her for the role of entrepreneur. What she lacked in skill, she acquired by participating in several trainings that were offered by a Hyderabad-based organization that supported female entrepreneurs. Also, in Annapurna's case, the business environment was instrumental in enterprise growth. She engaged in discussions with various government ministries and received widespread technical support from relevant agencies in the State. In her story, she acknowledged institutes and organizations that made her upgrading story possible. As compared to other upgrading stories in this series, the business environment clearly made the difference in her case.

This chapter is organized as follows. We begin with an overview of the Indian economy, explaining how rapid economic growth is met by the challenge of inequality and extreme poverty. This is followed by a glimpse of the Indian agricultural sector, a sector that continues to provide livelihoods to the poorest, including women. The section on Indian business environment highlights female Indian entrepreneurship and how social restrictions trap female entrepreneurs into traditional entrepreneurial activities. After a short description of the methodology, we continue with her upgrading story, told in her own words. This is followed by a section analyzing her story with the help of the Onion model. We conclude with lessons learned and conclusions.

The Indian Economic Context

The 1.2 billion people of the Republic of India form the world's fourth-largest economy and democracy as of today. India's development is generally regarded as one of the most remarkable and significant transfor-mation stories of our times: from independence until present, the country transformed from a net importer to a net exporter of food, a strong middle class has emerged and advanced information technology as well as software industries and pharmaceutics find favorable conditions for their businesses (The World Bank 2016; PwC 2016).

In the past 15 years India enjoyed strong economic growth with an average growth rate above 7% and peak years of more than 10% growth (The World Bank 2016a). Market liberalization began in the mid-1980s and more fundamental reforms since 1991 have fully transformed India to a free market economy (Ahluwalia 2002; OECD 2014). These trends were accompanied by a sharp reduction of poverty: while 46% of the total population lived from less than US$1.90/day in 1993, this number declined to 38% in 2004 and to approximately 20% in 2011 (The World Bank 2016a). However, these figures obscure the fact that due to India's enormous population growth, the absolute number of people in poverty increased, which is projected to result in a population expected to overtake China's in 2028. This population growth has ambivalent consequences: on the one hand, it will make India the largest workforce worldwide with an emerging, mostly urban, middle class, whose demand for consumption will increase income and create prosperity, but on the other hand, it puts Indians who just escaped poverty at risk of falling back into it. Further challenges to the Indian economy are rapid urbanization, which puts massive pressure on infrastructure, housing, the creation of jobs and the environment, but also huge needs in rural infrastructure investments to connect the population to markets, electricity, health services and education (Indian Planning Commission 2012; McKinsey 2010).

Today the rural population still accounts for ~67% of the total population, agriculture is still the main source of employment (~50% in 2013), while the share of the agricultural sector of the GDP just accounts for 17% in 2014 and for 10% of the overall exports (The World Bank 2016, 2016a). Furthermore, India's general development heads towards a service-oriented urbanized economy. One major constraint is social inequality. Although discrimination on the basis of the Hindu caste system is illegal now, old power structures have persisted and corruption prospered. This inequality is also highly evident in income distribution. Firstly, there are large regional disparities for example, growth rates and income per capita in Orissa are generally smaller than in Gujarat (Agarwalla 2011). Secondly there are large disparities within the society; approximately 30% of the income share is held by the highest 10% (The World Bank 2016a). The average income per capita in 2011 was US$1410, but the poorest states in India like Bihar have the run of just US$294 (The World Bank 2016, 2016a).

These figures are reflected in the Human Development Index at which India ranks in the 130th position. This positioning indicates that India is a medium human development country in contrast to the surrounding low human development countries like Pakistan and Myanmar (UNDP 2015). Thus, India must cope with rapidly changing social, economic and environmental conditions, facing many opportunities and challenges.

The Agricultural Sector: Agribusinesses in India

Agriculture is undeniably the largest livelihood provider in India as still half of the population is dependent on agriculture (Indian Planning Commission 2012). Although the overall Indian economy has experienced a boost in the last decade, productivity in the agricultural sector fell and the sector has remained underdeveloped, especially for small-scale farmers in remote areas (Landes 2008). Despite the Green Revolution and its accompanying shift from extensive to intensive agriculture, net farm income per hectare is lower for small-scale farms, which account for more than 80% of all holdings (Dev 2012). The situation today seems paradoxical: 250 million people in India regularly suffer from hunger, while the export of staple crops reached 40 million tons in 2014 (Sharma 2014). Additionally, India is the second largest fruit exporter in the world and the largest producer of milk, accounting for almost 19% of the dairy production worldwide (Indian Ministry of external Affairs 2015; IBEF 2016). Other main agricultural products for export are cotton, soybeans, rice, sugar, spices, coffee, tea, tobacco but also dairy products, eggs and meat (FAO 2011).

There are various challenges that the agricultural sector in India is currently facing and which need to be tackled to reduce poverty and to handle the enormous pressure of producing more food in the future (Tambe 2015). Low income levels and the inherent lack of economic access to food, fertilizers, etc. are the major obstacles for small-holders in remote areas (Dev 2010). Secondly, more sustainable management practices are needed. Models that highlight more sustainable use of water are sought after because agriculture accounts for 80% of the current water consumption. Also, the mostly rain fed (~56%) agriculture could be designed in a more efficiently and more environmental friendly manner (Indian Planning Commission 2012). More sustainable management practices are also needed to counteract the fragmentation of landholdings as the average farm size has fallen below 1.2 ha in 2011 (Birthal *et al.* 2015). The compensation of regional disparities is a further challenge for India. Poor infrastructure and market inefficiency inhibit the access to markets, credits, knowledge, fertilizer, seeds and subsidies for the majority of the poor (Tambe 2015; Landes 2008). In addition, land is distributed extremely unevenly with some households possessing less than a hectare of land (The World Bank 2012; Dev 2012). Furthermore, small-scale farmers face new challenges of integration into new value chains, meeting the requirements of supermarket standards, handling market volatility and adapting to climate change (Dev 2012).

Both women and men face these generic constraints in Indian agribusiness. Although owning land and decision making regarding cultivation and marketing are traditionally men's duties, the role of women in agriculture is growing: 83% of rural women work in agriculture in contrast to just 63% of rural men (Dev 2012). Women also face gender constraints when becoming an entrepreneur (Anitha 2015). To evade these disadvantages women start founding collectives and producer's groups to overcome constraints of small and uneconomic land holdings.

Future agribusiness investments are needed in post-harvest infrastructure such as ware-housing and cold storage. Those investments would reduce transaction costs and post harvest losses and would also increase employment (Indian Ministry of external Affairs 2015; Indian Planning Commission 2011). Additional agribusiness investments are needed in production of high-yielding seeds, organic farming and retailing (Acharya 2007). Moreover, since agribusinesses in India mainly produce fresh food, a future shift towards more semi- or full-processed foods might be more profitable (Anitha 2015).

The Business Environment – A Woman's Perspective

In the Doing Business Report 2016 India ranks above the regional average of South Asia (130 out of 189) but ranks much lower in comparison to its neighbor China (84). To start a business (rank 155) it takes approximately one month and 14 interactions with external parties, which is far above the regional average (7.9) and the OECD average (4.7). Major obstacles for small businesses are Paying Taxes (rank 157), Enforcing Contracts (rank 178) and the costs of Getting Electricity (rank 70), which is 442% of the income per capita. On the contrary, India compares favorably regarding the overall score of starting a business, Getting Credit (rank 40) and Protecting Minority Investors (rank 8) (The World Bank 2016b).

In general, doing business in India is currently particularly attractive because it has become Asia's biggest buying economy with the world's largest growing middle class, which will probably reach one billion within the next two decades. This middle class provides a well-educated and skilled workforce and unlike in Europe, this middle class will be young. The largest uncertainty for foreign investors has been the high inflation since 2008 (PwC 2012). As each Indian state is as big as a European country, Kashyap (2013) advises entrepreneurs to develop products and marketing strategies state-wise and to adjust them to local needs.

However, as stated earlier, a general distinction between rural and urban entrepreneurship needs to be made. While wealth has reached urban areas, rural areas are still facing severe difficulties regarding access to power, markets and other infrastructures (Indian Planning Commission 2011). Through the Micro, Small and Medium Enterprise Act of 2006 the government supports the formalization of businesses specifically in rural areas (Williams and GURTO 2011). Another distinction needs to be made between women and men entrepreneurship. Although gender discrimination is prohibited in India (Indiacode 2016), gender inequalities continue and there are no far reaching changes in sight (UNDP 2016). The domination of men in most spheres of society is a tradition deeply rooted in Indian society. Therefore, women face social and cultural restrictions in starting and running a business. They mostly do not have access to institutional credits and land. Moreover, discrimination by local authorities is commonplace. Women tend to stay in their traditional activities like selling flowers, selling fruit or textiles, which are mostly adjusted to household needs. Thus, it is difficult to distinguish between business and household work. The income from these combined businesses is essential for the survival of many households, but and this kind of work is not valued within society (Williams and Gurtoo 2011).

Methodology

The identification of the upgraded entrepreneur, Ms. Annapurna Kalluri, was conducted in cooperation with the Foundation for Micro Small and Medium Sized Enterprise Clusters (FMC). The FMC is a Delhi-based non-governmental and nonprofit organisation that contributes to the competitivenesss and sustainability of micro- small- and medium-sized enterprise clusters in India and the region. The FMC began by contacting two pro-active and prominent entrepreneur associations in the city of Hyderabad: the Confederation of Women Entrepreneurs (COWE) and the Association of Lady Entrepreneurs of Andhra Pradesh (ALEAP). These associations were known to have a good number of food processing units among their membership base. Therefore they were considered as good "first stops" to obtain leads for identification of an upgraded innovative entrepreneur.

COWE provided us with a list of entrepreneurs who had set up successful businesses such as bakeries and home-made sweets in the State. However, after an initial scoping, we soon found out that none of them had very innovative models, products, or approaches. Following that, ALEAP was contacted. They provided a number of excellent suggestions. Among their suggestions, the entrepreneur Ms. Annapurna Kalluri stood out as a good choice for a case the study due to following reasons mentioned by the association:

1. She had developed the equipment for making processed food from millet grains on her own,
2. She sought the help of several organizations to help her innovate, and
3. She actively participated in entrepreneurship development programs of the state and of ALEAP.

Annapurna started Mathesis Food Products company in 2008. However, to be considered an upgrader for our study, her enterprise should have surpassed two quantitative and qualitative thresholds:

- Have grown from a micro or small enterprise into a small or medium sized enterprise,
- Increased employee number by at least 10% in the last five years,
- Made documented efforts to innovate, and
- Grown significantly faster than its competitors.

After hearing her initial story, we ascertained that the development of the equipment that she needed to process millet grains and the introduction of millet-based processed food into the market are two innovations that allowed Ms. Annapurna Kalluri to upgrade her enterprise. Also, records showed that she has grown faster in terms of income and employee size than her competitors in a short span of time. In the next section, we will hear in her own words, the story of how she led the upgrading of Mathesis.

The Story of Mathesis Food Products Company

> Food processing was one of my passions ever since I was young. One day I decided to do research on a possibility of a small project in food processing. I found that there was a lot of grain-based porridge in the market but very few millet-based products. Millets are like the Indian version of oats so if oats are widely consumed, why not millets? I though this is one of the lines that can become a business model for my family. Also at the same time we would also be creating impact somewhere because we can help address malnutrition in the community. I was very concerned about this because at that time I read a study that malnutrition is worse in urban than in rural areas. We lack protein and calcium in urban areas. Therefore, our thrust and purpose right from our company set up in 2008 are millet grains—for example, Ragi, Jowar, Bajra and Foxtail—that we believe are today, an alternative to conventional grains like rice and wheat that are grown and consumed in large numbers.

When I studied about nutritional values of food grains we found millets to be not only more nutritious than most grains and at that time, it was also extremely easy to propagate because it requires very little water. Unfortunately, there were not many manufacturers of millets based food and raw material was limited in availability. Many consumers find millet "tough" to chew and when we looked into the market we found just one or two suppliers of millets. I know that these grains were once a staple in traditional kitchens of the state so I set out to find the reason as to why they were not so much consumed anymore. Studies among small consumer groups informed me that although people were interested in consuming these grains, ignorance about or difficulty in millet cooking techniques were inhibiting factors. This strengthened my feeling of the need to bring back these grains that have been forgotten in most kitchens in urban areas.

The government through the Ministry of Agriculture at that time was publishing a lot of small articles about millets and how to obtain subsidies for its processing. They had an intensive millet promotion scheme going on. So even if I was an Electronics Engineering graduate with an MBA and was working for IBM for 4.5 years, I decided to quit my job and start millet processing.

I did not have any common training in food processing so I first decided to get information. I have been interacting with lots of scientists, researchers, dieticians and nutritionists from universities and institutes. I was trying to understand all I could about food processing and the things I need to learn about processing millets in particular. I was reading a lot of books on food and food technology, I attended the Goldman Sachs Women Entrepreneur Program and I also attended a course at night from the Indian Institute of Packaging to better understand food packaging mechanics. I also interacted with a lot of entrepreneurs, particularly women.

I am very fortunate that there is lots of support from the government for entrepreneurs in India. When I started, I approached the Ministry of Food Processing in Delhi and I easily received my subsidy in 2011 from them. There are actually a lot of subsidies available from the government for entrepreneurs; you just have to approach them. It is time consuming to search for them but they are all there! From the government I received technological support also. I also engaged with ICRISAT who helped me in recipe formulation, millet-based products that were gluten free. The Indian Institute for Millet Research also helped me during my testing phase. My ideal in my business was not to alter the grain so much to avoid nutritional loss. I wanted my product to be similar to the preparations of my grandmother.

When I started in 2008, I operated in this small set-up that was kind of like an enterprise incubation space of around 1400-1500 square feet. This was hosted within ALEAP offices in an industrial area in Hyderabad. At that time when I started, I had three employees, a machinery investment of 20-25 Lakhs and earned around 50,000 INR only per month. So even if I had a set-up which was not from home, it was a very small place. We were really struggling then.

After some years we needed to develop some more machineries specific to our product so we moved from ALEAP into an engineering unit and we stayed there while waiting for the development of the equipment. After that we shifted our entire unit to this place where we are now. We have a structure of a two-floor building with prefabricated boards and now we have 65,000 square feet for production. Now we have 26 employees.

When we are developing new products, we always employ food science students. They are already knowledgeable in the field and they want to earn additional income—the perfect qualifications. We develop things together as a team. For example, developing millet bread was in my mind for a long time but I was waiting for a well informed person to do it with me because I know that there is a lot of thinking needed to get into this product. So when we were starting millet bread I actually took two students for four months into my unit and I was telling them what output I need. I was very specific about the product that I wanted: it has to be multi grain and it has to be composed of at least 50-60% millets, not 20% or 10% millet-based that they sell in the market. I bring up those ideas and these students work with me to develop the products. We do a lot of research and I file all the ideas and information. We test the products too, especially for shelf life. Then we take it to the market to test for consumer feedback whenever we have fairs or expositions. We do a lot of studies on how customers responded to it. After all of this information we compile and develop it into one product before we finally launch it into the market. This is actually what we do for all other products. Product development durations depend on the type of food product but we see an average of 1.5 to 2 months from idea to the first prototype. There are certain snacks that take longer, for example, 4-5 months, because it requires a lot of research to reach consistency in the product.

When we started my enterprise we were only in Hyderabad and now we are also selling in the neighboring states of Tarnaka and Tamil Nadu. I am eager to explore other markets. My membership at ALEAP and Confederation of Indian Industries (CII) has helped me in my expansion. We do direct marketing and supplying to schools, colleges and universities. We also have our stalls in the colonies (residential subdivisions) and have an online store. We also now supply to NGOS, to midday meal programs and to corporate hospitals such as the cancer institute here in Hyderabad. We now are happy that many health stores in Hyderabad feature our products. Always coming up with new products has allowed us to easily penetrate the market, but the real boost was when the hospital started accepting our millets into their meals, it boosted our turnover and our business.

The first products rolled out were snacks called "Energy Bytes," which is an extruded millet snack. We also came up with millet-based porridge mixes. Today we have expanded our product line into 35 different items ranging from snacks to Ragi, Jowar porridge and upma mixes, flakes and muesli, to idli and dosa mixes. I consider my enterprise as a successful venture due to the fact that turnover which was at Rs. 50,000 a month in the initial year has now increased manifold to Rs.8-9 lakhs a month.

It looks easy but I encountered several challenges in my enterprise when I was just beginning. First was the lack of specialized equipment for millet processing. My father is also an engineer who worked at a food processing center in Telangana. He helped me develop my machineries. Together we invented a machine that saved us a lot of time in processing. We call it the "extruder" and the product comes out pre-cooked. This is the machine that we used to create our Energy Bytes. Before that we went to various agencies to ask for machines and the officers always said they don't have those kinds of machines. We were recommended to import it for 50 Lakh—they would support us in importing it—but that is too much money for us. So I collected books on extruders and gave them to my father and we discussed the specifications of the extruder machine that we developed ourselves. We also later developed a roller flaking and de-hulling machine by improvising on machinery available for processing other grains. This in-house machinery development required a concerted effort of 7-8 months. Even this would not have been possible if I did not have the required expertise of my father. My father helps with maintenance of the machines now.

My second challenge was the lack of consumer knowledge about millet benefits in general and millet products in the market. There was simply no awareness on millet grains. Selling products through major retail chains and supermarkets in cities was unthinkable due to high charges for shelf space. These rents, running into lakhs of rupees (in addition to retailer margins), was not something a small scale entrepreneur like me could afford. We therefore set off on direct marketing of our products through organizing talks and awareness drives in schools, colleges and housing colonies, where we also educated people on the nutritional value of millet grains. Every year we were always invited and always participated in various millet or grain based festivals.

Aside from these, I think the third and biggest challenge in my business was being a woman and trying to enter a market where millions and millions of men are there. Earlier, wherever I went they always ask: "Why your husband doesn't come?" This discrimination was something that was always there whenever I went to the discussions. But finally

I think people realized that I have a product to offer. There is still discrimination there but I think I proved them all wrong. I am happy there are currently more producers of millet and more food processors. I heard that a woman acquaintance started making millet noodles and three more entrepreneurs are producing millet crispies.

Analysis of Upgrading Strategy

In this section, we analyse the upgrading strategy of Annapurna Kalluri using the Onion model. We begin from the outside shell and work towards the inner shells of the Onion model. This means we begin by discussing the business environment first, followed by networks, enterprise characteristics and finally, entrepreneur characteristics. As the following section will show, the business environment, through the assistance of various agencies, played a very strong role in the development and upgrading of Annapurna's business. In addition, Annapurna's social class - discussed at the level of entrepreneurs' characteristics - meant that she was equipped with the education, financial capital, and the confidence to lead her business to sustainable growth.

A. Business environment

Indian millet production has been on the decline in the past years, the reason the government has been eagerly supportive of Annapurna's enterprise. Around the time that Annapurna decided to start her venture, a drastic reduction in the cultivation, production and consumption of millet grains at the national level was occurring. Between 1961 and 2009, there was a dramatic decrease in cultivated area for millets: a reduction of 80% cultivated area for small millets, 46% for finger millet, 59% for sorghum, and 23% for pearl millet. There was also a dramatic decrease in total production of small millets: 76% less harvest for all India (DHAN foundation 2012). Many farmers were opting to exit millet cultivation due to decreasing productivity, low returns and low demand. Annapurna's strategy was to approach the government, an institution that she trusted, that she knew could help her the most. And it paid off. From collecting information to gathering technical advise to obtaining subsidies and to collaborating in product development, Annapurna approached and received support from the government.

The state of Andhra Pradesh and neighboring Telangana, being one of the foremost millet producing states in the country, received much support from the Central and State government as well as research institutes and universities for promotion of millet cultivation, processing and value addition.

> The government through the Ministry of Agriculture at that time was publishing a lot of small articles about millets and how to obtain subsidies for its processing. (-Annapurna Kalluri)

She used this campaign to her advantage and approached several government-based institutions for support. She identified four agencies that were instrumental in her upgrading, which we listed here:

IIT Kharagpur - When she was beginning to gather literature on creating machineries for her millet processing, she found intensive research on extrusion machinery from IIT Kharagpur. The Indian Institute of Technology in Kharagpur West Bengal is one of the leading universities in the country in terms of research and development for industries. They offer support to enterprises by devoting pillars of their research activities on entrepreneurship and innovation.

INSIMP - The Initiative for Nutritional Security through Intensive Millet Promotion Scheme (INSIMP) was initiated by the government in 2011-2012 under the Rashtriya Krishi Vikas Yojana (RKVY) project to demonstrate better production and post-harvest technologies to increase millet production in the country. Besides increasing production of millets, the Scheme also aimed to develop processing and value addition techniques in order to generate consumer demand for millet-based food products. Three universities in the state of Andhra Pradesh were tasked to investigate better cultivation techniques, to develop more efficient distribution of inputs to local producers and to establish centers of excellence for product development technology. They were also tasked with entrepreneurship training and establishment of market linkages between processors and producers. For aspiring millet product entrepreneurs, the programme also attempted to bridge the gap of machinery supply by offering subsidized machinery (flaking and pulverizing machine, roaster) for entrepreneurs.

Annapurna was a beneficiary as well as contributor to this scheme. Since her unit was one of the first entities to develop specialized millet processing machinery, she is also now a licensed supplier of millet processing machinery to the INSIMP program whereby the machinery developed by her is now being supplied to other INSIMP beneficiaries, while also availing the subsidy for set up of the same machinery at her unit.

MPIC - The Millet Processing and Incubation Centre was set up at Professor Jayashankar Telengana State Agricultural University in July 2013 to popularize millet-based foods under the RKVY scheme. The Centre addressed several of the bottlenecks faced by many entrepreneurs including the development of equipment for manufacturing products like noodles, pasta and biscuits out of millets as these are not readily available in the market. The MPIC also retrofitted the equipment and developed their own millet processing technology. About 21 food products have been developed by the Centre so far that the center markets under its own brand name - "Millet Plus". It also provides its products and technology to entrepreneurs interested in marketing them or producing them. The technology is currently being sold by five entrepreneurs and 15 entrepreneurs are marketing its products. Annapurna has been a beneficiary of the technical support from the products and technology from the MPIC.

> I approached the Ministry of Food Processing in Delhi and I easily received my subsidy in 2011 from them. [...] From the government I received technological support also. I also engaged with ICRISAT who helped me in recipe formulation that was gluten free. The Indian Institute for Millet Research also helped me during my testing phase.
>
> (-Annapurna Kalluri)

ICRISAT - The agribusiness incubation platform at International Crop Research Institute for Semi Arid Tropics (ICRISAT) promotes agribusiness ventures through technology development and commercialization. The platform benefits farmers through assistance in the creation of competitive agri-business enterprises – providing incubation services in seed, farm, agri-biotech and innovative ventures. Value adding innovations based on millet grains was something they ventured into from 2007 after ICRISAT started the NUTRIPLUS Knowledge Program (NPK) funded by the Andhra Pradesh government. Here, ICRISAT started the food processing lab and conducted related research and development into food processing. Support offered for clients such as Annapurna include technology development, tie ups with experts in the relevant field for mentorship, access to laboratory facilities and design of business plans. In 2014 Annapurna developed muesli composed of Jowar and Bajra Indian flakes, nuts and honey with assistance in recipe formulation from the agribusiness incubation platform of ICRISAT.

B. Personal and professional networks

There are many factors which Annapurna considers to be her stepping stones to reach the comfortable position she is in today, and her family's support was the most important one. Apart from the technical expertise of her father for technology and equipment development, her supply of raw material was stabilized through millet production on their own agricultural land.

> My father is also an engineer who worked at a processing center in Telangana. He helped me develop my machineries. (-Annapurna Kalluri)

At the professional level, she is a member of the Association of Lady Entrepreneurs of India (ALEAP), a voluntary association that trains, guides and counsels aspiring women entrepreneurs. ALEAP has also established the country's first industrial estate for women in Hyderabad, from where Mathesis originally obtained space to operate. Annapurna has also received food processing and enterprise development training from the association.

> My membership at ALEAP and Confederation of Indian Industries (CII) has helped me in my expansion. (-Annapurna Kalluri)

This robust support system that developed technology and provided business incubation support for female entrepreneurs in her state has aided her in the upgrading of her enterprise.

C. Enterprise characteristics

The location of Annapurna's company in the state of Andhra Pradesh brought it under the radar of several government agencies that were actively reviving millet production and consumption in the state. Her location made it easier to avail of a host of government support. Also, her company's location in the State proved advantageous for easy transportation of raw material supply. Annapurna's decision to hire postgraduate students as co-developers of her products provided her with a "cheaper" source of educated and skilled workforce. She described her postgraduate student-workers as an extremely dedicated team who stay with her from the inception of an idea to its realization. She recognized them as a major strength for the company.

> When we are developing new products, we always employ food science students. They are already knowledgeable in the field and they want to earn additional income. We develop things together with them.
> (-Annapurna Kalluri)

One strategy that differentiates Annapurna from most entrepreneurs is her product portfolio. She and her team have managed to create 35 different products out of millet and other grains in such a short span of time. Recently she has started to process food from other types of cereals and has successfully tested them in the market. Aside from food processing, Annapurna is also into the development and sale of millet processing machinery. She cooperates with her father and with INSIMP in this venture.

D. Entrepreneur characteristics

Annapurna is a classic example of an upgraded entrepreneur that has been endowed with human capital. She is highly educated and possessed the relevant work experience at a leading firm that gave her insights on office and employee management. She might have initially lacked entrepreneurship skills, but she made up for it by linking up with ALEAP, engaging with academics and researchers and availing of trainings and courses that prepared her for her role as proprietor.

I also attended a course at night from the Indian Institute of Packaging to understand food packaging mechanics. (-Annapurna Kalluri)

While the specifics of her caste membership were not discussed, it is believed that Annapurna comes from a higher social class in the Indian society. This assumption was made in light of her high education as an Engineer and her father's similar education before her. Land ownership and her work experience at IBM contributed to the notion that her social background allowed her access to resources that most start-up entrepreneurs could not have. She mentioned however that she had to put up with gender discrimination, particularly during the earlier stages of her enterprise. This is not uncommon. Successful female entrepreneurs in Ghana were found to have similar experiences in terms of gender discrimination and had to find creative ways to overcome this challenge (see Hampel-Milagrosa 2011).

Lessons Learned and Conclusions

This case study evaluated the upgrading story of Annapurna Kalluri, a young mother and owner of the Mathesis Food Products company of Hyderabad. Kalluri creates snacks and other food products from millet, a cereal whose production and consumption is being promoted by the state of Andhra Pradesh. The analysis of Annapurna's upgrading was conducted within the framework of the Onion model that looked at four strands of factors affecting sustainable enterprise growth, namely: business environment, personal and professional networks, enterprise characteristics and entrepreneur characteristics.

The analysis showed that the three main constraints to the growth of Annapurna's enterprise was the lack of specialized technology for millet processing, the general low levels of awareness about millet in Andhra Pradesh and elements of gender-based discrimination. The first constraint forced her to conduct extensive research and to approach various government agencies for help. Unfortunately, those agencies did not have the necessary technology yet offered to support her in case she decided to import the machines. In the end, she and her father decided to innovate and create the local technology themselves. The second constraint was the lack of awareness and thereby, low consumption levels of millet in her immediate market of Andhra Pradesh. Consumers were not aware of the health benefits of millet and the proper methods on how to cook it. Millet-based foods are still marketed as niche health products for urban consumers and are not viewed as potential alternatives for the more widely consumed rice and wheat. The visibility of millet-based products is still low as these are available only in select retail stores and not in major supermarket chains. It is for this reason that she and her marketing team decided to conduct direct marketing in schools, colleges, hospitals and residential colonies. She eagerly held talks and awareness-drives to educate consumers about the nutritional value of millet. The third constraint of gender-based discrimination is a systemic issue among micro-, small-, and medium-sized entrepreneurs in the private sector. Fortunately, her social background (which allowed her to have a high education and work experience) and determination to succeed helped her overcome her experiences of gender-based discrimination.

Looking back, there are two important factors that allowed Annapurna to create her upgrading strategy to overcome her constraints. These two factors are business environment and social background and arise from the two extreme layers of the Onion model.

After the government's support, cities like Hyderabad Bangalore, Chennai and Pune are now witnessing an increasing number of start-ups offering millet-based snacks. There are now several millet-based restaurants in south India. This rise is also being fueled by increasing consumer awareness on health issues and increasing consumer demand for healthy food in convenient, packaged formats. But although a lot of entrepreneurial activity is being witnessed in the region, not all startups are as endowed with human capital as the case of Annapurna. Not all entrepreneurs would have the patience nor the courage to approach experts, institutions and agencies to seek support. This is where her social background makes a difference.

Annapurna's social background meant that she would have received excellent education like her father and that her family would have owned properties. This also meant that financial resources to support her new enterprise would be available. Her education and work experience meant that she would be confident in discussing technical issues with experts and in requesting support from government agencies. As a female entrepreneur in India, gender-based obstacles to doing business abound and society is sometimes insensitive or immune to many challenges that women entrepreneurs face. The state-level government in this regard is commendable because of its tireless support to proprietors like Annapurna. Indeed, the business environment was the most influential in her upgrading story. Information, technical support for machinery development and training—all of these were made available to Annapurna through the concerted efforts of state-level agencies.

In closing, this case has important implications for policy makers seeking to create a favorable business environment for private sector development. If an entrepreneur that is endowed with human capital and access to resources still requires the support that the business environment provides, what about the majority of entrepreneurs that are less educated or less skilled? Annapurna Kalluri's case highlights the critical role that the business environment plays in providing the necessary boost that micro and small entrepreneurs need, particularly in the earlier stages of their enterprise.

References

Acharya, S. S. 2007. Agribusiness in India: Some facts and emerging issues. *Agricultural Economic Review.* **20**. pp.409-24.

Agarwalla, A. 2011. *Regional Income Disparities in India and Test for Convergence -1980-2006.* [Online]. Ahmedabad: Indian Institute of Management. [Accessed 11 July 2016]. Available from: https://web.iima.ac.in/assets/snippets/workingpaperpdf/2011-01-04Agarwalla.pdf.

Ahluwalia, M. S. 2002. Economic Reforms in India Since 1991: Has Gradualism worked? *The Journal of Economic Perspectives.* **16**(3). pp.67-88.

Anitha, V. 2015. Agribusiness – Employment opportunities for women entrepreneurs in India. In: Miryala, R. K. and Aluvala, R. ed(s). *Trends, Challenges & Innovations in Management.* Hyderabad: Zenon Academic Publishing, pp. 237-43.

Birthal, P. S., Roy, D. and Negi, D. S. 2015. *Agricultural Diversification and Poverty in India.* [Online]. Washington, D.C.: International Food Policy Research Institute (IFPRI). [Accessed 7 July 2016]. Available from: https://www.ifpri.org/publication/agricultural-diversification-and-poverty-india.

Dev, S. M. 2010. *Food Security in India: Performance, Challenges and Policies.* [Online]. New Delhi: Oxfam India. [Accessed 7 July 2016]. Available from: https://policy-practice.oxfam.org.uk/publications/food-security-in-india-performance-challenges-and-policies-346637.

Dev, S. M. 2012. *Small Farmers in India: Challenges and Opportunities.* [Online]. Mumbai: Indira Gandhi Institute of Development Research. [Accessed 7 July 2016]. Available from: http://www.igidr.ac.in/pdf/publication/WP-2012-014.pdf.

DHAN Foundation. 2012. *Supporting Millets in India Policy Review & Suggestions for Action.* [Online]. Krishnagiri: DHAN Foundation. [Accessed 26 November 2017]. Available from: http://www.dhan.org/smallmillets/docs/report/Millet_Support_Policies.pdf.

FAO (Food and Agriculture Organization). 2011. *Exports: Commodities by country.* [Online]. [Accessed 7 July 2016]. Available from: http://faostat.fao.org/.

Hampel-Milagrosa, A. 2011. The role of regulation, tradition and gender in Doing Business. Case study and survey report on a two year research project in Ghana. *German Development Institute Studies.* **60**(2011).

IBEF (India Brand Equity Foundation). 2016. *Agriculture in India.* [Online]. [Accessed 7 July 2016]. Available from: http://www.ibef.org/industry/agriculture-india.aspx.

Indiacode. 2016. *Part III Fundamental Rights.* [Online]. [Accessed 8 July 2016]. Available from: http://indiacode.nic.in/coiweb/coifiles/p03.htm.

Indian Planning Commission. 2012. *Faster, Sustainable and more inclusive growth.* [Online]. [Accessed 6 July 2016]. Available from: planningcommission.gov.in/plans/planrel/12appdrft/approach_12plan.pdf.

Indian Ministry of External Affairs. 2015. Agriculture. [Online]. [Accessed 7 July 2016]. Available from: http://indiainbusiness.nic.in/newdesign/index.php?param=economy_landing/213/2.

Kashyap, P. 2013. Strategies for Doing Business in Rural India. 23 June. *Ecopreneurist.* [Online]. [Accessed 7 July 2016]. Available from: http://ecopreneurist.com/2013/06/23/strategies-for-doing-business-in-rural-india/.

Landes, M. 2008. *The environment for agricultural and Agribusiness Investment in India.* [Online]. Washington, D.C.: U.S. Department of Agriculture. [Accessed 7 July 2016]. Available from: http://ageconsearch.umn.edu/bitstream/58628/2/eib37.pdf.

McKinsey. 2010. *India's Urbanization: A closer look.* [Online]. [Accessed 6 July 2016]. Available from: http://www.mckinsey.com/global-themes/urbanization/indias-urbanization-a-closer-look.

OECD. 2014. *Regulatory reform: Improving the business environment through effective regulation.* [Online]. France: OECD. [Accessed 6 July 2016]. Available from: http://www.oecd.org/india/India-Improving-Business-Environment-through-Effective-Regulation.pdf.

PwC (Pricewaterhouse Coopers). 2012. *Doing business in India.* [Online]. 3rd ed. Mumbai: PwC. [Accessed 7 July 2016]. Available at: https://www.pwc.de/de/internationale-maerkte/assets/doing-business-in-india.pdf.

PwC (Pricewaterhouse Coopers). 2016. *India.* [Online]. [Accessed 6 July 2016]. Available from: http://www.pwc.in/.

Sharma, D. 2014. Landwirtschaft in der Krise. 3 May. *Bundeszentrale für politische Bildung.* [Online]. [Accessed 6 July 2016]. Available from: http://www.bpb.de/internationales/asien/indien/189174/landwirtschaft-in-der-krise.

Tambe, P. R. 2015. Opportunities and Challenges in agribusiness in India. *International Journal of Combined Research and Development.* [Online]. **4**(9). pp.507-15 [Accessed 7 July 2016]. Available from: http://www.ijcrd.com/files/Vol_4_issue_9/5903.pdf.

The Economist. 2015. Farming in India: In a time warp. *The Economist.* [Online]. 25 June. [Accessed 6 July 2016]. Available from: http://www.economist.com/news/asia/21656241-india-reforming-other-bits-its-economy-not-farming-time-warp.

The World Bank. 2012. India: Issues and Priorities for Agriculture. 17 May. *The World Bank.* [Online]. [Accessed 7 July 2016]. Available from: http://www.The World Bank.org/en/news/feature/2012/05/17/india-agriculture-issues-priorities.

The World Bank. 2016. *Overview India.* [Online]. [Accessed 22 June 2016]. Available from: http://www.The World Bank.org/en/country/india/overview#1.

The World Bank. 2016a. *DataBank.* [Online]. [Accessed 6 July 2016]. Available from: http://databank.The World Bank.org/data/home.aspx.

The World Bank. 2016b. *Doing Business 2016: Economy Profile 2016 India.* [Online]. [Accessed 7 July 2016]. Available from: http://www.doingbusiness.org

UNDP (United Nations Development Program). 2015. *International Human Development Indicators.* [Online]. [Accessed 6 July 2016]. Available from: http://hdr.undp.org/en/countries.

UNDP (United Nations Development Program). 2016. *About India: Challenges.* [Online]. [Accessed 8 July 2016]. Available from: http://www.in.undp.org/content/india/en/home/countryinfo/challenges.html.

Williams, C. and Gurtoo, A. 2011. Evaluating women entrepreneurs in the informal sector: Some evidence in India. *Journal of Developmental Entrepreneurship.* **16**(3). pp.351- 69.

Printed in the United States
By Bookmasters